07/08

UNIVERSITY OF

D1612305

Re-Use
Architecture

Re-Use Architecture

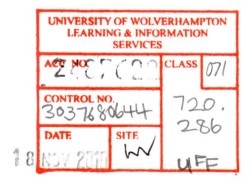

Chris van Uffelen

BRAUN

CONTENTS

6 Preface

Culture

12 **The Garden Museum**
Dow Jones Architects

16 **Jahrhunderthalle Bochum 'Montagehalle für Kunst'**
Thomas Pink | Petzinka Pink Architekten

20 **Philharmonie**
Frits van Dongen, de Architekten Cie.

24 **The North Wall Arts Center**
Haworth Tompkins

28 **Castellanza Civic Library**
DAP studio

32 **Consol 4**
TOR 5 Architekten

36 **Store 8B**
Arturo Franco Architect

40 **Store 17c**
Arturo Franco Architect

42 **Alvéole 14**
LIN Finn Geipel + Giulia Andi

44 **Centro de Monitorização e Interpretação Ambiental**
EMBAIXADA

48 **Max Ernst Museum**
ARGE van den Valentyn Architektur, SMO Architektur

52 **Dance Center**
3LHD Architects

56 **The Maria Helena Ship**
FloS und K architektur + urbanistik

60 **Louis Hartlooper Complex**
Vertex Architectuur en Stedenbouw

64 **CarriageWorks Contemporary Performing Arts Center**
Tonkin Zulaikha Greer

68 **Modern Museum Malmö**
Tham & Videgård Arkitekter

72 **Drents Museum**
Erick van Egeraat, Frank Huibers

74 **Bread Museum and Ilópolis Mill**
Brasil Arquitetura Studio with Anselmo Turazzi

78 **Danish Maritime Museum**
BIG

80 **Contemporary Jewish Museum**
Studio Daniel Libeskind

84 **Danish Jewish Museum**
Studio Daniel Libeskind

Hotel, Restaurant, Café

90 **The White Rabbit**
Takenouchi Webb

92 **Café-restaurant OPEN**
Pi de Bruijn, de Architekten Cie.

96 **Espressofabriek**
Studio Ramin Visch

100 **Kruisherenhotel**
SATIJNplus Architecten

102 **Court Hostel**
24H architecture

104 **Les Cols**
RCR Arquitectes

108 **Andel's Lodz**
Jestico + Whiles

112 **Grand Hotel Casselbergh**
BURO II & ARCHI+I

114 **The Tote**
Serie Architects

118 **Stayokay Hostel**
Personal Architecture BNA

Living

124 **Living in a Townhall**
Format Architektur

128 **Former auditorium**
hks Architekten + Gesamtplaner

132 **Lant Street**
Dow Jones Architects

134 **New River Bank Barn**
Blackburn Architects

138 **Hirschkron / Camacho apartment**
MANIFOLD.Architecture Studio

142 **Kiln House**
Swaney Draper Architects

146 **Retirement Home 'Matthäushof'**
Werkgemeinschaft Quasten + Berger

148 **Living and work in a former bank house**
Architektur Büro Jäcklein

150 **The Coach House**
David Archer

154 **Rosellenturm**
van den Valentyn Architektur

158 **Art in the Bunker – Living in the Tower**
binnberg design

162 **1800 am Gerzensee**
Halle 58 Architekten GmbH with smarch Architekten

164 **The Dairy House**
Charlotte Skene Catling

168 **Märchenring Residence**
baurmann.dürr architekten

172 **Monroe Park**
Sergei Tchoban Architekt BDA nps tchoban voss A. M. Prasch, S. Tchoban, E. Voss

176 **Siloetten / The Sil(o)houette**
C. F. Møller Architects with Christian Carlsen Arkitektfirma

180 **DJ's Garden**
rooijakkers + tomesen architecten

184 **Lafayette Lofts**
Hacin + Associates, Inc.

186 **Yale Steam Laundry Condominiums**
John Ronan Architects

190 **Living in the Above Ground Bunker**
Luczak Architekten

194 **Ludgerhof**
Atelier PRO architekten

198 **Living in the former Jesuit monastery**
Franke Rössel Rieger Architekten

200 **Apartment on the Top of a Grain silo**
Szymon Rozwałka (C+HO_aR), Tomas Pejpek

202 **Tikkurila Silk Mill**
Davidsson Tarkela Architects

204 **Silos Apartments**
Tonkin Zulaikha Greer

208 **Biscuit Company Lofts**
Aleks Istanbullu Architects

212 **Carré at Dolderse Hille**
Paulus van Vliet architects
with Blok Kats van Veen architects

214 **Senior residence Carl-Fried Haus**
Angelis+Partner Architekten

Mixed-use

220 **experimenta Science Center**
studioinges Architektur und Städtebau

224 **Rote Halle**
Thomas Pink | Petzinka Pink Architekten

228 **Ideenbotschaft**
Thomas Pink | Petzinka Pink Architekten

232 **District Office Oost-Watergraafsmeer**
Dirk Jan Postel (Kraaijvanger • Urbis)

234 **The Docks Dombasles**
Hamonic + Masson

236 **Ernst-Reuter-Haus**
Sergei Tchoban Architekt BDA nps tchoban voss
A. M. Prasch, S. Tschoban, E. Voss

240 **Picanol Site Reconversion**
BURO II & ARCHI+I

242 **Renovation of Rahova Commodities Exchange**
RE-ACT NOW Studio

246 **The Hangar**
diederendirrix

250 **Lamot**
51N4E

254 **FP3**
Hacin + Associates, Inc.

258 **The Village Office**
Inbo

260 **Ford Ching**
XTEN Architecture

264 **Fuller Lofts**
Pugh + Scarpa Architects

268 **Walden Studios**
Jensen Architects, Jensen & Macy Architects

272 **The Green Building**
form, environment, research (fer) studio LLP

Office

278 **Redevelopment headquarters Essent**
Pi de Bruijn, de Architekten Cie.

282 **Architekturbüro [lu:p]**
Architekturbüro [lu:p]

286 **Werbeagentur Djermester / Lindner**
oliv architekten

290 **House Benois**
Sergei Tchoban Architekt BDA nps tchoban voss
A. M. Prasch, S. Tchoban, E. Voss

292 **Water Tower Office**
Christoph Kalb Architekt ARB DipArc BSc

296 **Pionen – White mountain**
Albert France-Lanord Architects

300 **3ality Digital**
Fung + Blatt Architects, Inc.

302 **Architecture in a Container**
L6 studio

304 **Office Van Alckmaer voor Wonen**
Klous + Brandjes Architecten bna

308 **Kraanspoor**
OTH, Ontwerpgroep Trude Hooykaas

312 **VTT Valimo**
Davidsson Tarkela Architects

316 **Harris & Ruble Law Offices**
Aleks Istanbullu Architects

320 **Maison de l'Architecture**
chartier-corbasson

Various functions

326 **Ílhavo City Library**
ARX PORTUGAL, Arquitectos Lda.

330 **Siobhan Davies Company**
Sarah Wigglesworth Architects

332 **L'OREAL Academy**
m2r architecture

336 **Thermae Bath Spa**
Grimshaw

340 **Royal and General Archive of Navarra**
Rafael Moneo

342 **MTV Networks Benelux**
Max van Aerschot architect bv

346 **Restoration Center**
UTARCHITECTS

350 **Synagogue Münstersche Straße**
Sergei Tchoban Architekt BDA nps tchoban voss
A. M. Prasch, S. Tchoban, E. Voss

354 **St. Elisabeth**
fischerarchitekten

358 **WellnessSky**
4of7 architecture

362 **Children's Toy Library**
LAN Architecture

366 **bastard store**
studiometrico

370 **Licantén Public Library**
Emilio Marin + Murúa-Valenzuela

372 **Hubertusburg**
Ipro Dresden, Büro Böhme + Schönfeld

374 **Lieven de Key-building Handicraft School**
Gijs van Thienen Architecten

376 **Library of Special Collection**
Atelier PRO architekten

380 **Jigsaw**
Pugh + Scarpa Architects

384 **355 11th Street: Matarozzi / Pelsinger Building**
Aidlin Darling Design

388 **Mediatheek**
Dok architecten (Liesbeth van der Pol) and
AEQUO Architects (Aat Vos)

392 **SAC Federal Credit Union Ames Branch**
Leo A Daly

396 Architects Index

407 Picture Credits

408 Imprint

Breathing new life into old bones

by Chris van Uffelen

Building conversion is not a new phenomenon, but in the context of the ongoing discussion about soil sealing and recycling it is more topical than ever before. Existing buildings were being converted to new uses already in the Middle Ages, when the Porta Nigra of antiquity became a chapel, or in Córdoba when the shaft timbers of the existing mosque were used as the radiating chapel of the cathedral and the new building with its contemporary plateresque style was located in the middle of the existing Islamic structure. Since the plateresque style was an amalgam of the vocabulary of the outgoing Gothic and the nascent Renaissance, but also Islamic architecture, the contrast was moderated a bit. The cathedral with the greatest area in the world, at more than 23,000 square meter of floor space, was the result. However this conversion, which began under the emperor Karl V in 1523, was a sign of the victory over the Moors – even if it took place more than 300 years after the reconquest of territory that had been occupied by the Moors. The emperor himself led a crusade against Tunis only twelve years later.

↖↖ | **Córdoba, Cathedral,** a gothic church built into an existing Islamic mosque
↖ | **Paris, Conciergerie,** transformation from royal palace to Palace of Justice to prison and back to Palace of Justice
← | **Lucca, Piazza Anfiteatro,** a Roman amphitheater capable of welcoming 10,000 spectators became a plaza with houses

The impact of such a conversion on the affected religion is still an explosive political issue today. However it must be borne in mind that with their Mezquita (beginning in 786 A.D.) the Moors built over the Visigoth cathedral of Saint Vincent of Saragossa, reusing different parts of it. The Visigoth building itself had a prehistory as a Roman temple. The emperor was reportedly disappointed upon seeing the new building in the midst of the old one: "I didn't know what was going on here. Because if I had, I would not have permitted them to touch the old building. They did what was possible to build something that already exists somewhere else, and in the process destroyed something which was unique in the world."

The danger of incurring such a verdict confronts every architect involved in the conversion of historical building stock. Conversion always takes place in the conflict of interests representing conformity with the criteria of historical listing and radical new interpretation, and conscious inclusion of historical significance and the economical use of existing architecture as raw material. This book presents buildings which are distinguished by the fact that they have more or less undergone a significant change in species: an art center emerging from a swimming pool, a police station turning into a cinema, a bridge becoming a restaurant, an office occupying a bunker, a transformer station transformed into a synagogue and a former metal working shop revamped as a library.

In light of the transition from an industrial to a service society, former factories are especially prominently represented. Factories and industrial facilities were first classed as historically and architecturally worthy of preservation in this sense in the course of the 1970s. Just as the Jugendstil, which was "discovered" at about the same time, industrial buildings soon underwent an unforeseen Renaissance especially as

→ | **Paris, Louvre, sketch by Israël Silvestre, 1650,** perspective showing the former fortress transformed into a royal palace
→→| **Paris, Jeu de paume, sketch by Charles Hulpeau, 1607,** in the indoor tennis hall

loft apartments. The original structures can only seldom be used without a partial demolition, like the often redundant factory floors or warehouses or the halls of the Jeu de paume, a kind of indoor tennis from the annals of architectural history. This kind of hall can be adapted to the most varied uses by insertions. Many Jeu de paume courts became ballrooms, or churches, or libraries. The most famous, in Paris, became a museum.

Every architectural conversion changes the building not only materially but also from a standpoint of content, as the example of the cathedral in Córdoba explicitly shows. However on the other hand, when the decision has been made to include the old structure as an esthetic factor or as raw material instead of building a new one, then every future use will be juxtaposed to the tradition of the location. Evading the tradition of the location is only possible with a complete conversion which completely obliterates the historical substance or a by creating a symbolic act. In order to break through this historical tabu Christo and Jeanne-Claude, the "wrappers" wrapped the former Reichstag in Berlin before the Bundestag moved in. Similary, many unused sacred buildings are not only officially profaned (Catholic "deconsecrated", Evangelical "decommissioned"), they are assigned an artistic interim use before they can be used for secular purposes.

The chapter division of this book follows the new uses, so that the conversions of sacred buildings are found in different chapters as restaurants, museums, apartments and offices, while in the chapter "Living" one finds one after the other, a former city hall, an auditorium, a warehouse, a barn, a synagogue, but also a grain silo, laundry, bunker and even sacred buildings. Uses for "Living" and "Culture" are most often represented. The conversions in the area of "Hotel, Restaurant, Café" tend to play most freely with the existing building substance, while the "Office" use is determined to a great extent by economic and functional considerations. In the "Mixed-use" chapter one finds many large building inventories which had to be assigned a new use, while "Various functions" includes very different uses, whereby libraries are most prevalent.

Among the examples there are also buildings by well known older and younger architects. Among them is the Renaissance architect Phillip Vingboons, the master of the Modern, Alvar Aalto and Piet Bloms Baumhäuser, the icon of post-war architecture, because their buildings have also aged in the meantime and must either be restored or assigned a new use. In the case of architectural ornaments the role of the documentation of the existing building is especially important.

Although the majority of such buildings are anonymous, the conversions use the old building as a vehicle of expression, intervening with a vocabulary that either contrasts or conforms to the existing building substance, while rescuing architectural artefacts and referring to the history of the building in the process. The meaning of the existing building as part of the urban picture is very often the inspiration for the conversion, so that the conversion often involves the restoration of the original building, with or without an extension, as contrast or extension of the existing stock.

↗ | **Paris, Jeu de paume,** the ancient indoor tennis hall houses now a museum
↗↗ | **Berlin, Reichstag,** Christo and Jeanne-Claude wrapped the former Reichstag in Berlin before the Bundestag moved in – a symbolic act of transformation
→ | **Paris, Louvre,** the former royal palace is now one of the largest museums of the world

DEM DEUTSCHEN VOLK

CULTURE

Dow Jones Architects / Biba Dow, Alun Jones

↑ | Function space
→ | Main aisle to façade

The Garden Museum

London

In October 2007, the architects won an architectural competition to redesign the former Church of St Mary in Lambeth. The competition brief asked for a new gallery space where temporary exhibitions could be housed in secure and environmentally-controlled conditions. The guiding principle was to create a belvedere within the existing building in order to house the new galleries and provide a raised ground from which a new perspective of the existing building is attained. The belvedere structure made it possible to place the temporary gallery at ground floor level and move the permanent collection from its former location in the nave to the new first floor level. The Garden Museum is a gardener's delight, replete with riotous flowers and stained glass windows.

PROJECT FACTS

Address: Lambeth Palace Road, London, SE1 7LB, United Kingdom. **Client:** The Trustees of the Garden Museum. **Completion:** 2008. **Building type:** museum. **Gross floor area:** 700 m^2.
Original building: architect unkown. **Client:** Diocese of Southwark. **Completion:** 1800s. **Building type:** church. **Gross floor area:** 500 m^2.

↑ | **Permanent exhibiton space**
← | **Elevation**, west

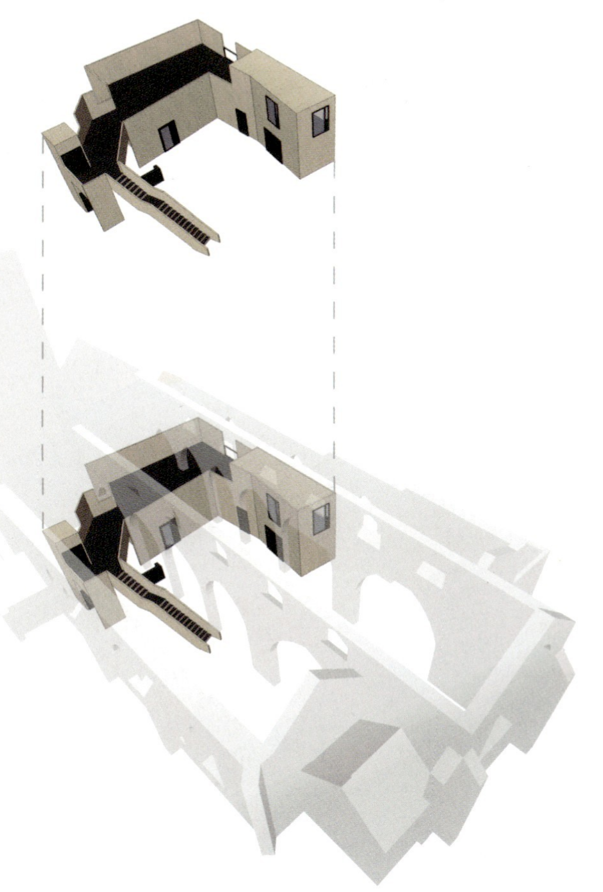

← | The free-standing timber structure
↓ | Permanent exhibition space

Thomas Pink | Petzinka Pink Architekten

↑ | **Bar,** first floor

→ | **Main entrance and view into the bar**

Jahrhunderthalle Bochum 'Montagehalle für Kunst'

Bochum

The Jahrhunderthalle industrial monument is located in the Westpark district of Bochum. A central event venue was created here for the RuhrTriennale. The planning goal was the preservation of the overall historical impression in dialogue with new architectural elements, high quality technical, acoustical and indoor climatic stage equipment and the technological realization of energy concepts. In order to reactivate the monument as an 'Assembly Hall For Art' the statics were stabilized by an innovative coupling of the halls with newly erected flanking building elements. The historical craneways were equipped with new crane bridges, contributing the decisive precondition for the flexible use of the halls.

PROJECT FACTS

Address: An der Jahrhunderthalle 1, 44793 Bochum, Germany. **Client:** LEG Landesentwicklungsgesellschaft NRW GmbH, Dortmund. **Completion:** 2003. **Building type:** event hall. **Gross floor area:** 18,000 m².

Original building: H. Schumacher. **Client:** Bochumer Verein. **Completion:** 1903. **Building type:** exhibition hall, then: turbine hall. **Gross floor area:** unknown.

↑ | **Event hall**
↙ | **Ground floor plan**
↓ | **Bird's-eye view,** building process

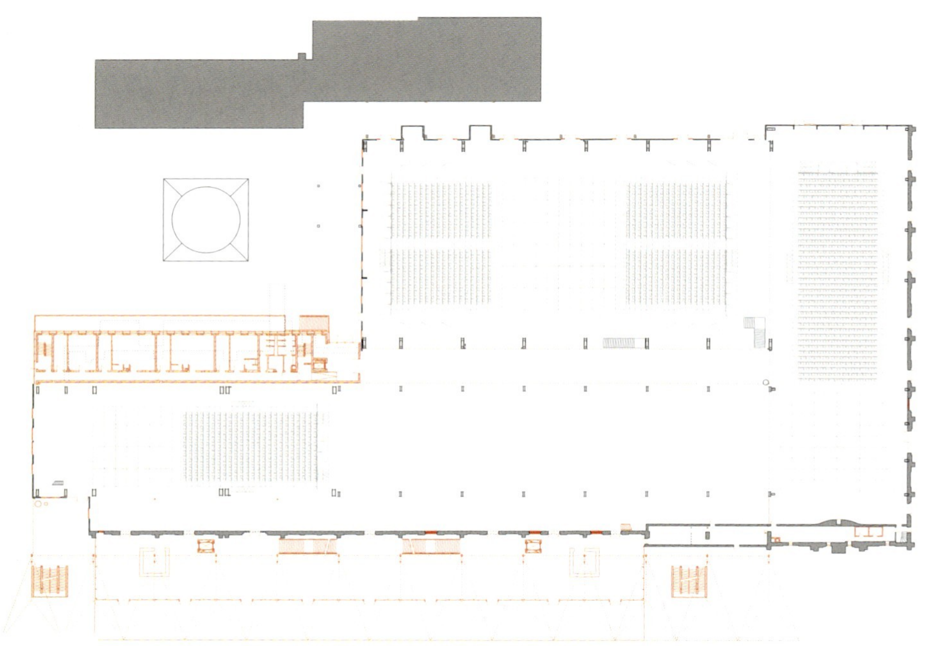

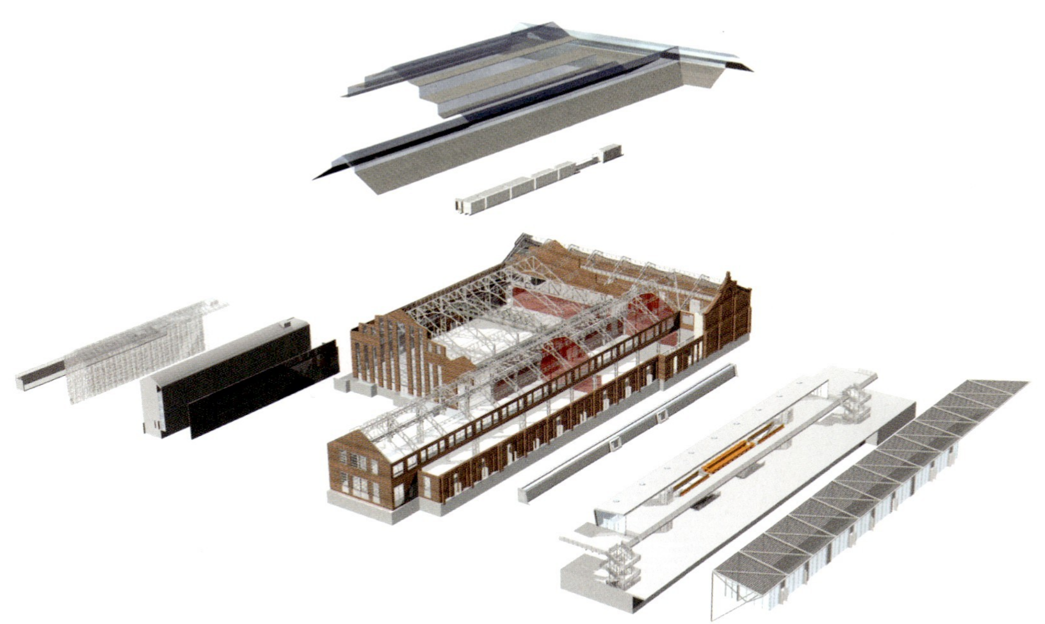

← | **Exploded isometry**
↓ | **Supporting framework**, south

Frits van Dongen,
de Architekten Cie.

↑ | Street elevation
→ | Foyer

Philharmonie

Haarlem

The new music center has a simple, clear-cut and logical layout. The main hall has been extended lengthwise and the stage has been enlarged. An acoustic that ranks among the best in Europe has been achieved by deepening the hall, making the balconies into one continuous whole, and restoring classic ceilings and detailing. The new small concert hall seems to float, a structure that "hangs" in the foyer. Its rounded forms and the use of wood lend it an intimate, warm atmosphere. The foyer forms the centerpiece of the building, connecting old and new and providing cohesion between the different spaces. In addition to the main hall for symphonic music and the small hall for modern music, three classical music salons were created.

PROJECT FACTS

Address: Lange Begijnestraat 11, 2011 HH Haarlem, The Netherlands. **Client:** City of Haarlem. **Completion:** 2005. **Building type:** concert hall. **Gross floor area:** 6,200 m².

Original building: Adriaan van der Steur. **Client:** Sociëteit Vereniging. **Completion:** 1878. **Building type:** society's building. **Gross floor area:** 4,700 m².

↑ | **Van Beinum music salon**
← | **Connection** between new and old building
↓ | **Routing foyers**

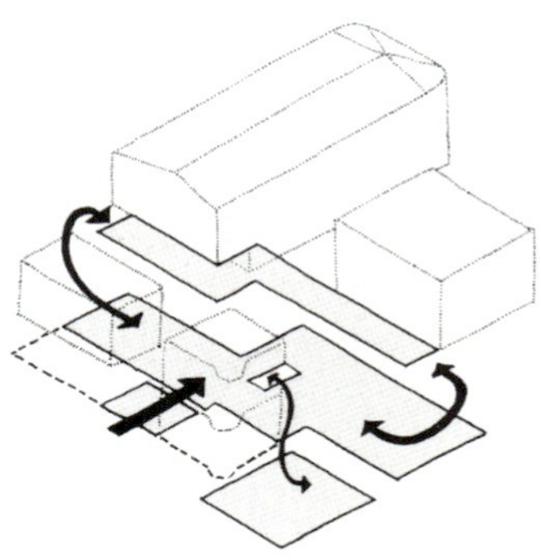

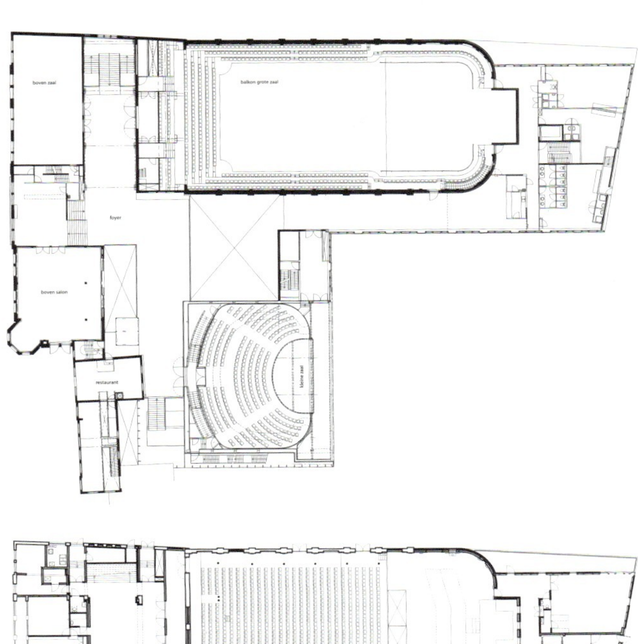

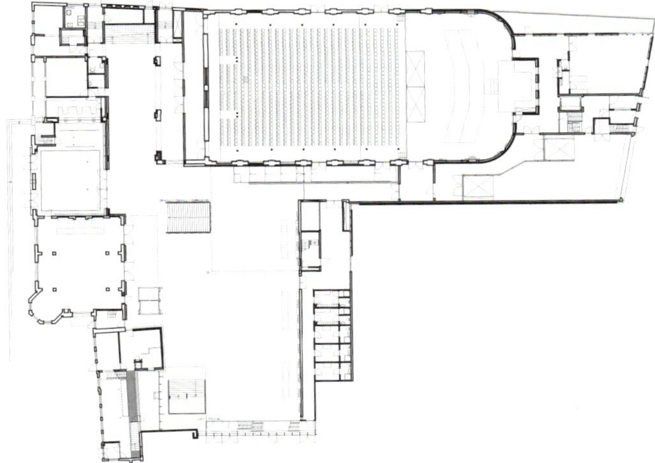

↖ | First floor plan
← | Ground floor plan
↓ | Small concert hall

Haworth Tompkins

↑ | South facing elevation
→ | South facing courtyard elevation
↓ | Previous northern exterior

The North Wall Arts Center

Oxford

Built on the grounds of St Edward's School, the Center is shared by the school and town. It houses a flexible 300-seat theater, a rehearsal space, dance studios and an art gallery. The design unites an ancient stone boundary wall, a Grade 2 listed Victorian former swimming pool and a new building to form a carefully scaled streetscape to the public side and a new courtyard to the school. The scheme has been envisaged as a linear series of connected "barns" built against the weathered stone boundary wall. Vernacular forms, con-mporary detailing, and traditional but unfamiliar materials emphasize the building's as a place for innovation and creativity within an historic environment.

PROJECT FACTS

Address: St Edward's School, Woodstock Road, Oxford, OX2 7NN, United Kingdom. **Client:** St Edward's School. **Completion:** 2006. **Building type:** performing arts center. **Gross floor area:** 1,250 m². **Original building:** William Wilkinson. **Client:** St Edward's School. **Completion:** 1888. **Building type:** victorian swimming pool. **Gross floor area:** unknown.

↑ | **Dance studio**
← | **Gallery / foyer**
↓ | **Section**

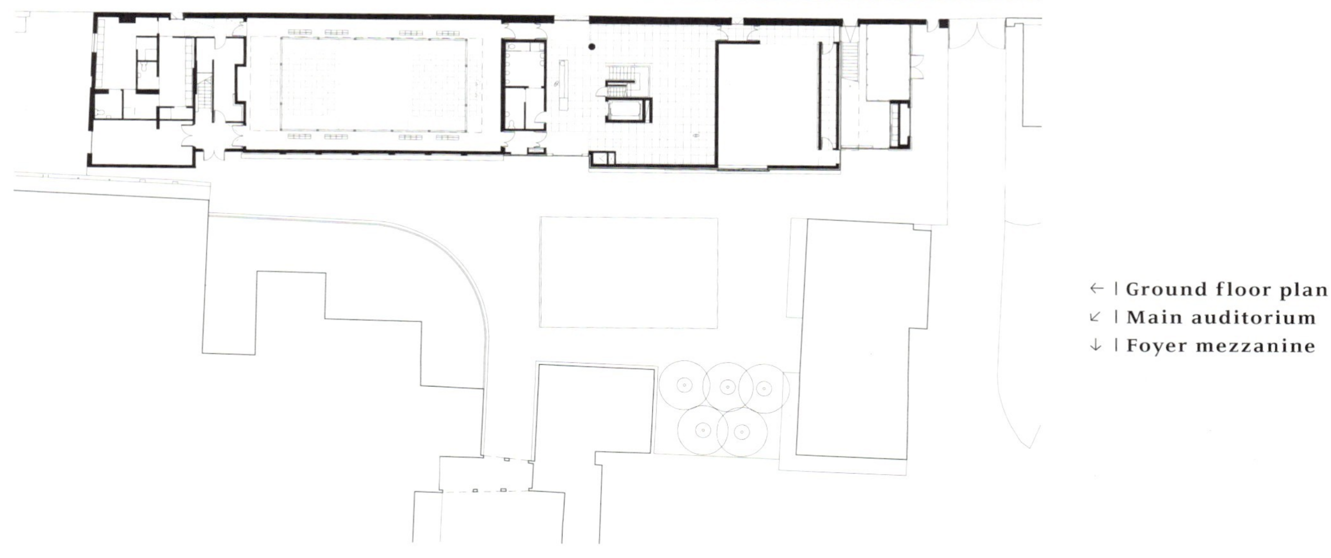

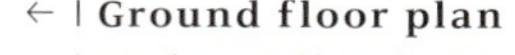

← | Ground floor plan
↙ | Main auditorium
↓ | Foyer mezzanine

DAP studio / Elena Sacco, Paolo Danelli

↑ | **Exterior view,** restauration preserved the original brick image
→ | **Stairs,** underlining the continuity between the ground floor and the first floor

Castellanza Civic Library

Castellanza

Part of a more extensive plan to redevelop the area, the new Civic Library is housed inside an old industrial building facing onto the river Olona. The project leaves the factory structure exactly as it was: a simple flat-roofed brick body on two floors that has been restored by bringing out its distinctive elements. The new projecting steel bow windows are the elements that characterize the new intervention, creating a strong relationship between inside and outside. They replace preexisting fixtures and are now used for communication and exhibition purposes or as simple colored light boxes: the windows in fact are distinguished by a lighting that gradually changes its color.

PROJECT FACTS

Address: Piazza Castegnate, 21053 Castellanza (Varese), Italy. **Client:** City of Castellanza. **Completion:** 2004. **Building type:** library. **Gross floor area:** 1,850 m².
Original building: architect unknown. **Client:** Tosi factory. **Completion:** 1870. **Building type:** factory. **Gross floor area:** 1,850 m².

↖ | **Conference and exhibition room**
↑ | **Interior view**
← | **The "functional islands"** floating in a free structure and standing out through their contrasting colors and materials

↖ | **Elevation**
← | **Sections**
↓ | **The study room** ensures privacy without losing visual contact

TOR 5 Architekten / Herfried Langer, Markus Wüllner

↑ | **Exterior**
→ | **View of training room,** southwest

Consol 4

Gelsenkirchen

This project involved the conversion of the historically listed machine hall including the concrete shaft tower situated on Pit 4 into a music rehearsal center. The central idea was the revival of the pit as a unit: the shaft tower and machine hall belong together and were functionally reconnected. 40 solidly constructed 25 square meter music rehearsal rooms were installed in the machine hall, at a distance from the existing structure. Like an ice cube floating in a glass, the upper floors of the machine hall glisten behind a green glass wall. The shaft and the hall are connected by an exterior, expanded metal clad stairway.

PROJECT FACTS

Address: Consolstraße 3, 45889 Gelsenkirchen, Germany. **Client:** City of Gelsenkirchen. **Completion:** 2005. **Building type:** culture center. **Gross floor area:** 2,500 m^2.
Original building: W. A. Görgen. **Client:** Ruhrkohle AG, Deutsche Steinkohle AG. **Completion:** 1956 (power house), 1958 (shaft tower). **Building type:** industrial. **Gross floor area:** 1,000 m^2.

←←| **Entrance by night,** rock lobby and galery
← | **Interior of stair tower**
↓ | **Fourth floor plan**

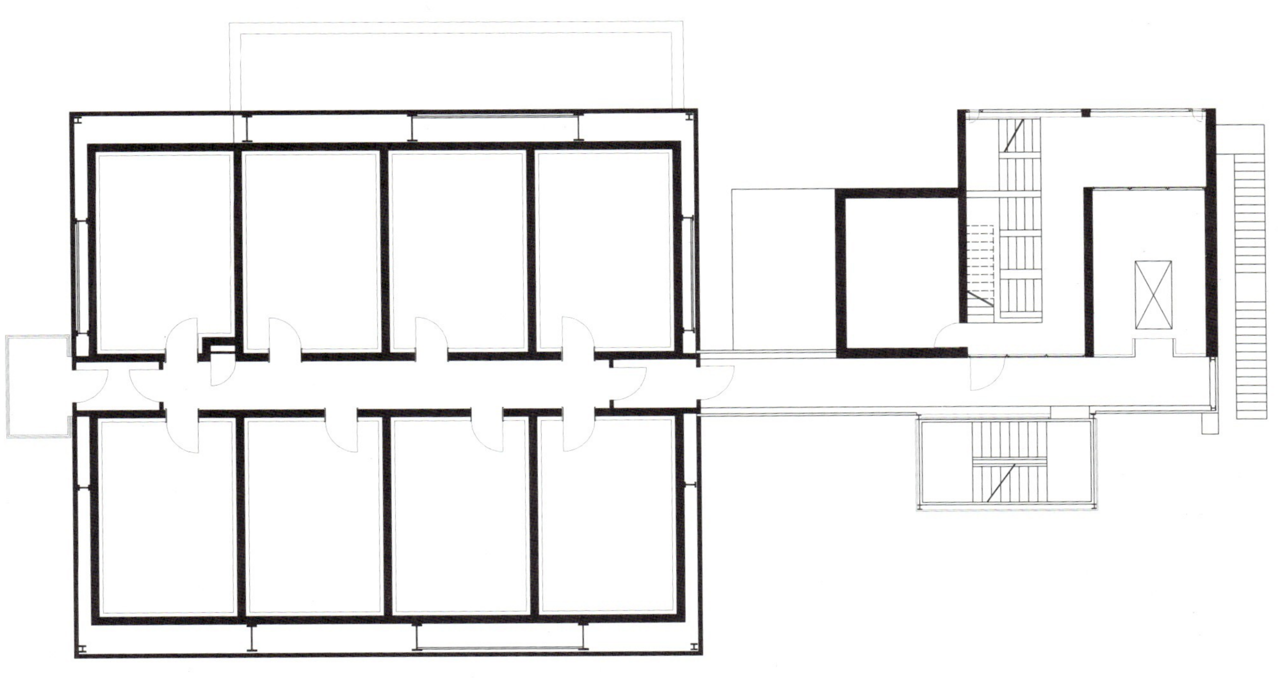

Arturo Franco Architect

↑ | Exterior
→ | Interior

Store 8B

Madrid

In the former warehouse 8B the tiles in bad condition have been removed from the roof, been stacked and been put inside to solve a problem. That is the summary of the intervention. The priority was to replace a roof of flat shingle tiles over boards and a patchwork of hollow bricks, to structurally reinforce the whole ensemble and to revamp the interior, thermally and acoustically, so as to provide service to the new users. This procedure had been followed before in other warehouses in the slaughterhouse with mountains of tile, timber, cladding and granite slab rubble piling up as a result.

PROJECT FACTS

Address: Paseo de la Chopera 14, 28008 Madrid, Spain. **Interior Design:** Diego Castellanos. **Co-Architecture:** Yolanda Ferrero. **Client:** Madrid Council. **Completion:** 2010. **Building type:** cultural center. **Gross floor area:** 1,000 m^2.
Original building: Luis Bellido. **Client:** Madrid Council. **Completion:** 1917. **Building type:** slaughter house. **Gross floor area:** 1,000 m^2.

↑ | Hall

← | Diagram

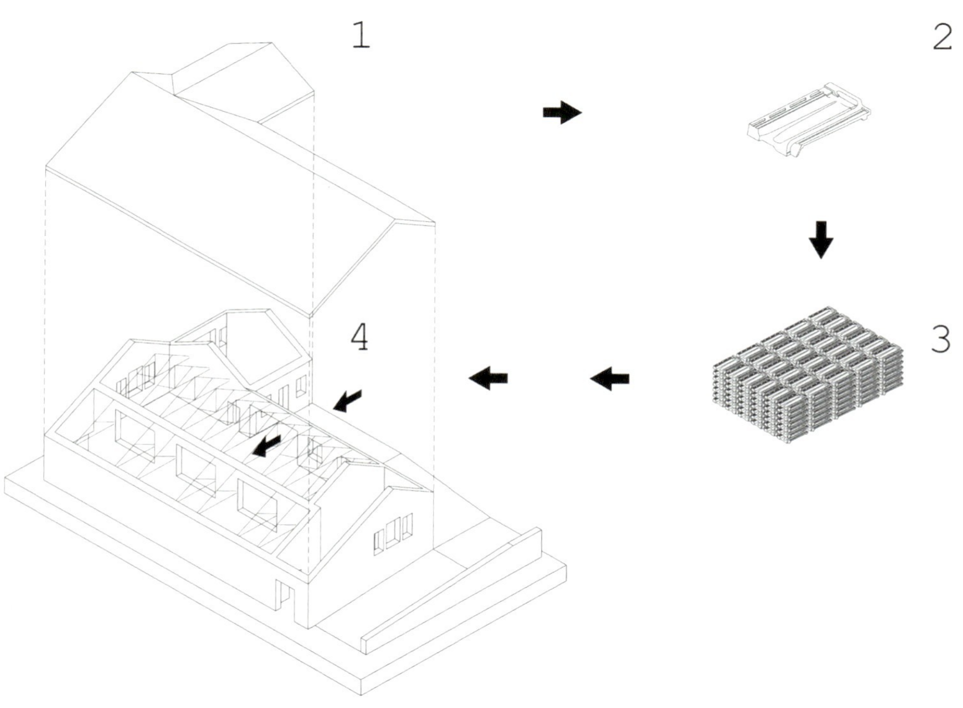

← | Tiles

↓ | Section, ground and first floor plan

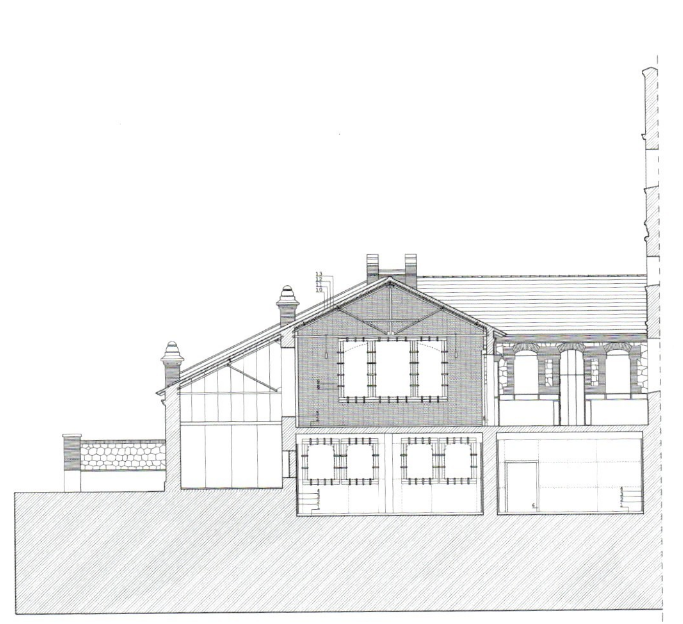

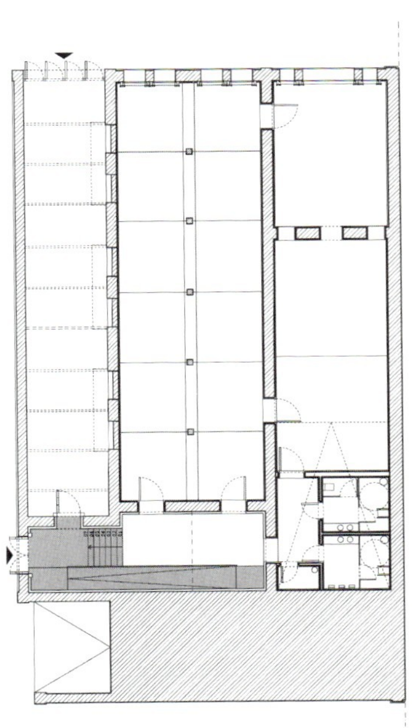

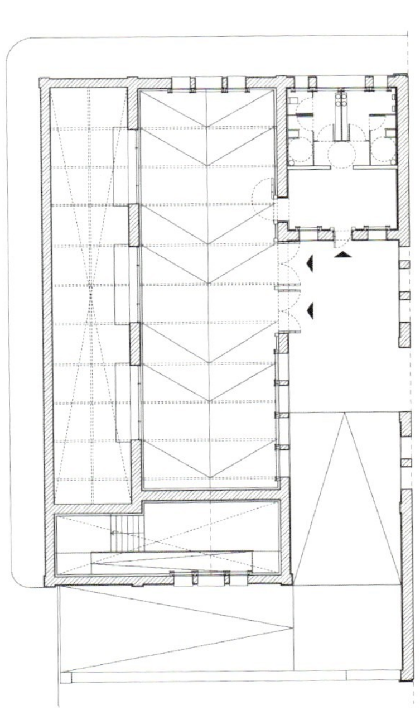

Arturo Franco Architect

↑ | Counter
↓ | Section and ground floor plan

Store 17c

Madrid

From the very beginning, the architects considered the intervention as an opportunity to explore the possibilities of refurbishment. In the context of historical legacy the point was to contribute an experience about the limits of non-intervention, of reducing such intervention to a bare minimum in a radical posture with a new attitude. In this project, the traditional insecurity and theoretical vagueness that persistently affects actual interventions into historical legacy with halfway results between what to do and what not to do, were absent from the very beginning. The architects decided to choose an idea and to explore it to the very end, without fear, with no inferiority complexes – to intervene in a radical manner.

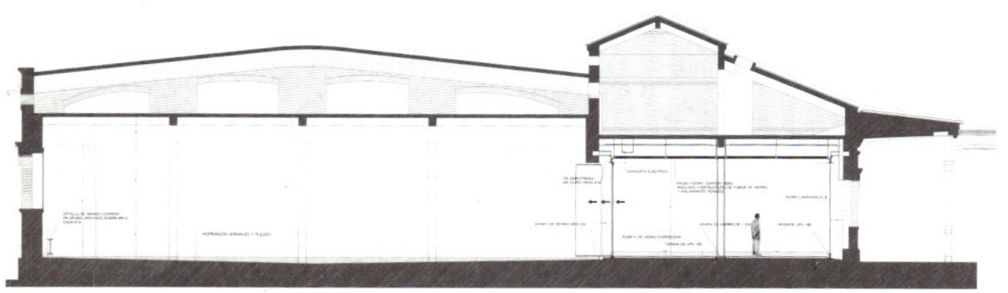

PROJECT FACTS

Address: Paseo de la Chopera 14, 28008 Madrid, Spain. **Interior Design:** Diego Castellanos. **Co-Architect:** Fabrice van Teslaar. **Client:** Madrid Council. **Completion:** 2007. **Building type:** cultural center. **Gross floor area:** 6,000 m².

Original building: Luis Bellido. **Client:** Madrid Council. **Completion:** 1917. **Building type:** slaughter house. **Gross floor area:** 6,000 m².

↑ | **Door in glass wall**
↓ | **Interior**

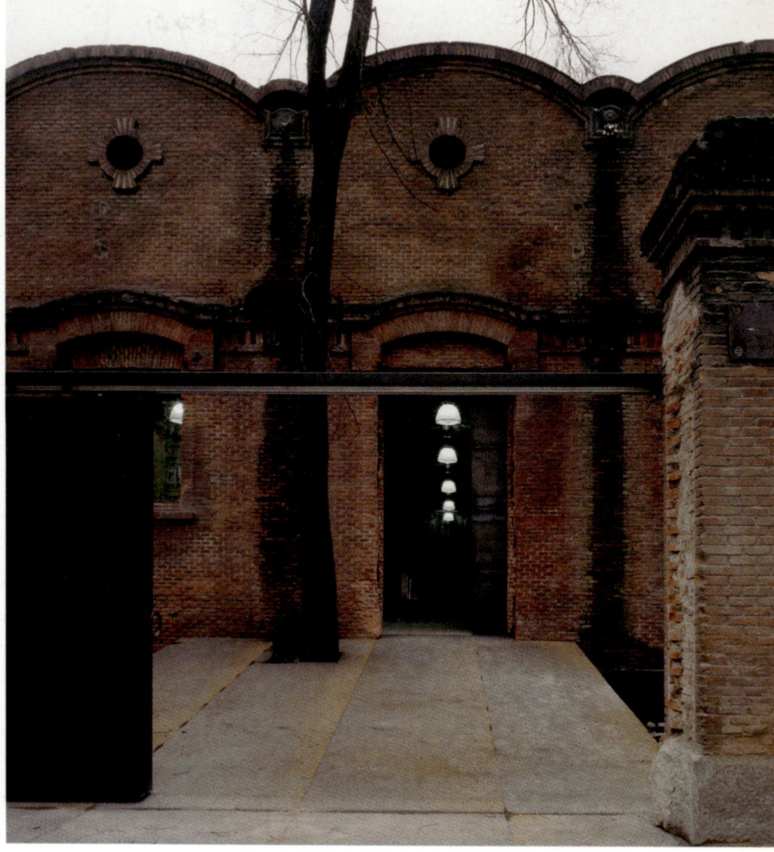

↑ | **Porch**

LIN Finn Geipel + Giulia Andi

↑ | General view

Alvéole 14

Saint-Nazaire

The submarine base of Saint-Nazaire is a raw and impressive structure, transformed with minimal interference. Two of its former cells were turned into cultural elements: LiFE and VIP. The hall for the international center for emerging art forms (LiFE) is a minimalistically equipped "Monospace", situated in a former submarine basin and opened up towards the harbour. VIP, a "venue for contemporary music", occupies one of the volumes inside the bunker. On the roof, a geodesic dome from the Berlin Tempelhof Airport serves as a "think tank" for art and music projects. A newly defined street with an enigmatic atmosphere traverses the entire base. It creates interaction between the various already existing spaces and the newly created ones.

PROJECT FACTS

Address: Base sous-marine, Alvéole 14, Bd. de la Légion d'Honneur, 44600 Saint-Nazaire, France. **Client:** City of Saint-Nazaire. **Completion:** 2007. **Building type:** public space for contemporary arts and music. **Gross floor area:** 5,570 m^2 (converted part).
Original building: Organisation Todt, Oberbauleitung Süd. **Client:** German Navy. **Completion:** 1943. **Building type:** submarine base. **Gross floor area:** 37,000 m^2.

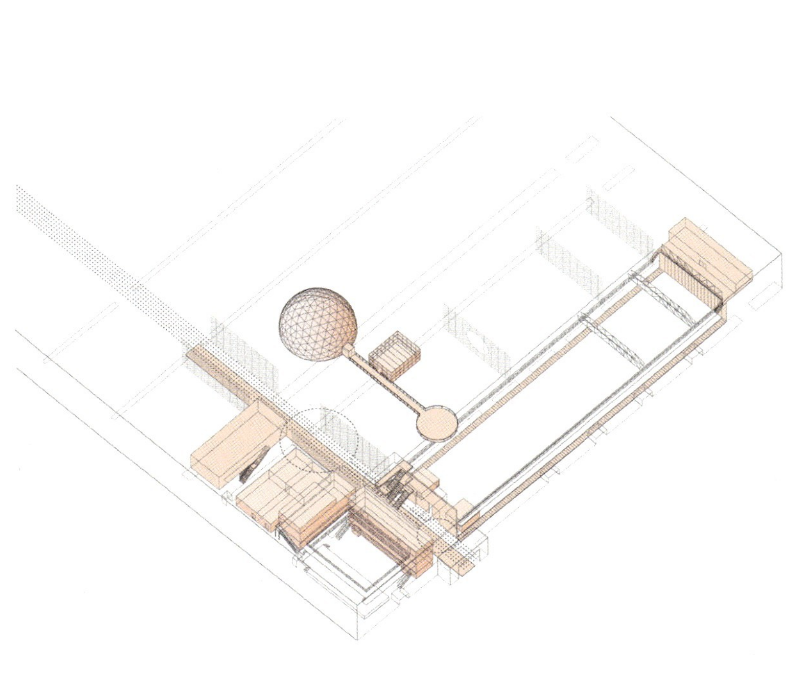

↑ | **Site plan**

↑ | **Interior view,** during an event
↓ | **Concert hall**

EMBAIXADA

↑ | **Interior view,** top floor
→ | **Entrance area,** atrium

Centro de Monitorização e Interpretação Ambiental

Tomar

This project is a reconstruction of an already existing, but run-down structure. The new program serves two distinct functions: providing a public area for exhibitions and a private area, consisting of lecture rooms and accommodation for invited artists. The design maintains the entire external perimeter construction. The private areas are volumetrically defined within the structure and optimized for habitation. The rundown interior has been totally renewed, allowing it to become the focus point of the building. The social life takes place in the interstitial space around the new structure, and is characterized by the programmatic events defined by the newly refursished structure.

PROJECT FACTS

Address: Praça Alves Redol nº 5 Tomar, Portugal. **Client:** Tomarpolis. **Completion:** 2006. **Building type:** cultural facility. **Gross floor area:** 980 m².
Original building: architect unknown. **Client:** Order of the Knights. **Completion:** unknown. **Building type:** storehouse for cereals. **Gross floor area:** 438 m².

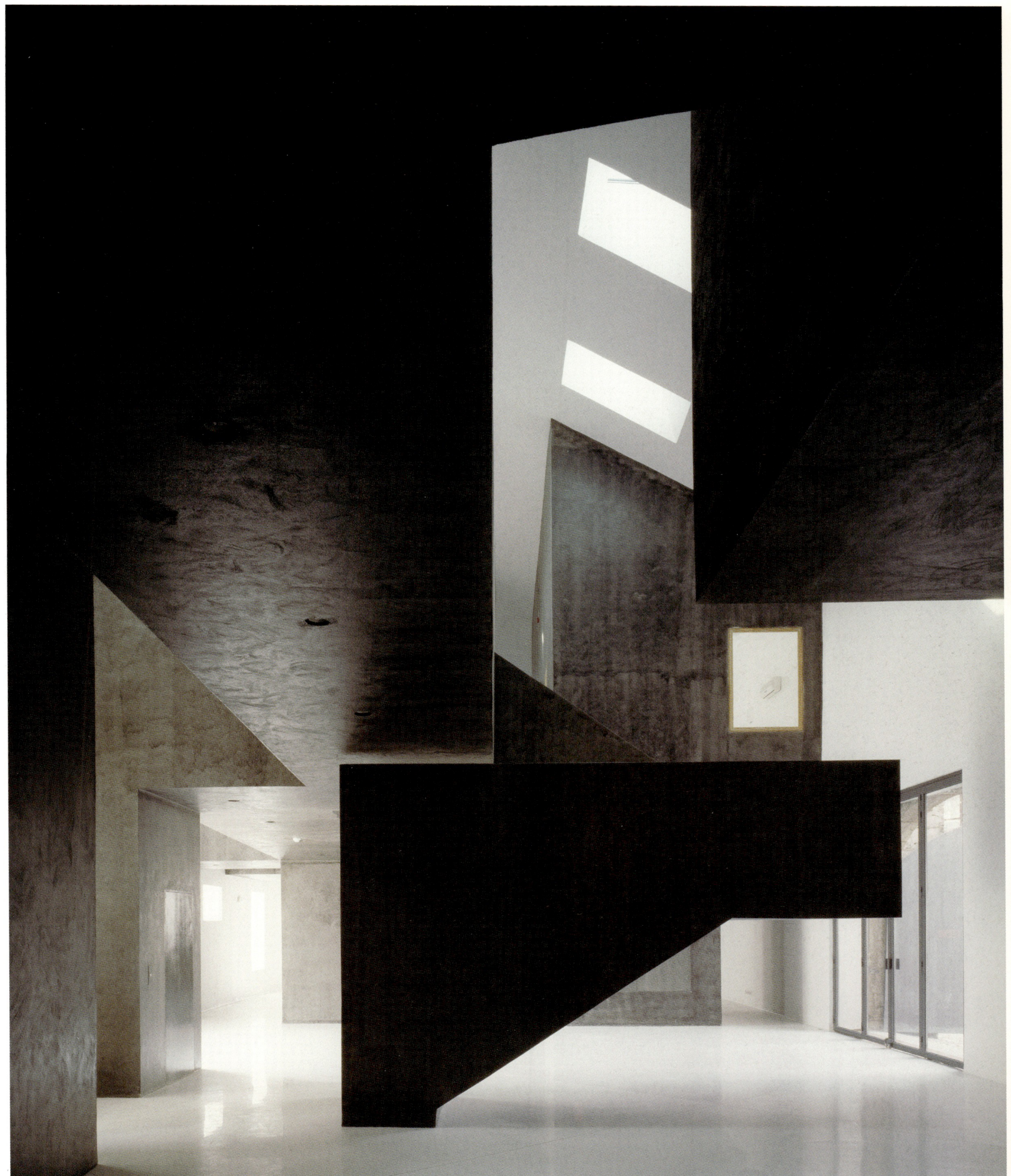

↖ | Interior view
↑ | Atrium
← | Longitudinal section

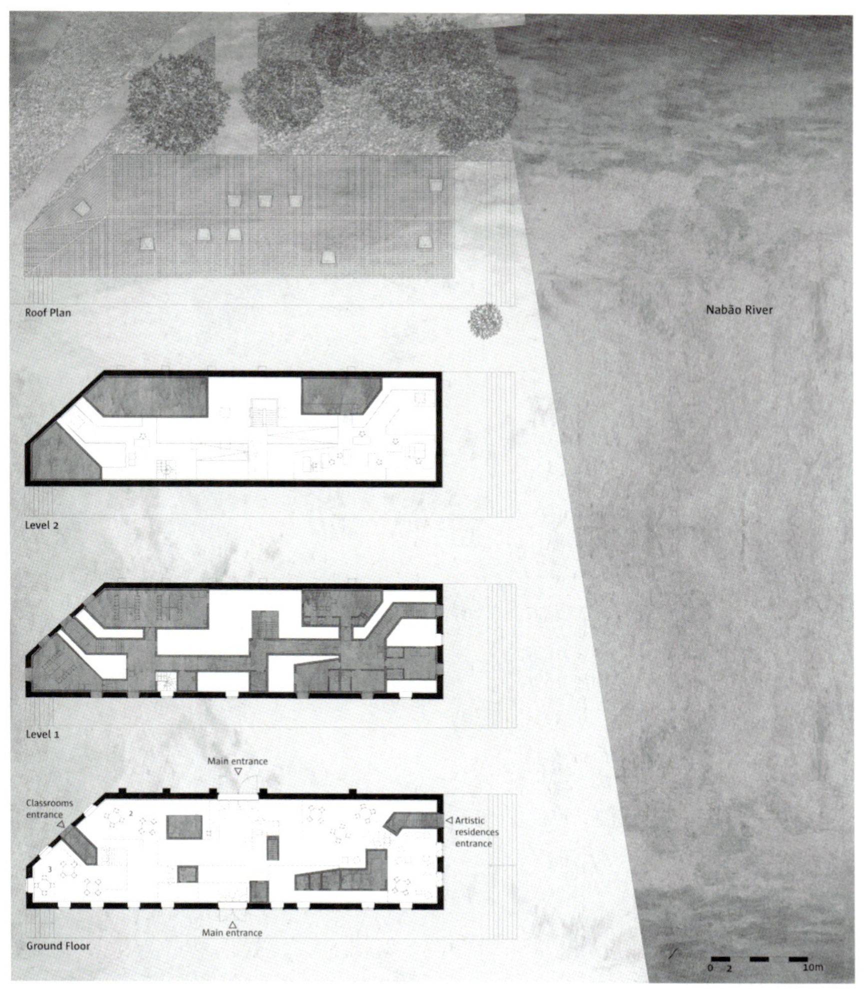

← | **Floor plans**
↓ | **Exterior view** from riverside

ARGE van den Valentyn Architektur, SMO Architektur

↑ | **South elevation**
→ | **Detail,** pavilion

Max Ernst Museum

Brühl

With all the annexes removed, the character of the classicistic three-wing complex, built around 1844, was maintained, and restored to its original form with the courtyard opening up to the park. The complex was augmented with a new, half subterranean building, the roof of which is reflected as a slightly raised natural stone plateau in the park. An entryway pavilion inserted in the courtyard constitutes the connecting link between old and new. It ushers the visitor down to the temporary exhibition via an open flight of stairs. The space is supplied with daylight by means of traversable skylights. The old structure is devoted for the most part to the art of Max Ernst, which has its home as a permanent collection in the main building.

PROJECT FACTS

Address: Comesstraße 42, 50321 Brühl, Germany. **Client:** City of Brühl. **Completion:** 2004. **Building type:** museum. **Gross floor area:** 5,400 m^2.

Original building: architect unknown. **Client:** Peter Granthil. **Completion:** 1844, 1870. **Building type:** Pavilion Brühl, dance hall, hotel. **Gross floor area:** unknown.

↑ | **Pavilion,** entrance area

↓ | **Ground floor plan**

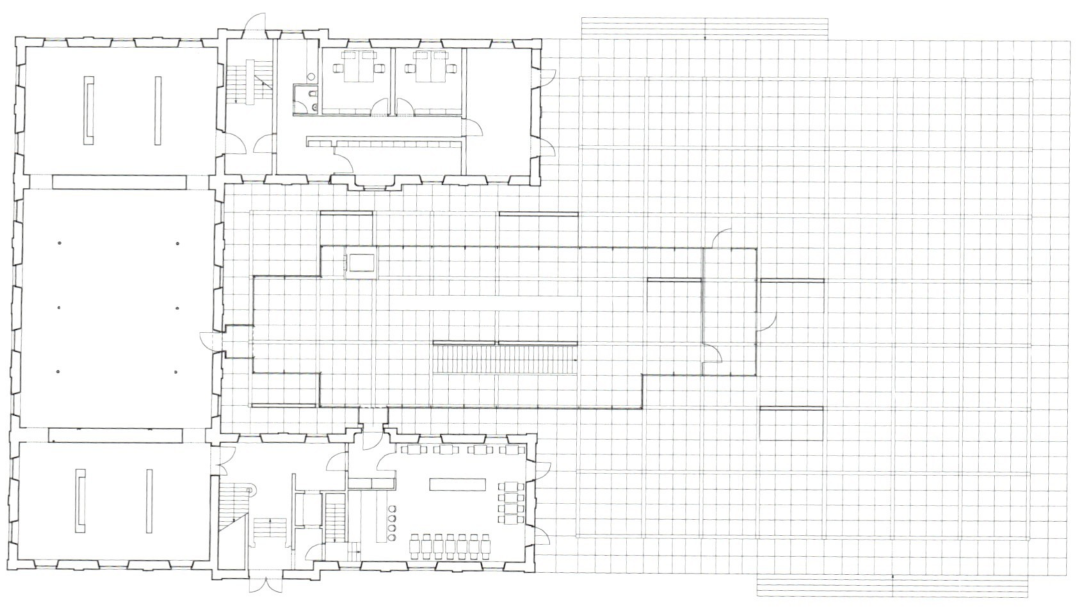

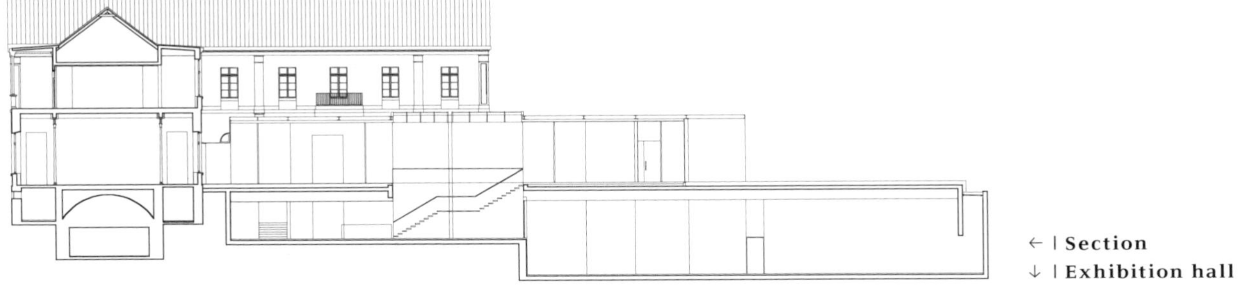

← | Section
↓ | Exhibition hall

3LHD Architects

↑ | **Exterior** of the Dance Center from the courtyard
→ | **Hallway** leading to Studio 3

Dance Center

Zagreb

The opening of movieplex cinemas in Zagreb has led to the dying out of old cinema theaters in the city. The city of Zagreb decided to reuse those spaces for new cultural facilities. The old Lika cinema was given the role of a dance center in the new scenario. It is located in a dilapidated block one hundred meters away from Zagreb's main square. The entire projects was placed in the old cinema shell. The only new architectural element is the entrance lobby, a communication and meeting space. The volume and its broken form suggest dance movement, creating a connection between the courtyard and the roof terrace which is an important part of the project of preservation and restoration of Zagreb's last open roof stage.

PROJECT FACTS

Address: Ilica 10, 10000 Zagreb, Croatia. **Client:** City of Zagreb. **Completion:** 2009. **Building type:** dance center. **Gross floor area:** 1,438 m^2.
Original building: architect unknown. **Client:** private ownership / City of Zagreb. **Completion:** around 1850. **Building type:** stables, then privately owned cinema. **Gross floor area:** 1,438 m^2.

↑ | **Interior view,** studio 3
↓ | **Section**

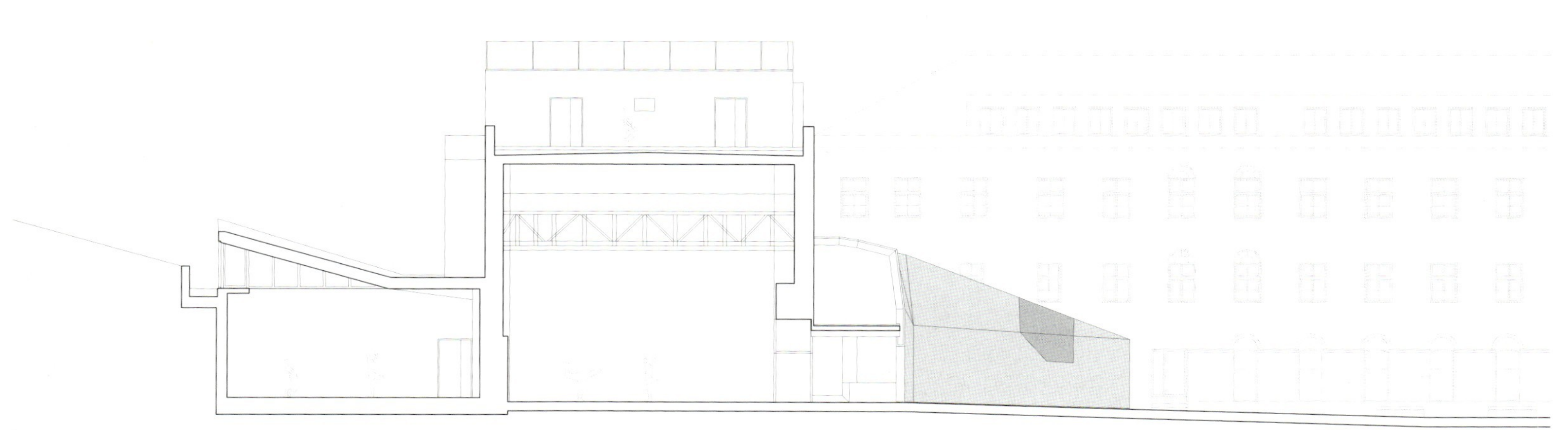

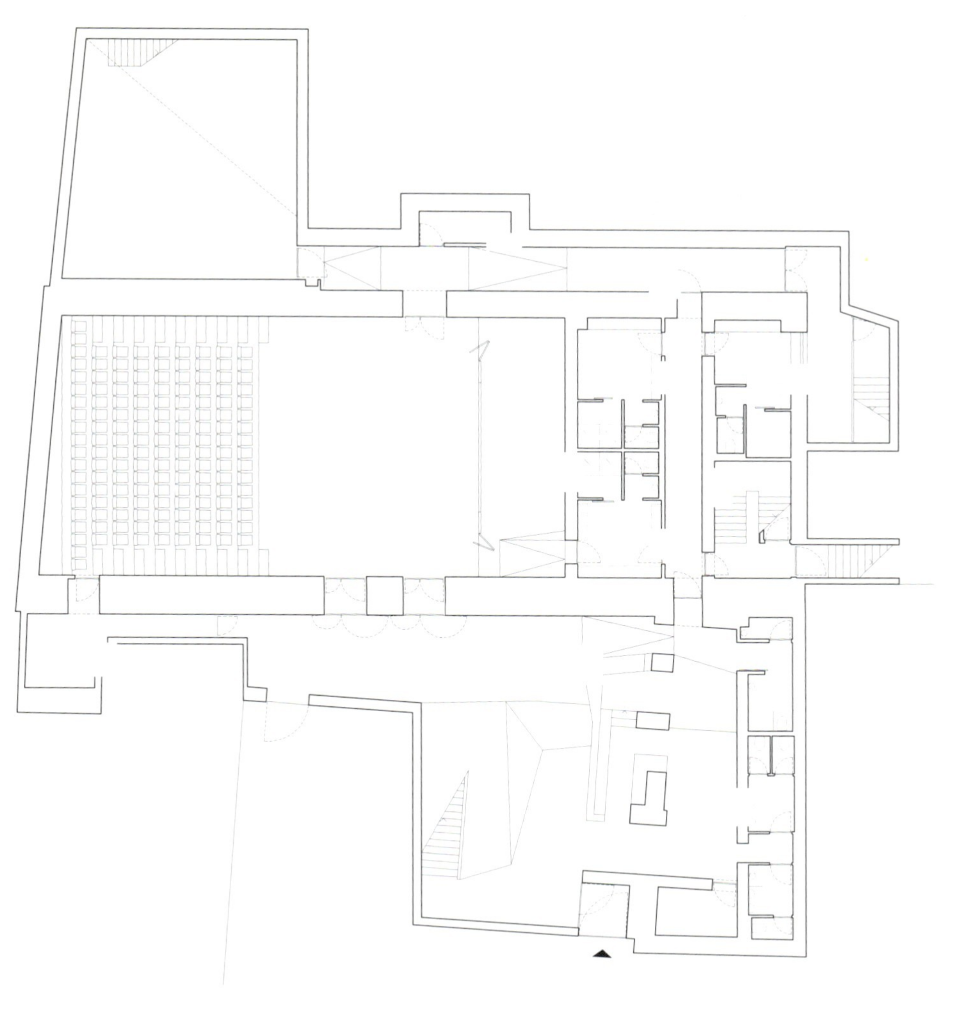

← | **Ground floor plan**

↓ | **Entrance lobby** and the gallery staircase

FloS und K architektur + urbanistik

↑ | View of the stage
→ | View of the theater boat

The Maria Helena Ship

Saarbrücken

The theater maker Frank Lion had the idea to turn an old pèniche into a theater ship. The challenge was to retain the character and charm of the old boat while completely changing its function. The conversion involved minimal changes in the exterior and the basic structure. Only the mobile corrugated steel plates which covered the stowage were replaced by a transparent construction and a new access to the theater space was opened in the upper deck. The old bulkhead walls, which are a striking feature of the interior, were emphasized by targeted lighting.

PROJECT FACTS

Address: Theaterschiff Maria Helena Liegeplatz Berliner Promenade, 66111 Saarbrücken, Germany. **Client:** Theaterkompanie Frank Lion. **Completion:** 2007. **Building type:** theater. **Gross floor area:** 215 m². **Original building:** architect unknown. **Client:** Frachtkahn (Pèniche). **Completion:** 1911. **Building type:** boat. **Gross floor area:** 245 m².

←← | **Entrance,** front
↙↙ | **Structure of entrance**
← | **Sidewall inside**
↓ | **Topview,** upper deck and lower deck

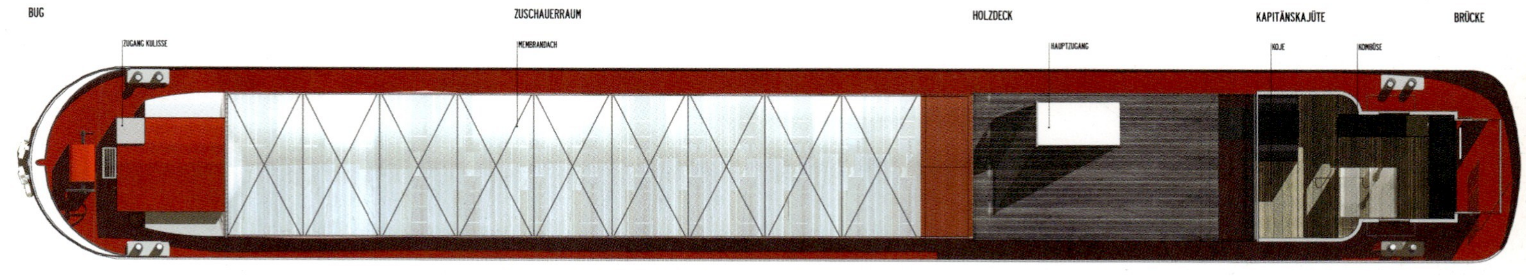

Vertex Architectuur en Stedenbouw / Otto Trienekens

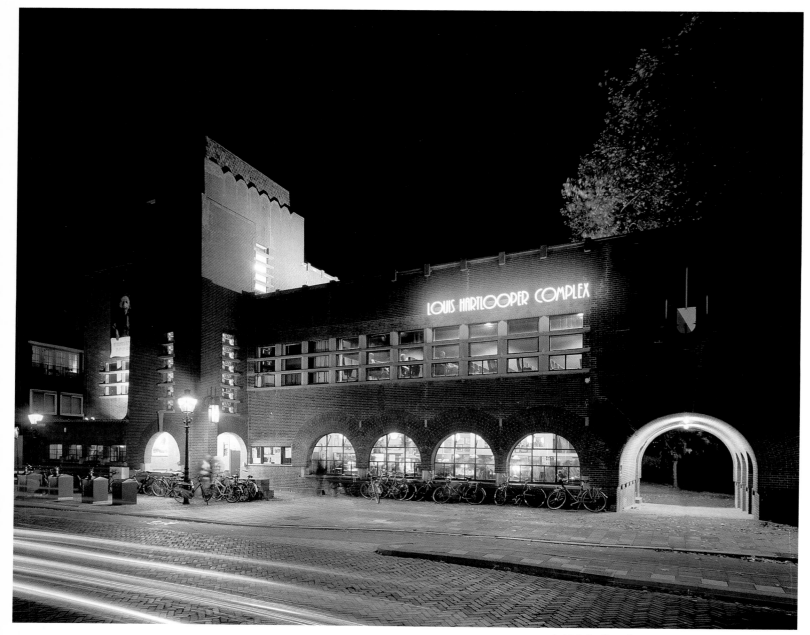

↑ | **Main façade**
→ | **Cinema 4 and cinema 1**
↓ | **Before conversion**

Louis Hartlooper Complex

Utrecht

The former police station enjoys the status of a national monument. Situated at the striking historical location where the medieval city gate once provided access to town, the building is part of the "Museums Quarter". Municipal policy focuses on reinforcing cultural and educational functions and providing public access to the cultural heritage of the developed environment. Thus the police station has been transformed into a center for cinema and culture, a public meeting place. Accommodation of the program implied a necessary redoubling of the floor space within the present boundaries of the lot. A two story and partly subterranean construction in the present courtyard contributes to this requirement.

PROJECT FACTS

Address: Tolsteegbrug 1, 3511 ZN Utrecht, The Netherlands. **Client:** Ledig Erfgoed b.v.. **Completion:** 2005. **Building type:** cinema. **Gross floor area:** 997 m^2.
Original building: Johannes Izak Planjer. **Client:** Municipality of Utrecht. **Completion:** 1928. **Building type:** police station. **Gross floor area:** 554 m^2.

↑ | **Hall**
← | **Section,** old situation
↙ | **Section,** new situation

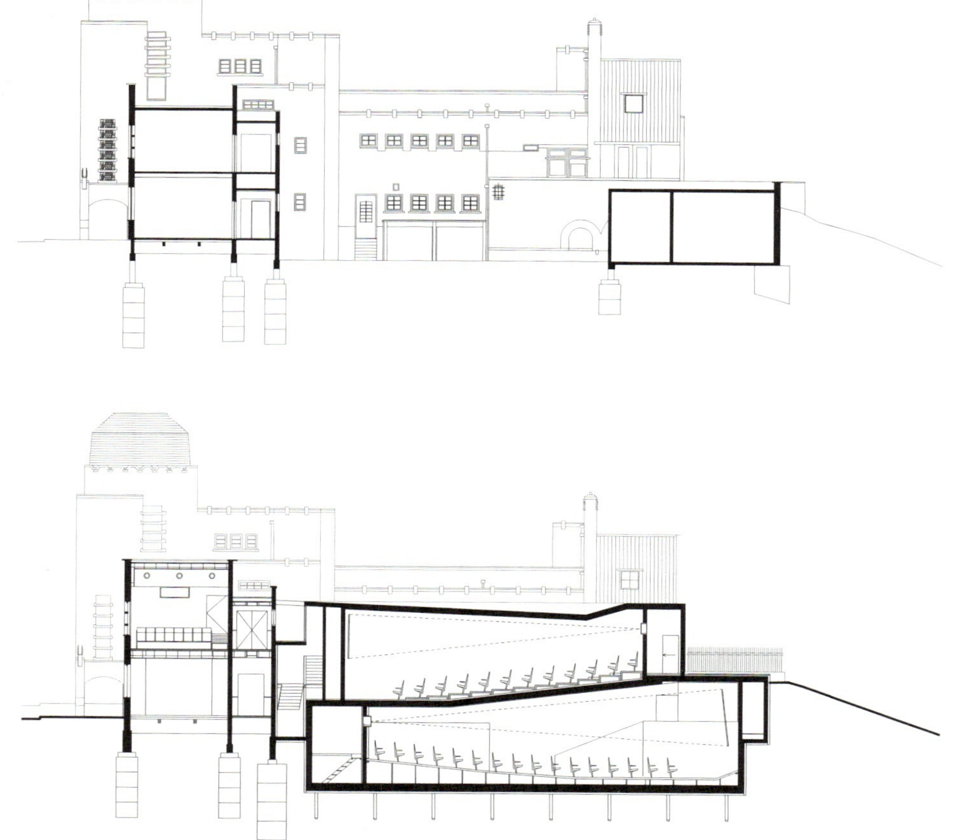

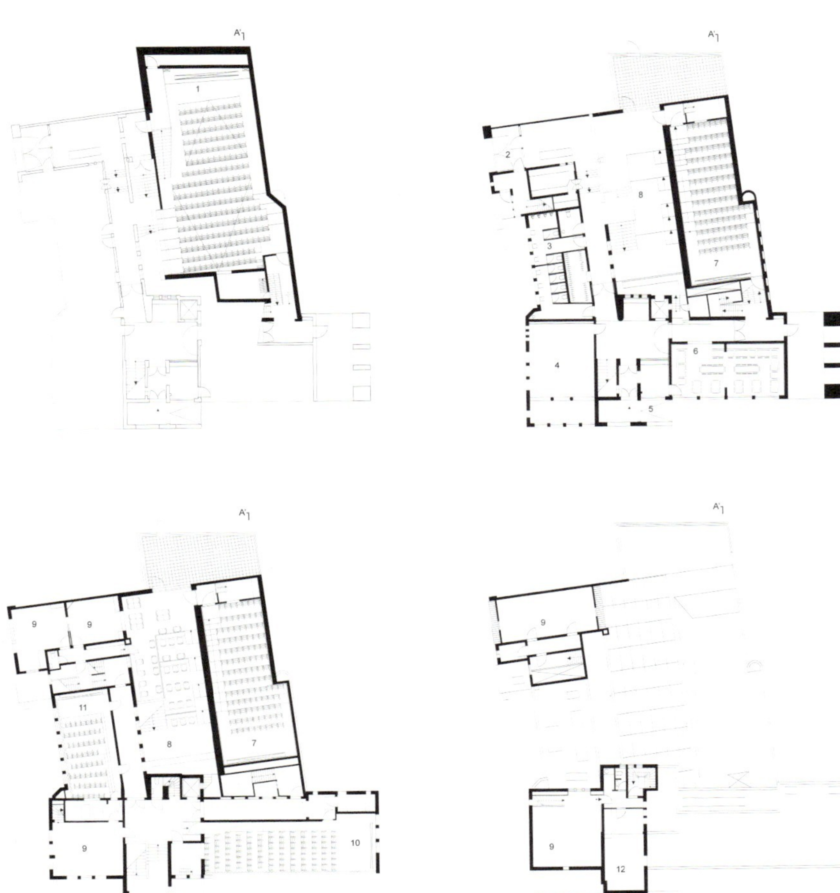

← | **Floor plans,** underground floor, ground floor, first floor, second floor
↙ | **Foyer,** inner court
↓ | **Foyer,** custom made furniture

CarriageWorks Contemporary Performing Arts Center

Eveleigh

↑ | **Main foyer,** the roof allows natural light to penetrate
↓ | **Historical view**
→ | **Interior view,** foyer

This former Carriage Workshop building has been transformed into an innovative center committed to the conception, development and presentation of performance. The architect's adaptive reuse embraces the past of the building whilst providing it with a bold new future. Three flexible theater spaces, rehearsal rooms, administrative offices, workshop space and amenities are housed in discrete concrete boxes, clearly articulated in the heritage fabric. The new forms stand free of rows of original cast iron columns, creating circulation routes in the interstitial spaces with views through the building. Linear entryway structures linking the theater spaces are like "ghosts" of the carriages that once moved through the building.

PROJECT FACTS

Address: 245 Wilson Street, Eveleigh, NSW 2015, Australia. **Client:** ArtsNSW. **Completion:** 2007. **Building type:** performing arts center. **Gross floor area:** 18,000 m^2.
Original building: George Cowdry. **Client:** unknown. **Completion:** early 1880s. **Building type:** railway workshops. **Gross floor area:** unknown.

↑ | **Interior view** from the upper level
↓ | **Sections**

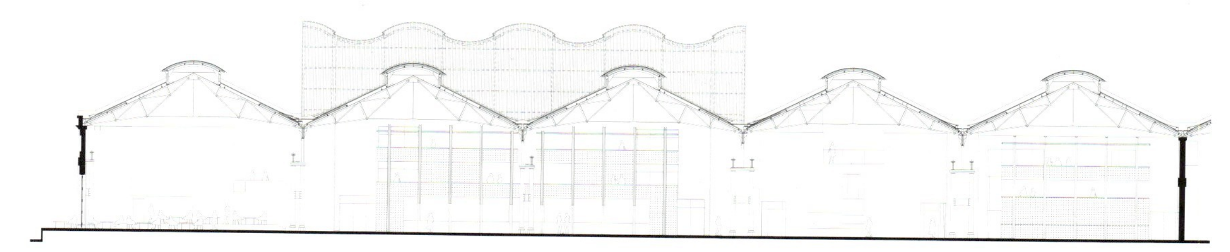

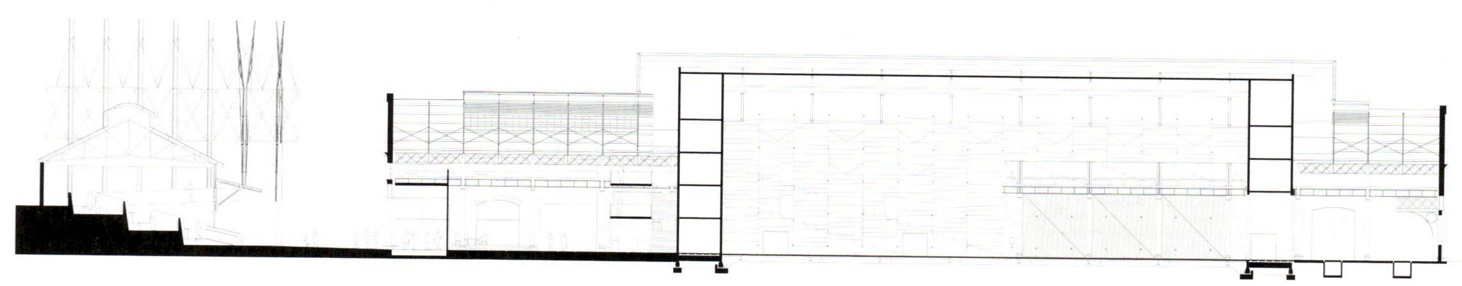

← | **New concrete surfaces** provide a canvas for playful shadows

↙ | **Exterior view by night,** new entry signage made from original trusses

Tham & Videgård Arkitekter / Bolle Tham, Martin Videgård

↑ | **Main façade**
↓ | **Section,** façade
→ | **Exterior by night**

Modern Museum Malmö

Malmö

This new art museum, housed within a former electricity plant, represents a rare opportunity to create a new focal point within the city, changing the urban balance and developing the surrounding neighborhood. In order to comply with the highest international standards for displaying art exhibitions, it soon became clear that a building within a building had to be built, a contemporary addition within the existing shell. This radical reconstruction provided a challenge as well as the opportunity to create something new. The extension provides a new entrance with a perforated, orange façade that connects to the existing brick architecture and introduces a contemporary element to the neighborhood.

PROJECT FACTS

Address: Gasverksgatan 22, 21129 Malmö, Sweden. **Client:** City of Malmö. **Completion:** 2009. **Building type:** museum. **Gross floor area:** 2,650 m^2.
Original building: John Smedberg. **Client:** Malmö stads Elektricitetsverk. **Completion:** 1900. **Building type:** electricity plant. **Gross floor area:** 2,430 m^2.

↖ | **Machine hall**
↑ | **Exhibition room,** "Monogram" by Robert Rauschenberg (1959)
← | **Plans**

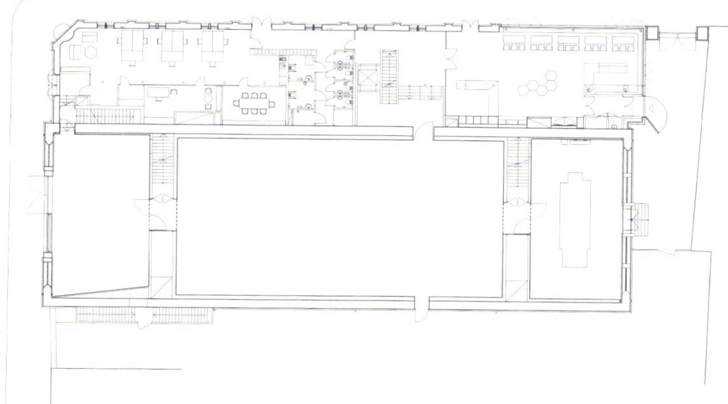

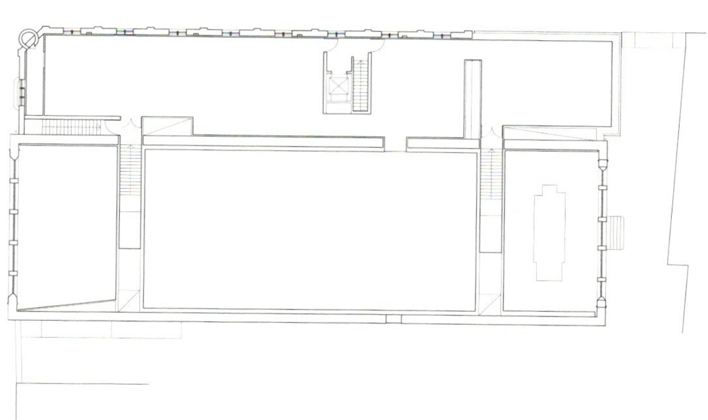

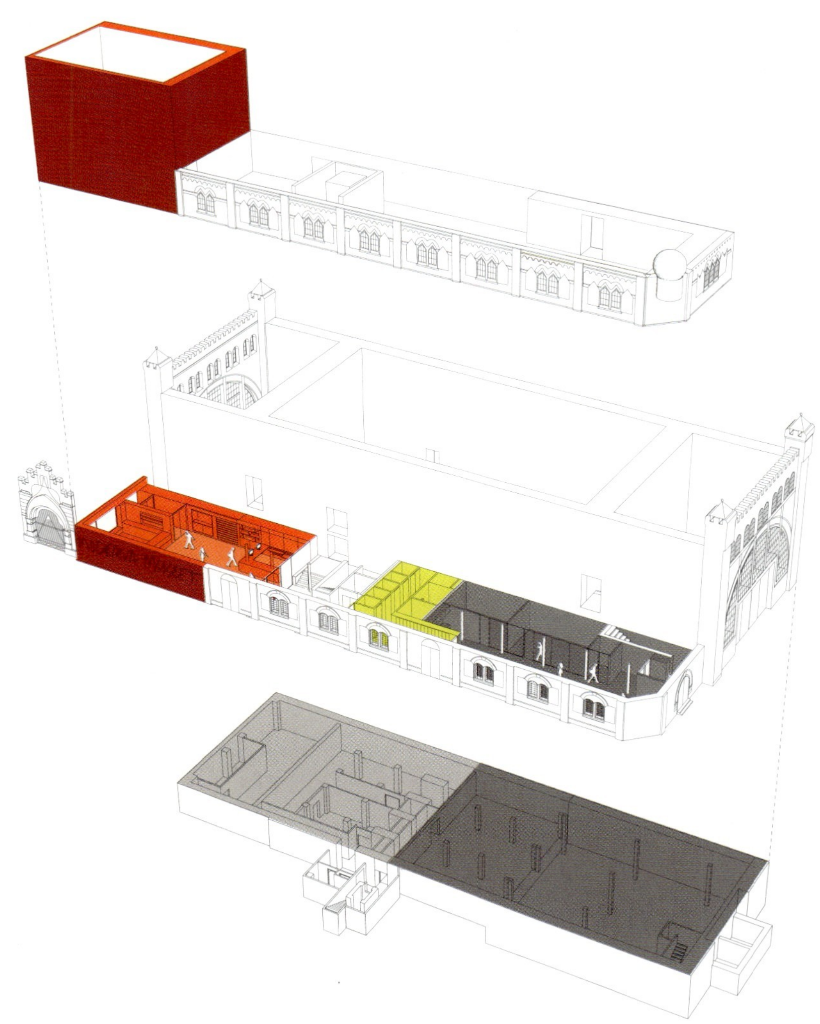

← | **3D drawing**
↓ | **Lettering of name of museum,** seen from café

Erick van Egeraat,
Frank Huibers

↑ | New entrance

Drents Museum

Assen

This new entrance and extension effectively integrate the museum into the fabric of the city, while a balanced play of building, landscape and water creates a new identity, emphasizing both the scenic character and the historic face of the city center. The new exhibition wing covers 2,000 square meters, all underground. Its staggered, organic roof consists of a public garden that connects to the existing city parks. The existing coach-house will serve as the new main entrance. Its historic facade will be left untouched, but the entire building will be lifted onto a spectacular glass plinth – allowing light to enter the building at daytime, and highlighting the building with interior lighting at night.

PROJECT FACTS

Address: Kloosterstraat, 9400 AC Assen, The Netherlands. **Client:** Province of Drenthe. **Completion:** 2011. **Building type:** museum. **Gross floor area:** 2,400 m^2.
Original building: architect unknown. **Client:** confidential. **Completion:** 1780. **Building type:** coach house. **Gross floor area:** 180 m^2.

↑ | Exterior view
↙ | Cross section

↓ | Exhibition hall

Brasil Arquitetura Studio with Anselmo Turazzi / Marcelo Ferraz, Francisco Fanucci

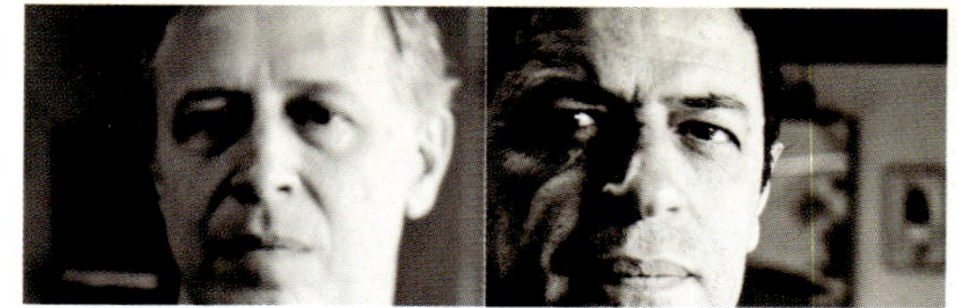

↑ | **New museum building**
↗ | **Interior of old mill,** with restored machinery
→ | **Old grain store,** transformed into a bar

Bread Museum and Ilópolis Mill

Ilópolis

This Bread Museum represents the founding stone of the "Route of the Taquari Valley Mills". The 100-year-old Ilópolis Mill was condemned to destruction after the miller's death, but has been given a neu life by the Bread Museum and Bakery Workshop, and has successfully been reintegrated into the small town's life. The new constructions were inspired by the old. The raw pine boards used as formwork for the exposed concrete, irreversibly left their marks upon the new. Here, museography and architecture arise simultaneously. The first exhibits are the old Mill itself, then the structure of the new volumes, their urban scale, the way the light enters, the materials, the timber walkways, the supports for the exhibits and, last but not least, the pieces on exhibition, collected from the region.

PROJECT FACTS

Address: Rua Padre Kolling, Ilópolis 95990-000, Rio Grande do Sul, Brazil. **Client:** Friends of the Taquari Valley Mills Association. **Completion:** 2007. **Building type:** museum. **Gross floor area:** new buildings 320 m², old mill 340 m².

Original building: Garibaldi Bertuol. **Client:** Tomasini & Baú. **Completion:** 1910. **Building type:** mill. **Gross floor area:** 330 m².

↑ | **Interior,** concrete and timber column in the museum
← | **Garden with mill stones**
↓ | **Ground floor plan**

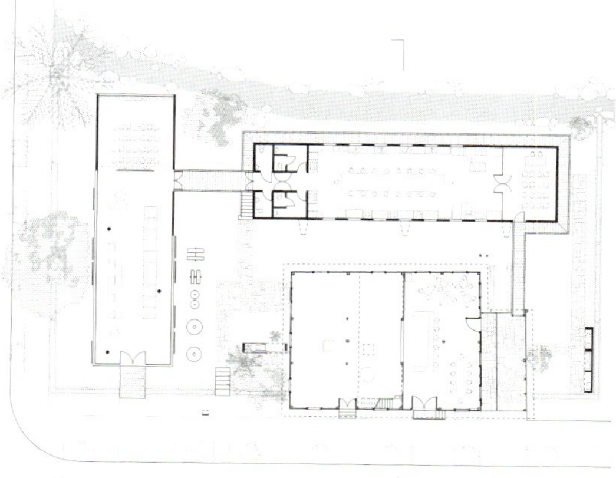

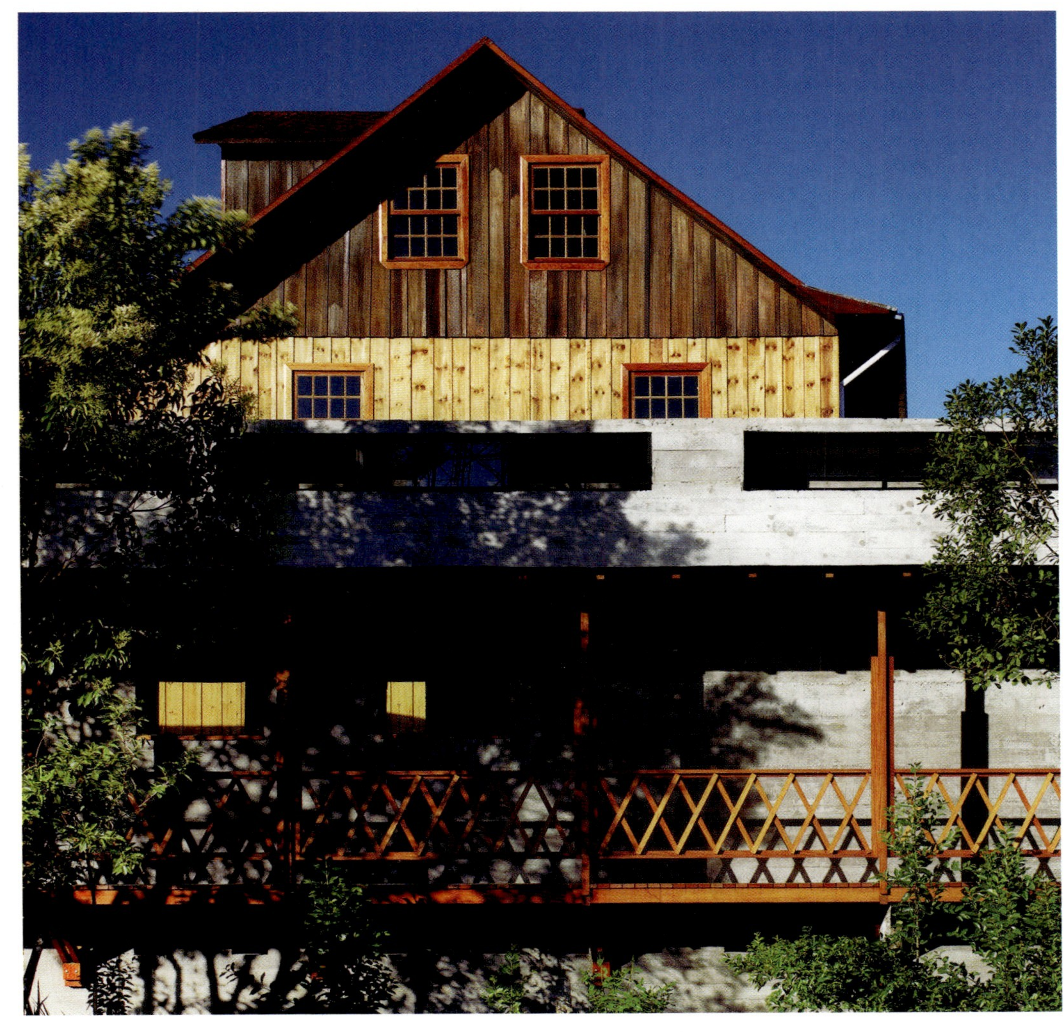

← | **Passageway outside of Bakery Workshop**

↓ | **Sketch of the main façade** of the museum and the old mill

BIG /
David Zahle, Bjarke Ingels

↑ | Overview of courtyard
↓ | Upper and lower level

Danish Maritime Museum

Helsingborg

The museum had to find its place in a unique historic and spatial context; between Kronborg Castle and a new, ambitious cultural center, while at the same time manifesting itself as an independent institution. In this context the building will be built as a subterranean museum around a former dry-dock that will be preserved as an open, outdoor display in order to maintain the powerful building structure as the core of the Maritime Museum. This is the basis of the layout of the entire museum. Bridges and ramps structurally and sculpturally traverse the air space, allowing visitors to penetrate the depth of the room.

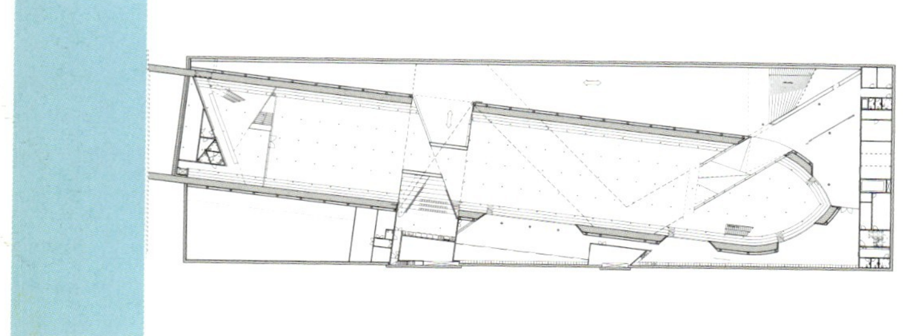

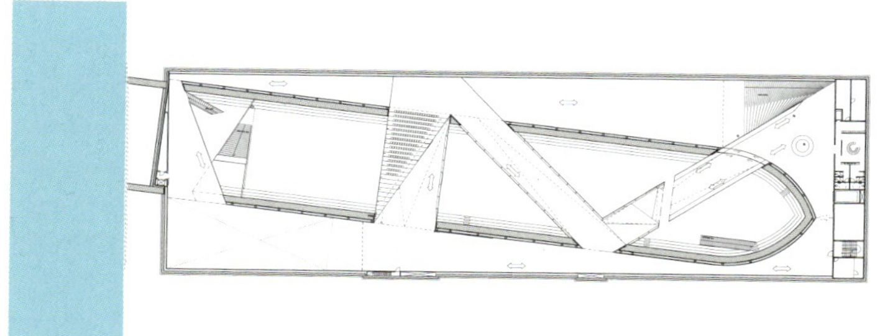

PROJECT FACTS

Address: Kronborgvej, 99999 Helsingborg, Denmark. **Client:** Maritime Museum Foundation. **Completion:** 2011. **Building type:** museum. **Gross floor area:** 7,200 m².
Original building: architect unknown. **Client:** Elsinore Shipyard. **Completion:** 1953. **Building type:** dry dock. **Gross floor area:** unknown.

↑ | **Staircase system in the museum,** view into the courtyard

↓ | **Subterranean courtyard**

Studio Daniel Libeskind

↑ | Evening view
↗ | Plaza
→ | Closeup of Yud and Plaza
↘ | Conversion process

Contemporary Jewish Museum

San Francisco

Housed in the abandoned late 19th-century Jessie Street power substation, updated in the first decade of the 20th century by Willis Polk, and landmarked in 1976, this museum literally creates visible relationships between new and old, between tradition and innovation, between the past, present and future, bringing together 19th, 20th and 21st century architecture into one building in the process. The CJM's design is based on the Hebrew expression "L'Chaim," which means "To Life." The building is based on new spaces created [illegible] tters of the chai: the chet provides an overall continuity for the exhibition and [illegible] spaces, and the yud, with its 36 windows, provides a pedestrian connector.

PROJECT FACTS

Address: 736, Mission Street, San Francisco, CA 94103, USA. **Architect of record:** WRNS. **Client:** The Contemporary Jewish Museum San Francisco. **Completion:** 2008. **Building type:** museum. **Gross floor area:** 5,850 m².

Original building: architect unknown. **Client:** unknown. **Completion:** unknown. **Building type:** power substation. **Gross floor area:** unknown.

↖ | **The Yud**, has 36 diamond shaped windows
↑ | **Lobby**
↓ | **Ground floor plan**

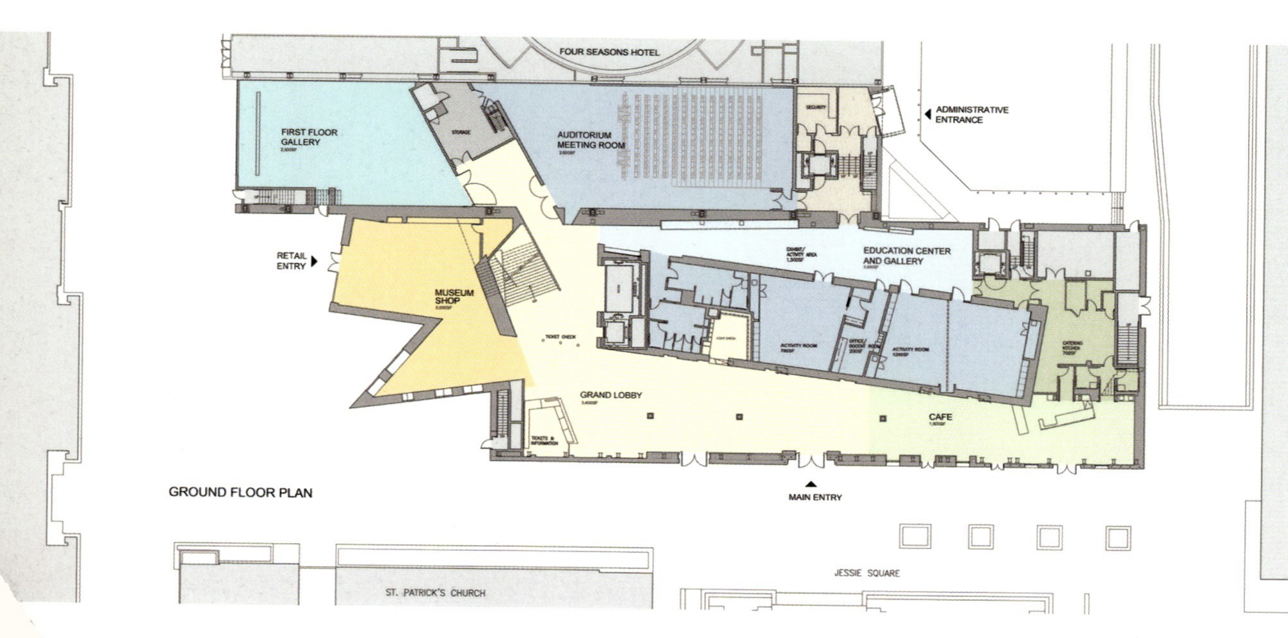

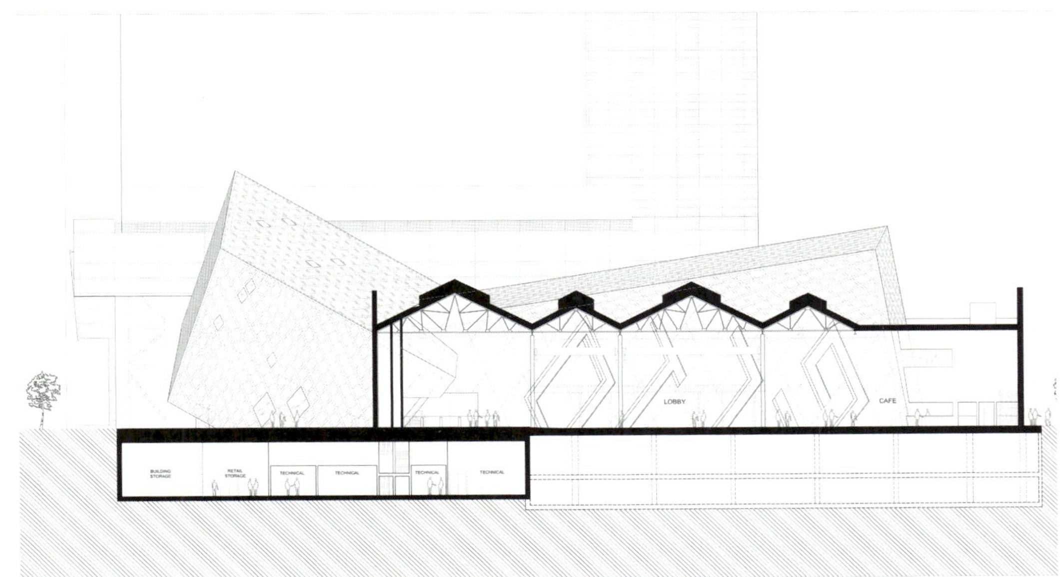

← | Longitudinal section
↓ | Gallery

Studio Daniel Libeskind

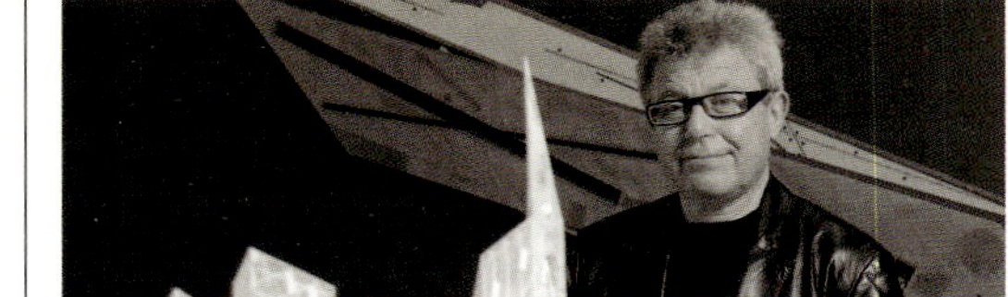

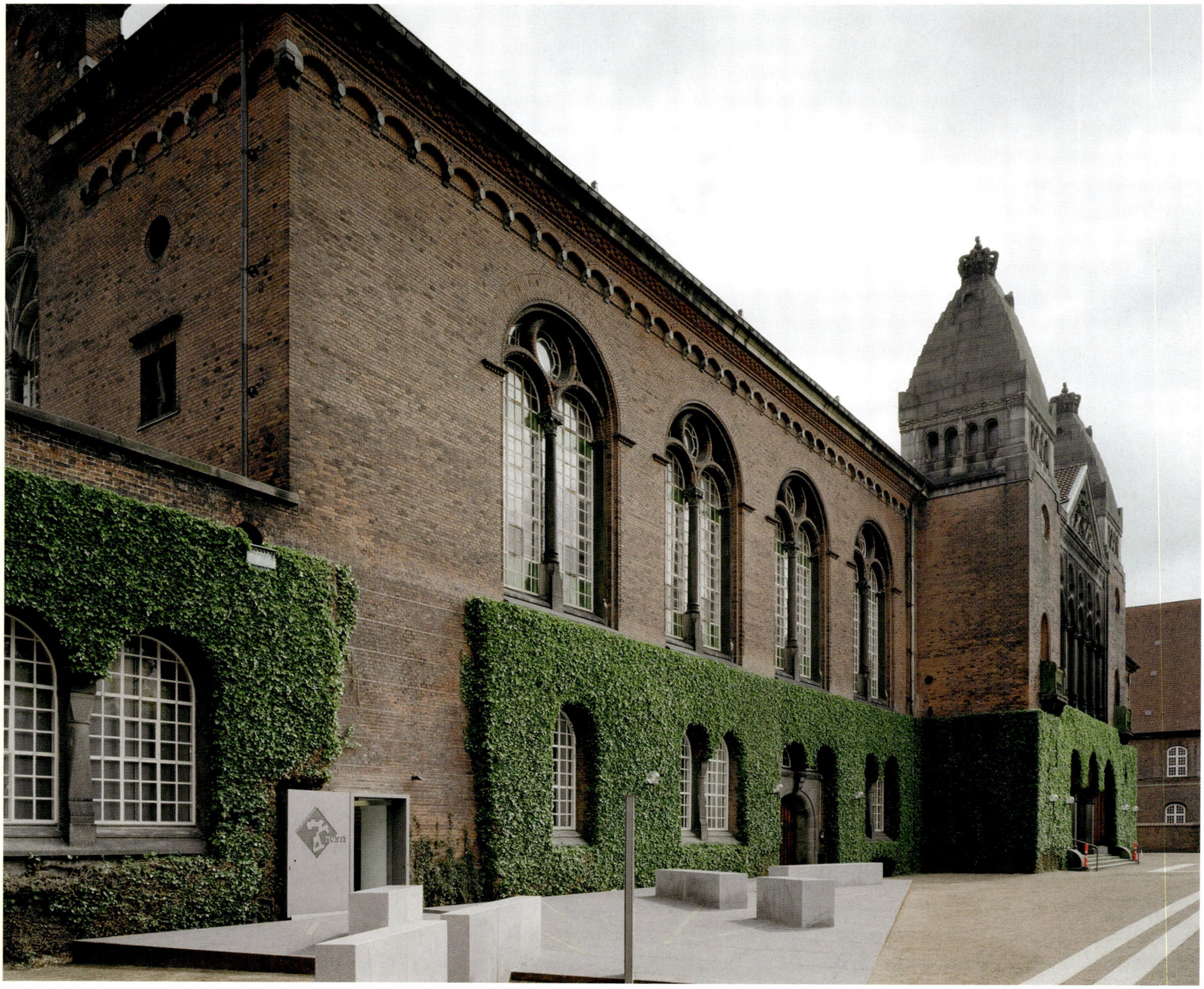

↑ | **Exterior view**
→ | **Exhibition,** ancient brick walls

Danish Jewish Museum

Copenhagen

This museum is dedicated to recording the history of Jewish life in Denmark starting in the 17th century. Located in one of the oldest parts of Copenhagen, the museum is housed in a 17th century structure, built by King Christian IV. The architects designed the museum's interior space while preserving the original building. Visitors enter an architectural structure in which the artifacts are seamlessly organized. The entire building has been conceived as an adventure, both physical and spiritual, in tracing the lineaments that reveal the intersection of different histories and aspects of Jewish culture.

PROJECT FACTS

Address: The Royal Library Garden, Proviantpassagen 6, 1218 Copenhagen, Denmark. **Renovation of Galejhuset:** Fogh & Følner Arkitektfirma. **Client:** Danish Jewish Museum. **Completion:** 2003. **Building type:** museum. **Gross floor area:** 450 m².

Original building: diffrent architects. **Client:** King of Denmark. **Completion:** beginning 17th century, 1906, end 20th century. **Building type:** royal boat house, royal library, black diamond. **Gross floor area:** unknown.

↖↑ | Exhibition space

← | Ground floor plan

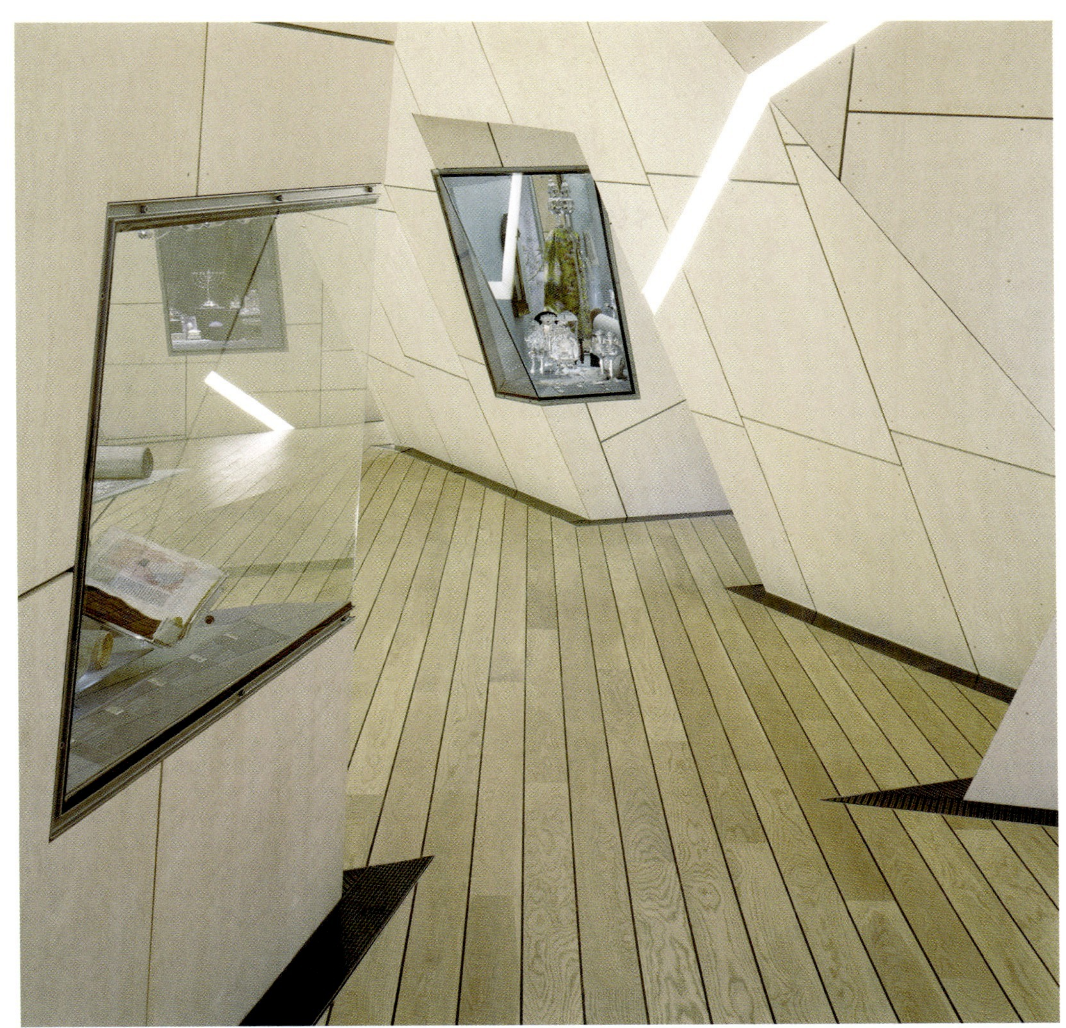

← | Detail of vitrine

↓ | Interior elevations and detail of vitrines

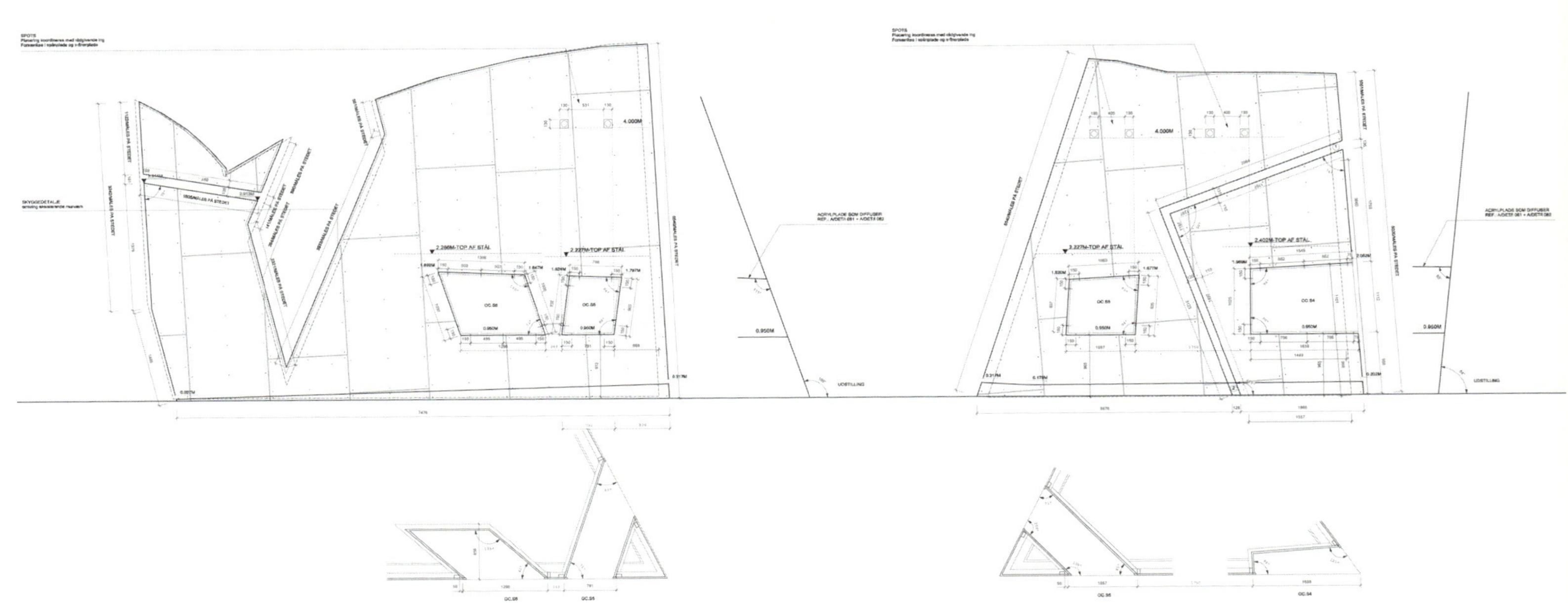

CAFÉ

HOTEL
RESTAURANT

Takenouchi Webb / Naoko Takenouchi, Marc Webb

↑ | Main dining space and bar

The White Rabbit

Singapore

The architects were inspired by traditional British public school dining halls and church buildings. The primary goal was to retain the simplicity and beauty of the existing space and restore as many of the details as possible. The solution was to draw a clear line between the old and new parts of the building by detaching the new elements away from the existing. The architects chose natural materials such as copper, steel, marble and timber, which were left as raw as possible to complement the texture of the existing building. The original ceiling soffit was replaced with identical paneling, the decorative steel window grilles restored with clear glass added to the openings. The original paintwork was matched and the mosaic floor cleaned and restored.

PROJECT FACTS

Address: 39C Harding Road, Singapore 249541, Singapore. **Client:** The Lo & Behold Group. **Completion:** 2008. **Building type:** restaurant. **Gross floor area:** 540 m^2.
Original building: architect unknown. **Client:** British Army. **Completion:** 1930s. **Building type:** church. **Gross floor area:** 360 m^2.

↑ | Conservatory

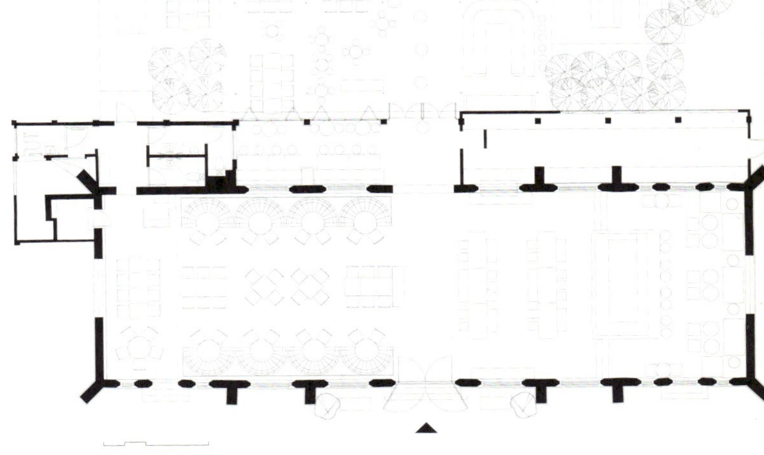

↑ | Floor plan
↓ | Lounge bar

Pi de Bruijn,
de Architekten Cie.

↑ | View from riverside
→ | View from platform

Café-restaurant OPEN

Amsterdam

OPEN café-restaurant is a pure, transparent, glass volume that fits precisely onto the existing bridge. It is composed of a floor, a roof and a glazed façade formed entirely by pivotal windows, all of which can be opened. The pivotal windows add a subtle refinement to the principle of the purist, modernist box, introducing the quality of elegant, undulating movement. Two detached green volumes inside contain the kitchen, cloakroom, toilets and bar. A pleated wooden ribbon meanders along the inside of the glazed façade, constituting in succession benches, a bar with seating, and railing. A staircase and a lift attached to the no longer functional brick pillar on the quayside, provide access to an outdoor serving area on top of it.

PROJECT FACTS

Address: Westerdoksplein 20-Brug, 1013 AZ Amsterdam, The Netherlands. **Client:** Stichting OPEN brug. **Completion:** 2008. **Building type:** café-restaurant. **Gross floor area:** 270 m². **Original building:** architect unknown. **Client:** unknown. **Completion:** 1922. **Building type:** railway bridge. **Gross floor area:** unknown.

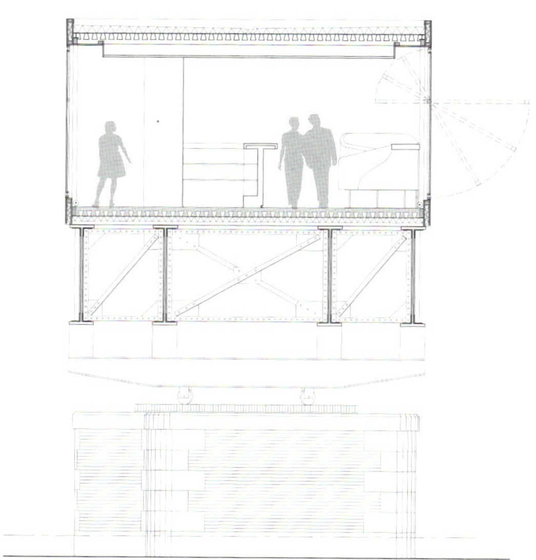

↖ | **The transparent glass volume** that fits precisely onto the existing bridge
↑ | **Cross section**
← | **Elevation**

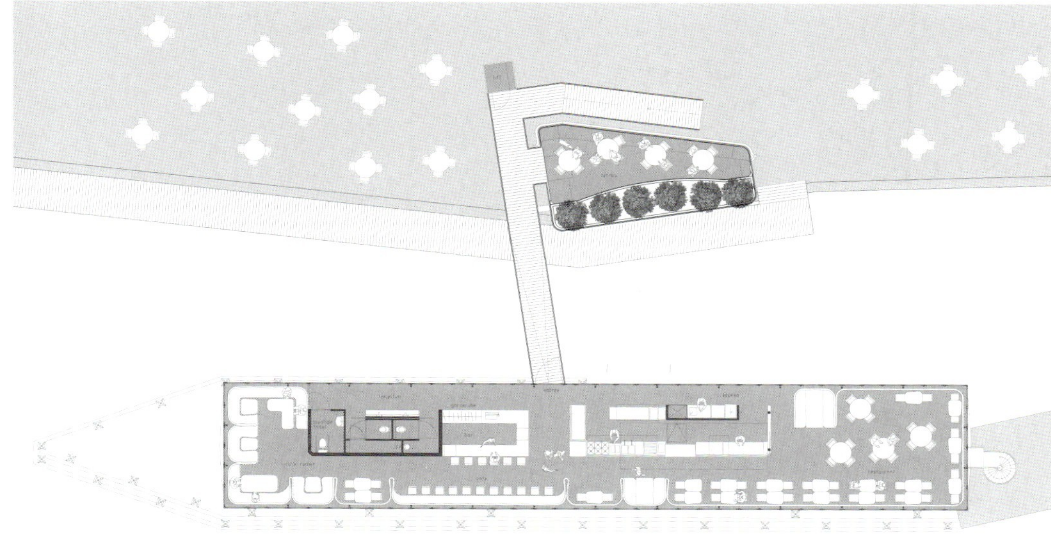

← | **Ground floor plan**
↓ | **Glazed façade,** formed entirely of pivotal windows, all of which can be opened

Studio Ramin Visch

↑ | Bar
→ | Bird's-eye view

Espressofabriek

Amsterdam

The architect has placed the new box lengthways with respect to the building, which is listed for preservation. There is storage space behind the bar and the entrance to the toilets is located at one end. Next to the building entrance, a staircase rises to the seating area above. Tables and chairs are grouped along the length of the space as well as above the bar. The relatively large height of the Meterhuis roof made it possible to create a second story beneath it. The materials of the box, with its surfaces treated with blackboard paint and a refreshment bar in stainless steel, contrast with those of the original architecture. Should the building ever be assigned a different function, the box could be extracted again without great effort.

PROJECT FACTS

Address: Gosschalklaan 7, 1014 DC Amsterdam, The Netherlands. **Client:** Rick W. Woertman. **Completion:** 2006. **Building type:** espressobar. **Gross floor area:** 76 m^2.
Original building: Isaaac Gosschalk. **Client:** GEB (municipal energy company Amsterdam). **Completion:** 1885. **Building type:** gas meter house. **Gross floor area:** 58 m^2.

↖ | **Bar area** with view to the entrance area
← | **Two-story bar**
↓ | **Sketch**

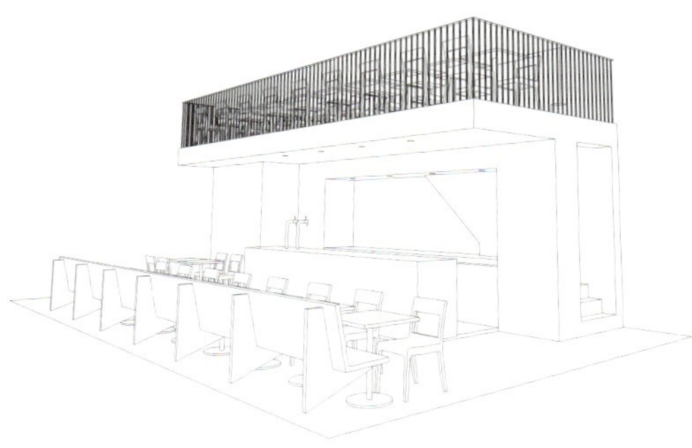

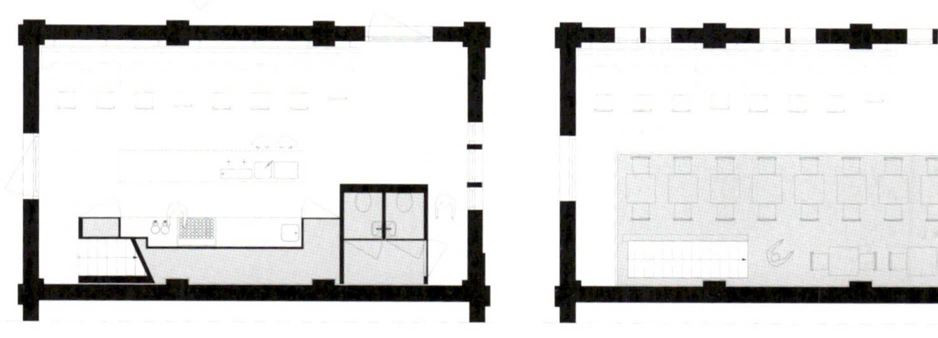

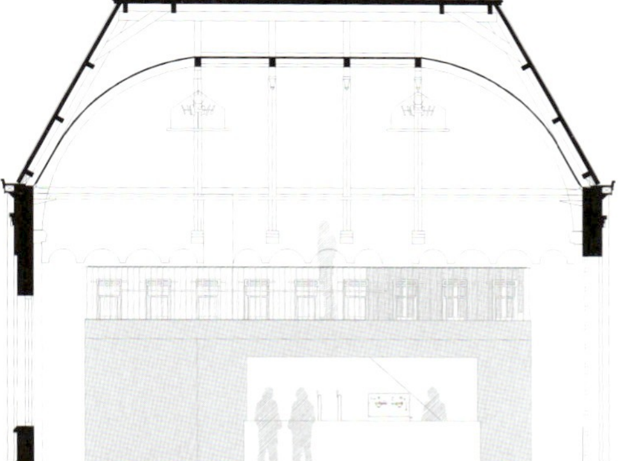

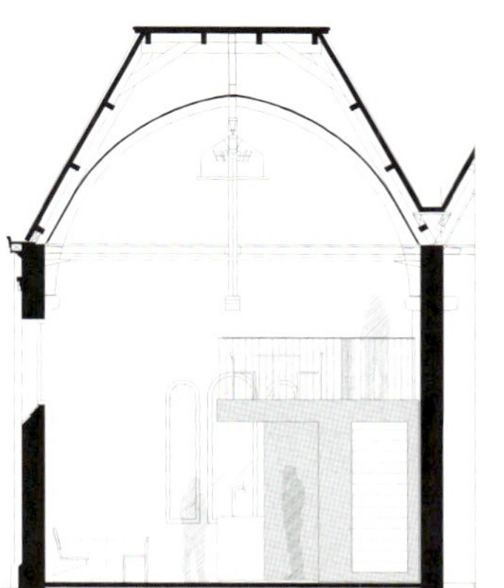

↖ | Floor plans
← | Sections
↓ | View from above

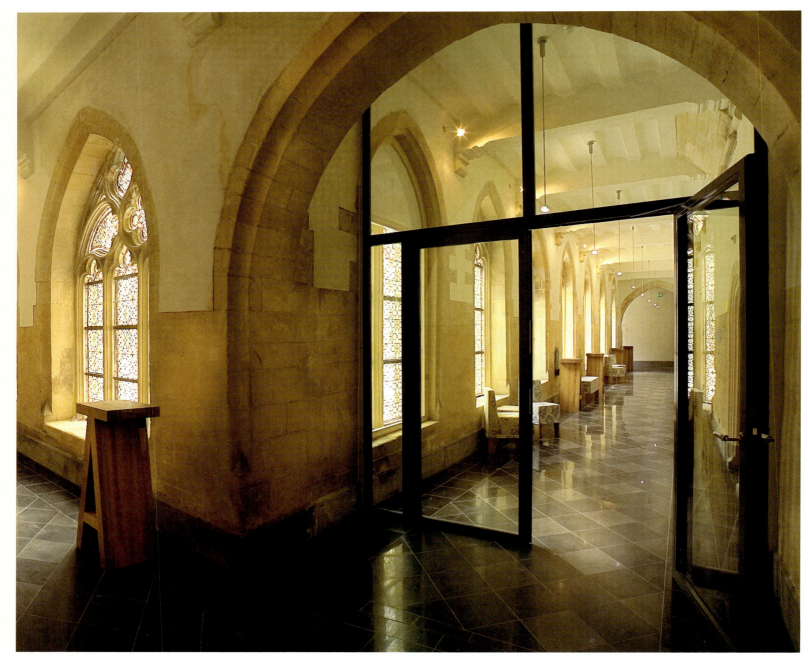

↑ | Gallery

Kruisherenhotel

Maastricht

The renovated monastery of the Crutched Friars is now a design hotel and offers a wealth of a veritable Gothic exterior with a sleek, modern interior. The complex consists of the original monastery, as well as a Gothic church, which now houses the reception area, including conference rooms, a library and a coffee bar. Many innovative solutions for structural challenges, like a glass elevator connecting the church to the monastery area, only confirm the notion that the sobriety of modern style forms a match for a late-medieval architectural expression of religious virtue. Another feature is the newly installed mezzanine which offers a spectacular view through the chancel windows.

PROJECT FACTS

Address: Kruisherengang 19–23, 6211 NW Maastricht, The Netherlands. **Interior designer:** Maupertuus / Henk Vos. **Client:** Stichting Monumentaal Erfgoed Limburg, Valkenburg a/d Geul. **Completion:** 2005. **Building type:** hotel. **Gross floor area:** 5,000 m².
Original building: architect unknown. **Client:** The Crutched Friars. **Completion:** 15th century. **Building type:** monastery. **Gross floor area:** 4,600 m².

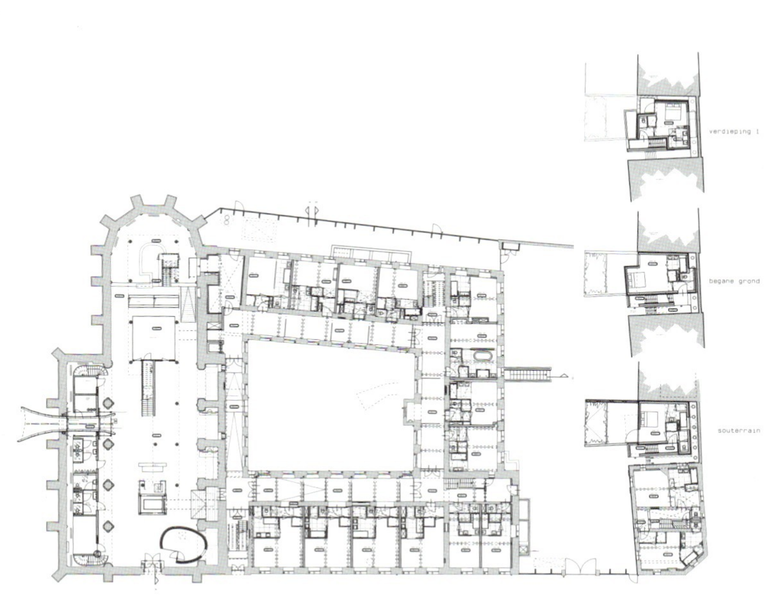

↑ | Ground floor plan
↓ | Mezzanine elevator

↑ | Mezzanine
↓ | Restaurant area

24H architecture / Maartje Lammers, Boris Zeisser

↑ | **Main façade**
↓ | **Reception**

Court Hostel

London

24H architecture developed the reconfiguration of a former courthouse with listed interior as a design-youth-hotel with 600 beds in the center of London. The main issue was to design the building access in order to provide guests with orientation. Main corridors are connected as a ring with sub corridors as wings. Each section has its own language and atmosphere to create vertical and horizontal differences. The rooms are designed according to themes. The internet room, lounge bar and reception are located in monumental former courtrooms and their design is related to each other with the new functions integrated in low-tech-looking volumes.

PROJECT FACTS

Address: 78 Kings Cross Road, London WC1X 9QG, United Kingdom. **Client:** Hostel UK Ltd. **Completion:** 2008. **Building type:** hostel. **Gross floor area:** 4,000 m².
Original building: architect unknown. **Client:** unknown. **Completion:** unknown. **Building type:** courthouse. **Gross floor area:** unknown.

↑ | **Historic decoration**

↑ | **Beds,** purple floor
↓ | **Section**

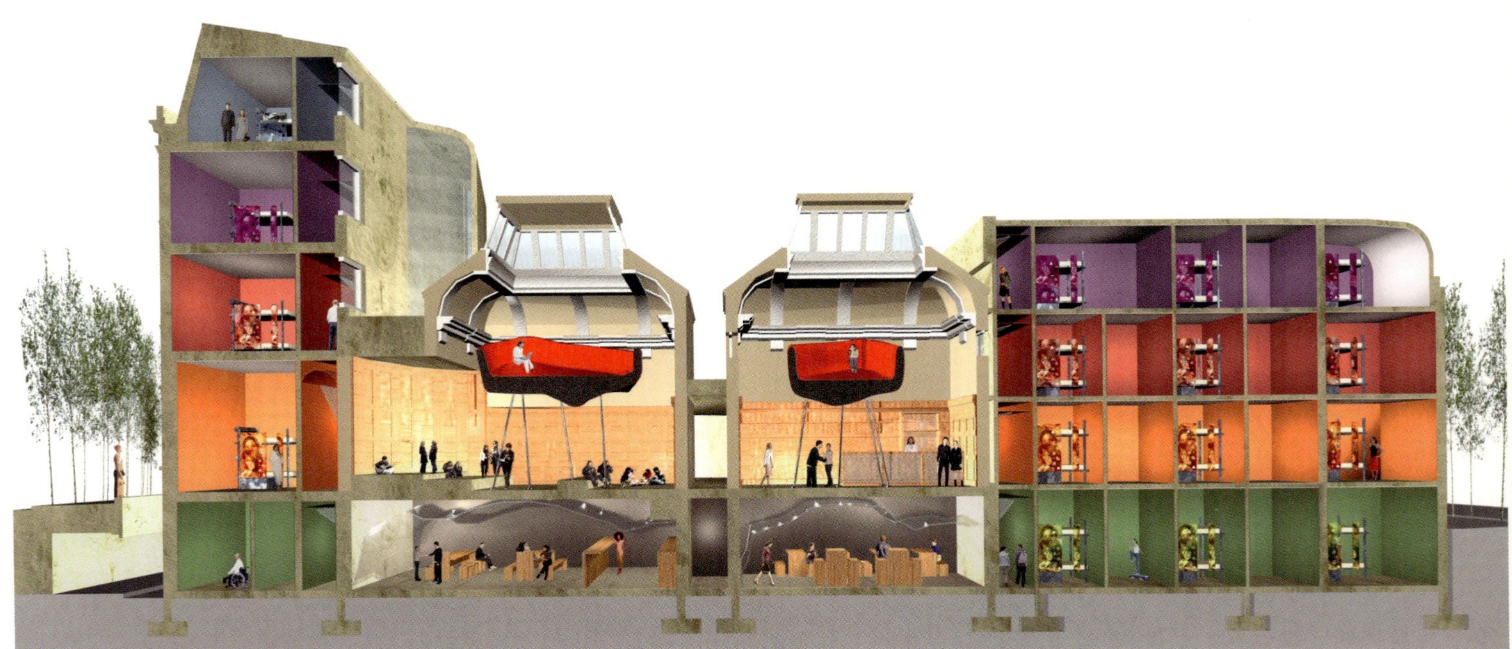

RCR Arquitectes

↑ | Exterior view
→ | View into restaurant

Les Cols

Olot, Girona

The architects have redesigned an old farmhouse, turning it into an esthetic and culinary experience. The traditional common room is reborn as an opulent banqueting hall whose walls and 20 meter-table are bedecked with gold. As its polar opposite, five hotel pavilions with minimalist glass architecture were built on the adjacent grounds. The construction of L-shaped steel supports allows for the walls as well as floors and ceilings to be designed as glass surfaces, hiding the furniture – except for the membrane of the mattress. A meditative space contained by semi-translucent glass shimmering in green is what emerges.

PROJECT FACTS

Address: Mas les Cols - Ctra. de la Canya, s/n, 17800 Olot, Girona, Spain. **Client:** Restaurant Les Cols. **Completion:** 2005. **Building type:** hotel, restaurant. **Gross floor area:** 225 m². **Original building:** architect unknown. **Client:** unknown. **Completion:** 17th century. **Building type:** farmhouse. **Gross floor area:** 223 m².

↑ | Banqueting hall

← | Sections

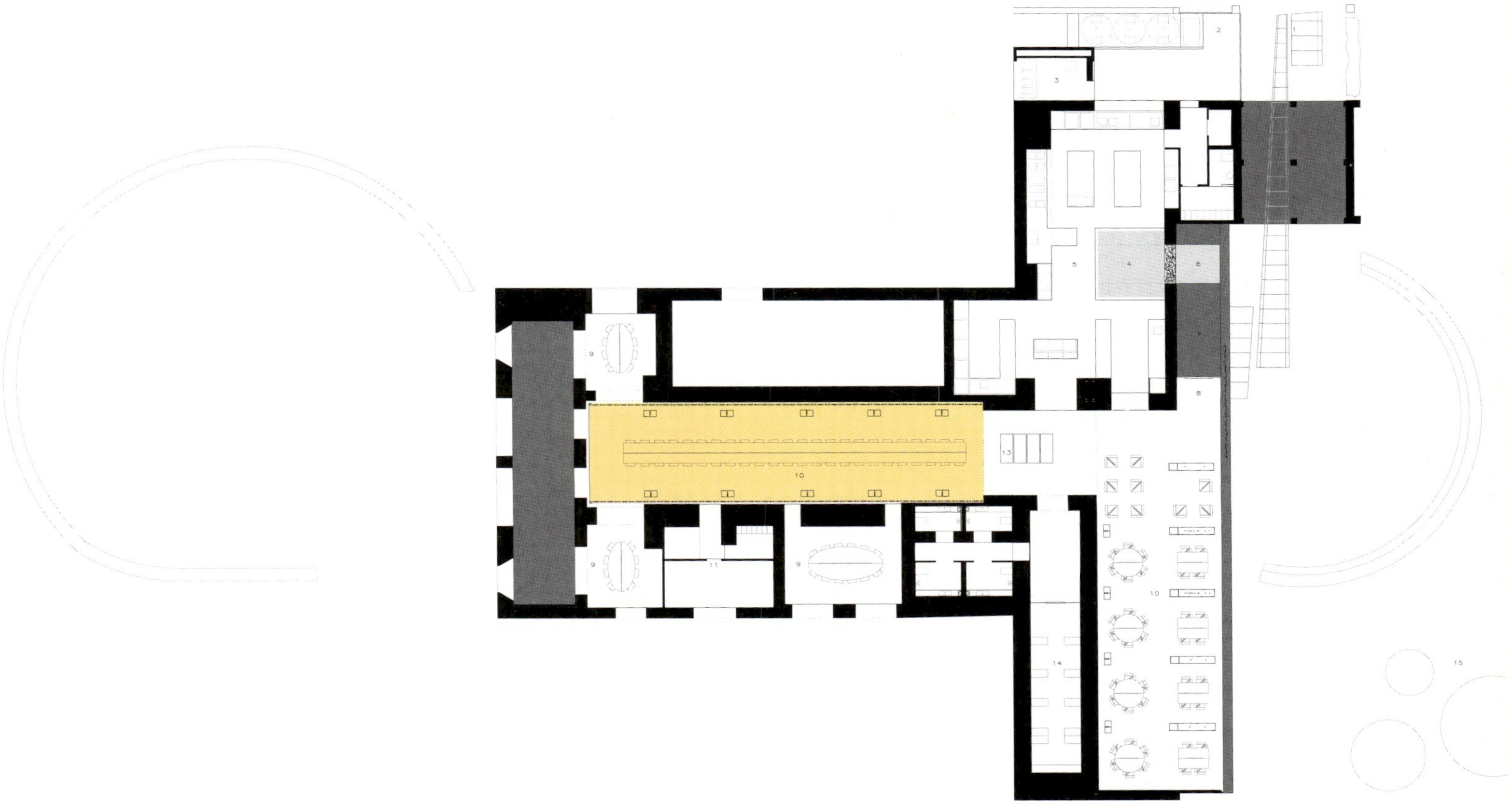

↑ | Ground floor plan
← | Detail of the golden wall

Jestico + Whiles /
James Dilley, John Whiles,
Vivien O'Brien

↑ | **Exterior,** entrance
→ | **Atrium**

Andel's Lodz

Lodz

The design has been developed in close consultation with the conservation authorities of Lodz and unlocks the true potential of the building. It blends a new, contemporary style and the existing arched ceilings, brick walls and cast iron frame to create a unique, elegant and inspiring hotel. The colors, textiles, art, sculptural features and furniture are conceived as contemporary interventions within the historic structure, transforming the factory into a gallery-like hotel which along with fun, excitement surprise and wit, also providescomfort and luxury. The hotel includes 180 bedrooms, 80 long stay apartments, a four level atrium, stylish bar, café, restaurant with a business center and a grand conference room for 600 guests.

PROJECT FACTS

Address: ul Ogrodowa 17, 91065 Lodz, Poland. **Interior Design:** Jestico + Whiles. **Client:** Warimpex. **Completion:** 2009. **Building type:** hotel. **Gross floor area:** 18,600 m^2.
Original building: Hilary Majewski. **Client:** Izrael Poznanaski. **Completion:** 1852. **Building type:** textile factory. **Gross floor area:** 18,600 m^2.

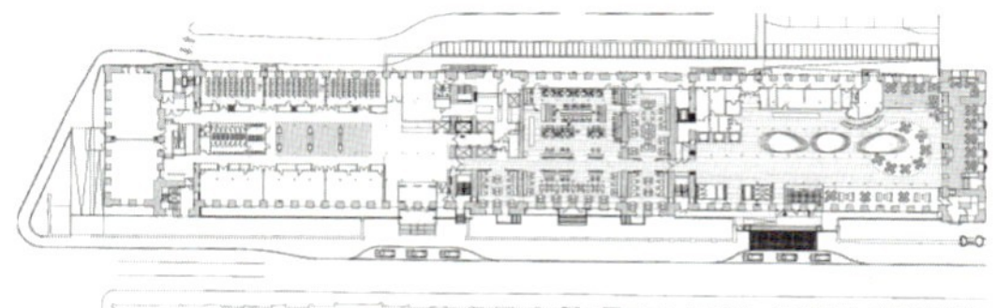

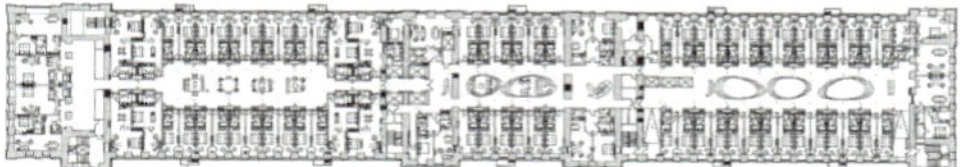

←← | **Superior Twin Room**
↙↙ | **Delight Restaurant**
← | **Plans,** first floor, ground floor
↙ | **Oscars Bar**
↓ | **Restaurant**

↑ | **Exterior view,** old and new rear elevation

Grand Hotel Casselbergh

Bruges

With its central location and rich history, this site is of major importance to the World Heritage City of Bruges. Tourism is an important engine of the local economy. The conversion of this building into a hotel with conference facilities will finally, after many years, remove an eyesore from the Hoogstraat. The project consists of two parts: the renovation of the three historic buildings and a new development. The modern development replaces a property of little value built in the 20th century. The new addition to the cityscape of Bruges is conceived as a bronze treasure chest set with gems. The architectural form of a box with a chamfered roof can also be found in the Bruge Belfort.

PROJECT FACTS

Address: Hoogstraat 6–8, 8000 Bruges, Belgium. **Client:** Project Planning Degroote nv. **Completion:** 2010. **Building type:** hotel. **Gross floor area:** 10,207 m².
Original building: architect unknown. **Client:** unknown. **Completion:** 14th century. **Building type:** townhouse. **Gross floor area:** 10,207 m².

↑ | **Elevation**

↑ | **Exterior view**
↓ | **Façade**

Serie Architects /
Chris Lee, Kapil Gupta

↑ | Banquet hall
→ | Detail tree structure

The Tote

Mumbai

A series of disused buildings from Mumbai's colonial past set within the Mumbai Race Course have been converted into a series of restaurant and bars. The conservation guidelines call for the preservation of the roof profile for three-quarters of the buildings and full conservation for the remaining one-quarter. However the most interesting aspect of the site lies in the open spaces covered by mature rain trees. These spaces are shaded throughout the year by the wide spread leaves of the rain trees, allowing almost the entire program to occur outdoors. The building attempts to continue this idea of a continuously differentiated space, with no clear boundary, into the envelope of the conservation building. A new structure within the old building envelope adopts that of a tree-branch.

PROJECT FACTS

Address: Keshva Rao Khadye Marg, Mahalakshmi, Mumbai 400 034, India. **Client:** DeGustibus Hotels Pvt. Ltd. **Completion:** 2009. **Building type:** banqueting hall, restaurant, bar. **Gross floor area:** 2,500 m². **Original building:** architect unknown. **Client:** Royal Western India Turf Club. **Completion:** 1890. **Building type:** betting stand and administrative offices. **Gross floor area:** 2,500 m².

↑ | **Exterior,** night view
↓ | **Ground floor plan**

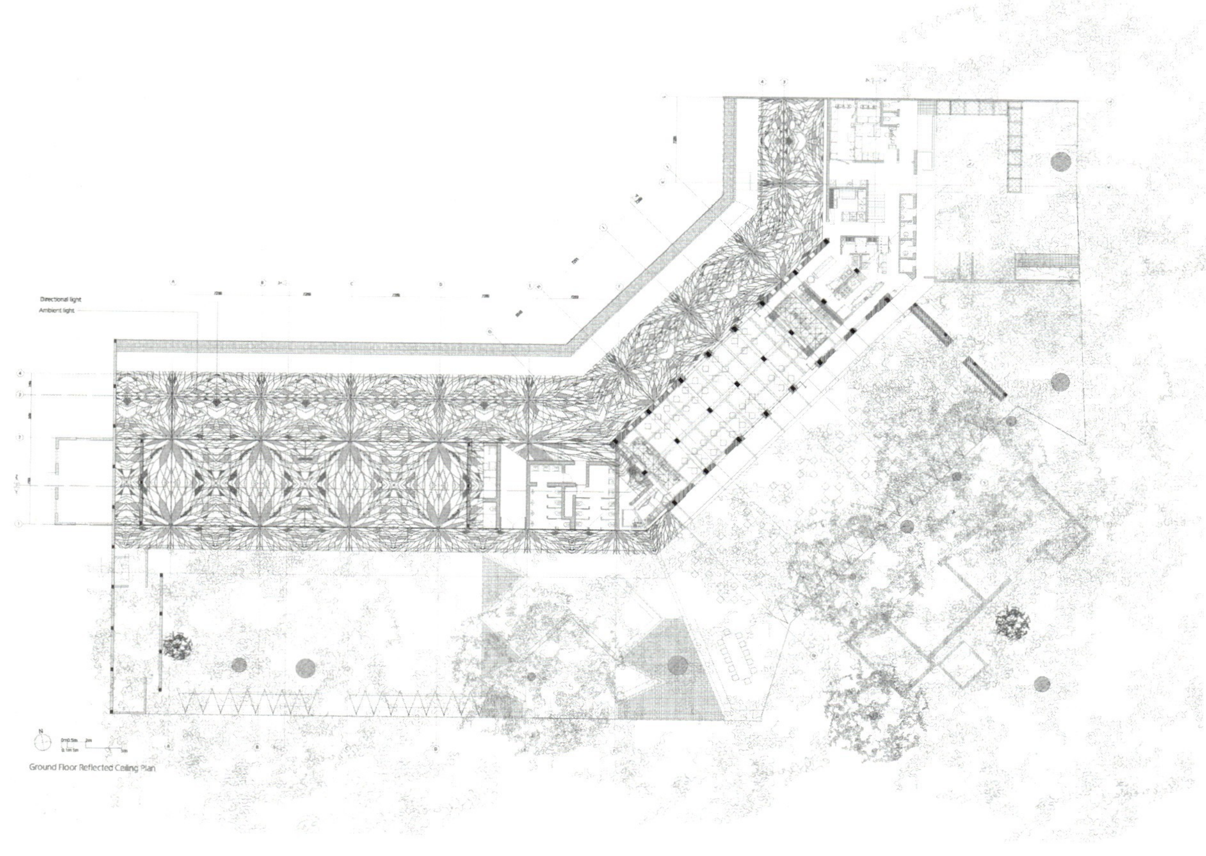

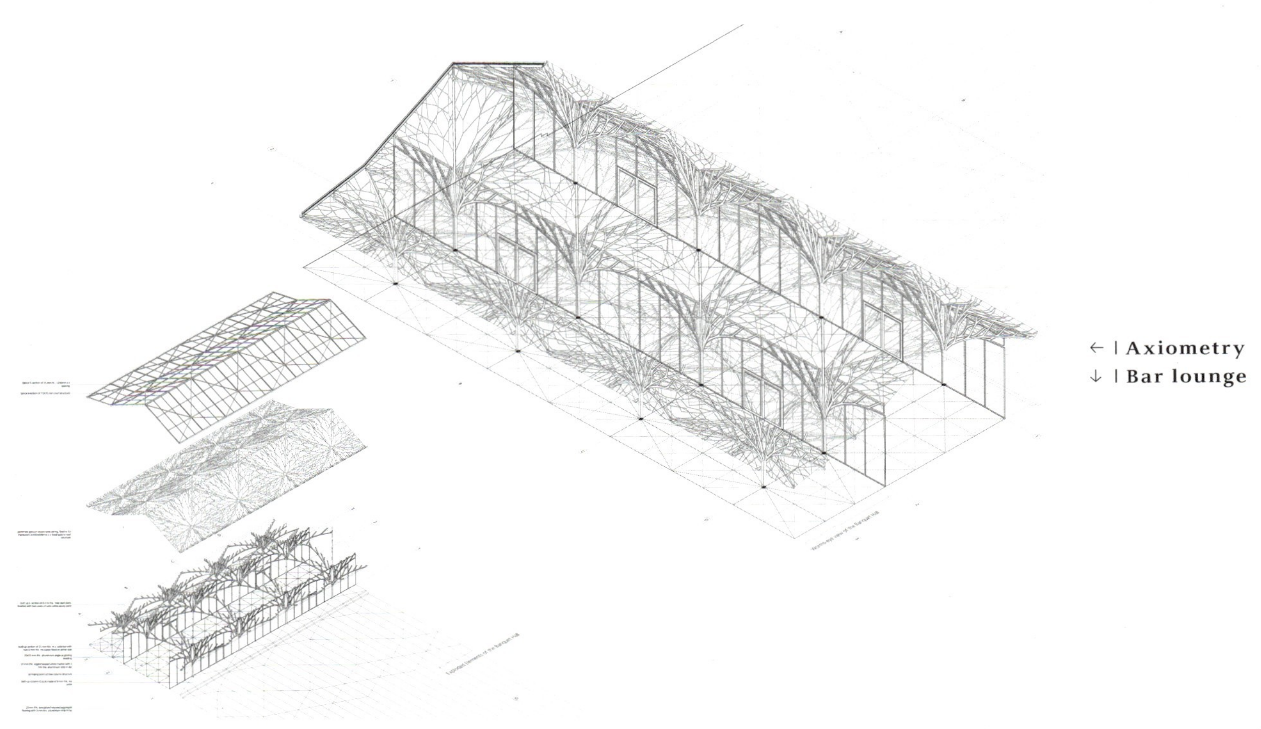

← | Axiometry
↓ | Bar lounge

Personal Architecture BNA / Sander van Schaik, Maarten Polkamp

↑ | **Bar**
→ | **Bedroom**

Stayokay Hostel

Rotterdam

The famous cube-complex by Piet Blom consists of 51 cube-form private dwellings and three "super cubes". Two of the super cubes originally housed the "Rotterdam Academy of Architecture" and have now been redeveloped into a hostel with 49 rooms, all different in size, atmosphere and view. The slanted faces of the cubes create unusual triangular and hexagonal floor plans. The complicated, disorienting geometry of the building requires a new, unambiguous circulation area. Corridors and sky bridges connect the rooms on the higher levels to a central void. An "interior cube", an abstract representation of the surrounding cube houses, is hung in the void to mark the central core of the building. A new elevator runs through the interior cube, enabling the guest to experience the full dimensions of the cubes. At night it is illuminated, making it a huge light sculpture.

PROJECT FACTS

Address: Overblaak 85, 3011 MH Rotterdam, The Netherlands. **Other creatives:** Architectenbureau Kees van Lamoen, SEVV. **Client:** NJHC beheer, Amsterdam. **Completion:** 2009. **Building type:** family hostel. **Gross floor area:** 2,830 m^2.

Original building: Piet Blom. **Client:** Hogeschool Rotterdam. **Completion:** 1982. **Building type:** school building. **Gross floor area:** 2,830 m^2.

↑ | Interior

← | First floor plan

↓ | Cube system

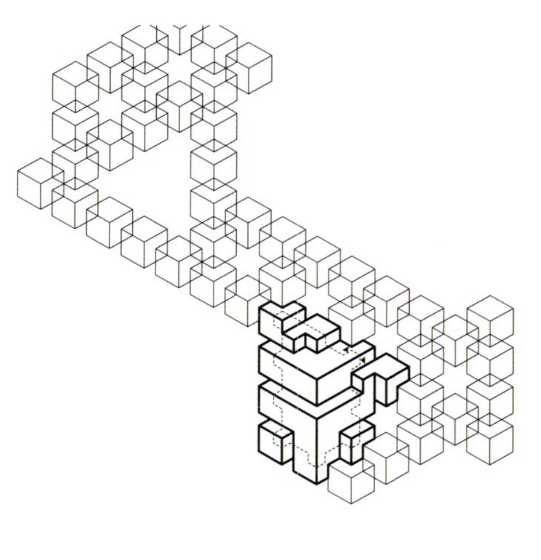

← | Exterior cube houses
↓ | Façade

LIVING

Format Architektur

↑ | Façade
↓ | Original building

Living in a Townhall

Cologne

Despite being planned as early as 1920, this town hall building was finally built in 1957. However, after the Rhineland Reform in 1972, the building lost its function as town hall and was later used to serve a number of temporary uses, include providing housing for asylum seekers. It wasn't until 2008–2009 that the building was bought and developed to provide community housing. From the beginning, the project focused on the importance of preserving the design of the original building. The building's façade was kept because of its historical and cultural importance the garden redesigned in the style of a traditional 1950s garden, and the L-shaped administration building was divided vertically to provide separate housing units.

PROJECT FACTS

Address: Lerschstraße 6–20, 50858 Cologne, Germany. **Client:** Raiffeisenbank Frechen Hürth eG. **Completion:** 2009. **Building type:** living. **Gross floor area:** 2,858 m². **Original building:** Hans J. Lohmeyer. **Client:** City of Weiden. **Completion:** 1957. **Building type:** townhall. **Gross floor area:** 2,858 m².

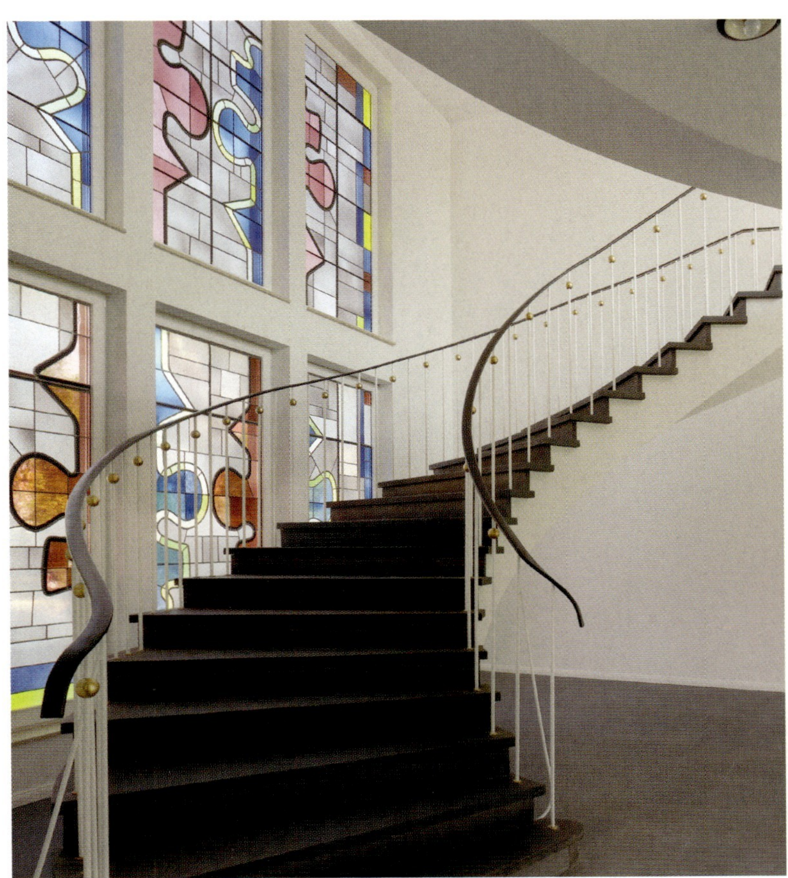

↑ | **Stairs,** with original stained glas windows

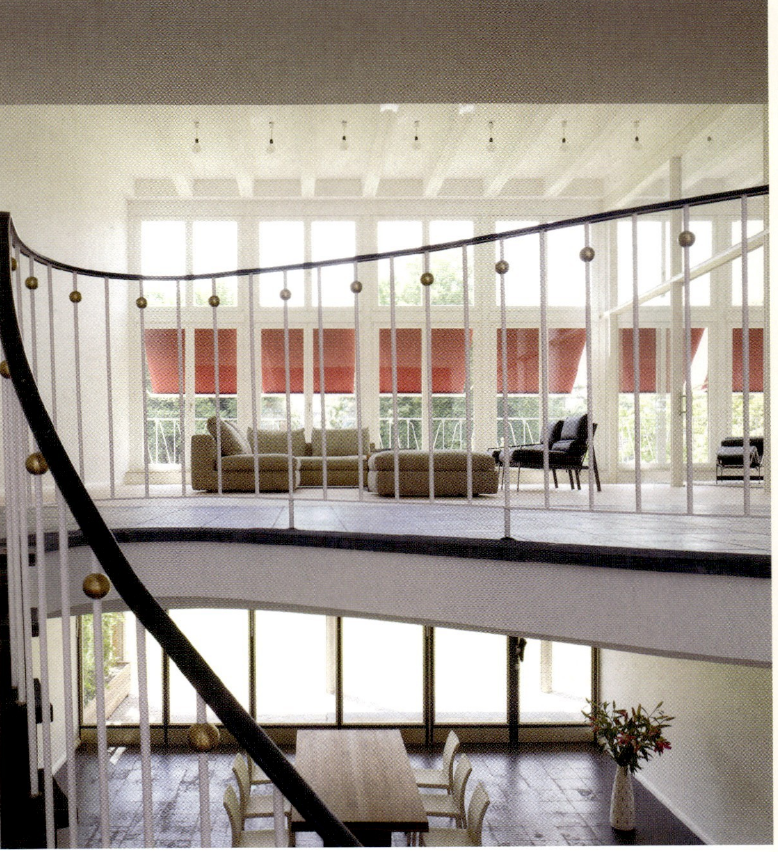

↑ | **Apartment,** living room and dining area

↓ | **Exterior**

↑ | **Exterior,** garden façade
← | **Ground floor plan**

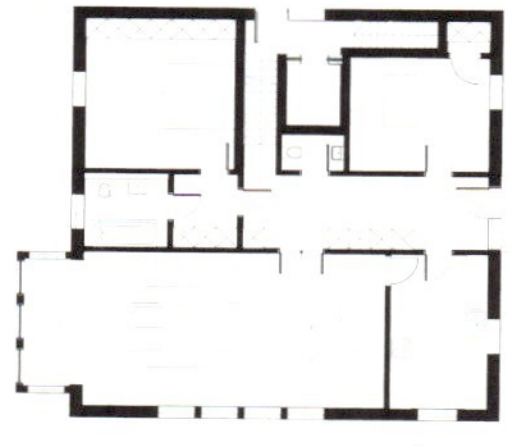

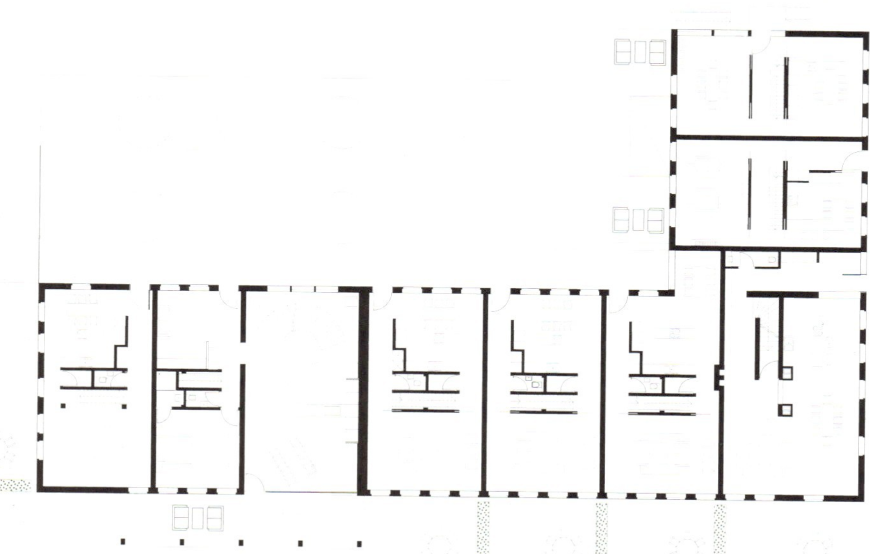

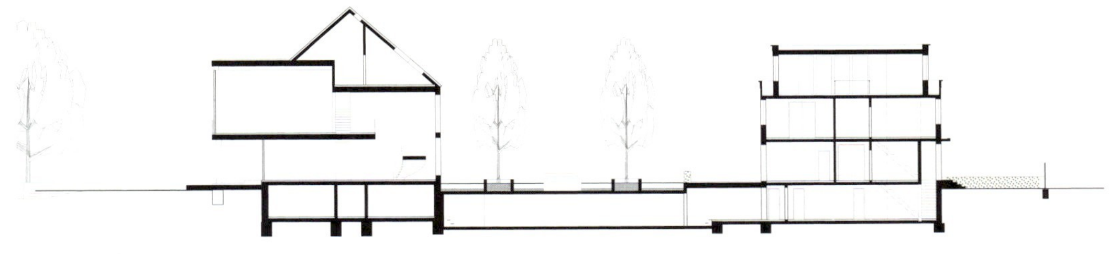

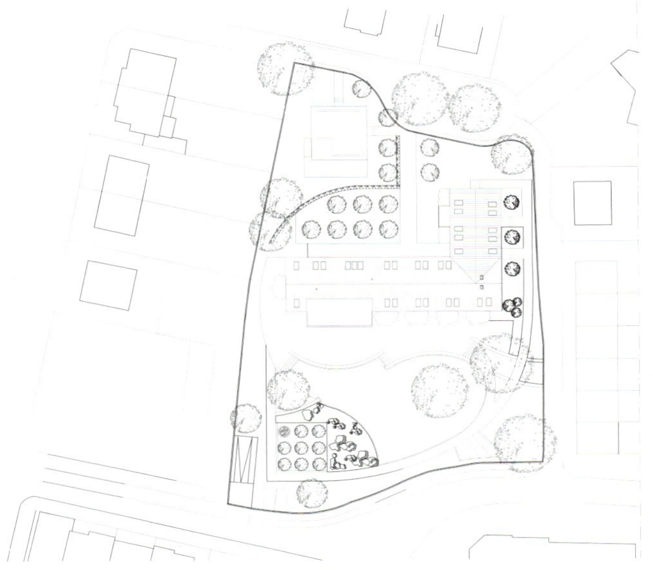

↖ | Section
← | Site plan
↓ | Interior

hks
Architekten + Gesamtplaner

↑ | **Street elevation**
→ | **Garden elevation** with balconies
↓ | **Before conversion**

Former auditorium

Erfurt

The "Alte Hörsaal" (Old Auditorium) in a central inner city location was renovated according to a conservation standpoint, preserving it as a structurally revamped historical building. The new division of the window elements creates a unity of construction and design. Ceilings and walls made of in situ concrete with building component activation installed in the volume of the former auditorium comprise the space for the new residential use. Two story rooms with gallery levels retain the multi-story character of the interior. The newly installed balconies are coordinated from a design as well as construction standpoint with the existing fall protection, fitting in with the garden façade.

PROJECT FACTS

Address: Gorkistraße 5, 99084 Erfurt, Germany. **Client:** Owner community Lindenlaub Rommel. **Completion:** 2009. **Building type:** townhouse. **Gross floor area:** 1,750 m^2.

Original building: Ludwig Adolf Lang. **Client:** gynecological hospital Erfurt. **Completion:** 1956. **Building type:** laboratory and classroom. **Gross floor area:** 1,200 m^2.

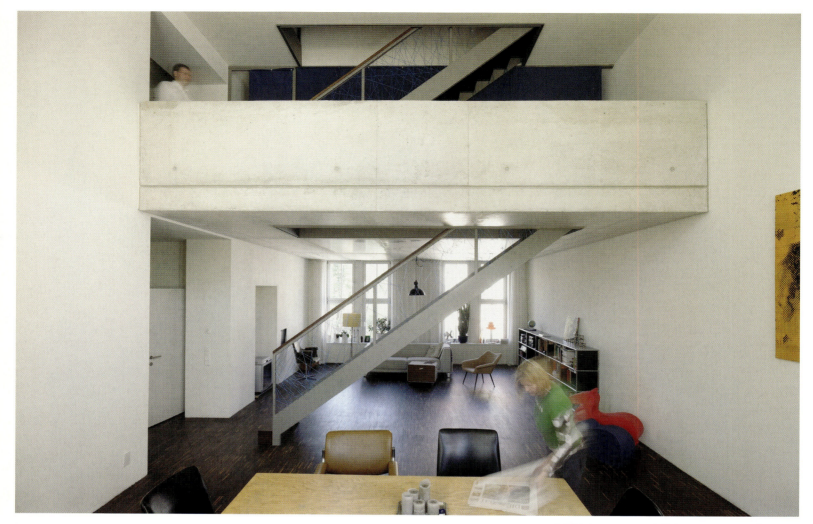

↑ | **Living area** and dining room, exposed concrete

↓ | **First floor plan**

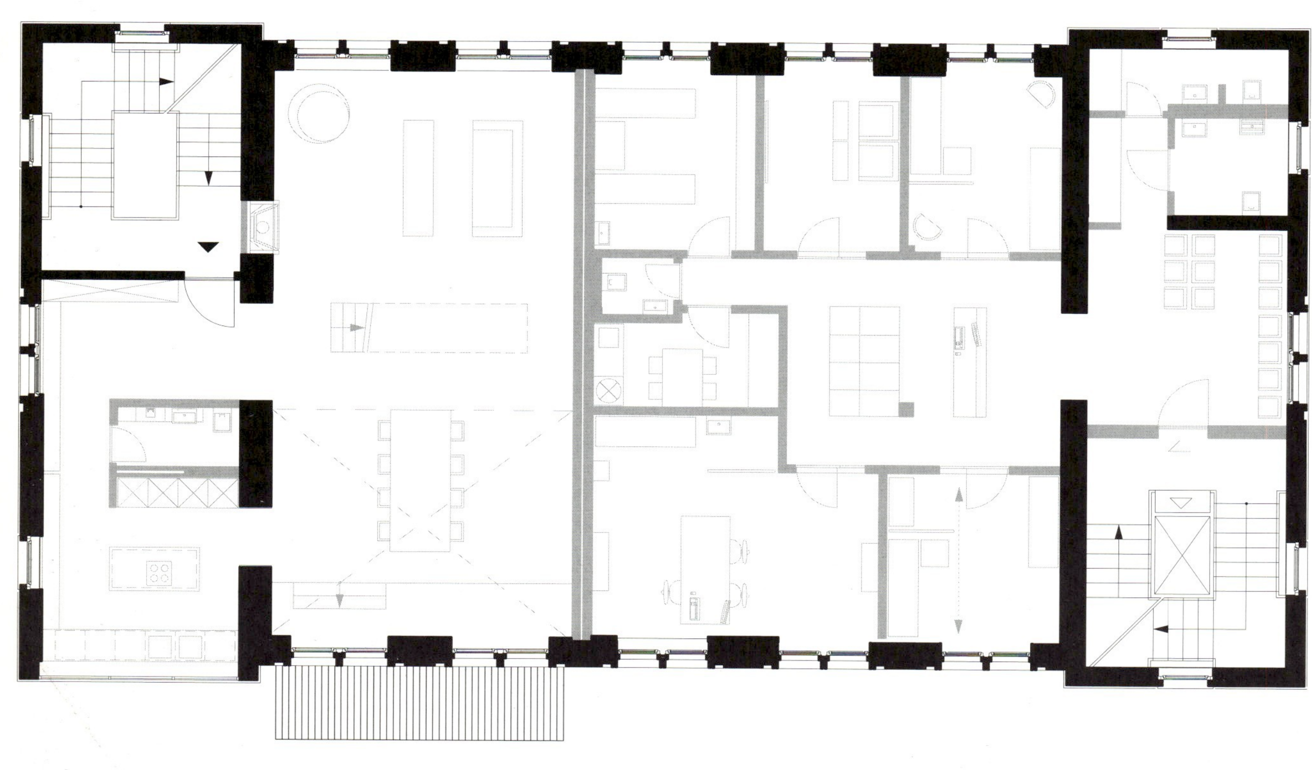

← | Longitudinal section
↓ | Stairs-landing-balcony

Dow Jones Architects / Biba Dow, Alun Jones

↑ | Roof garden

Lant Street

London

The project involved the conversion of the top two floors of a Victorian era clog-making factory as a home for a filmmaker. It creates a retreat in the city from a busy working life, a place of reflection which takes advantage of the city views around it. The existing ...f structure was removed and replaced with two habitable steel and timber box girders, ...he brick walls, establishing a new horizon at roof level. In addition to sup... ...f, the girders provide an organizational structure, marking out a terri... ...d screening. The space formed inside one girder is a rooftop "thinking ... over the terrace to the city beyond.

PROJECT FACTS

Address: 57A Lant Street, London, SE1 1QN, United Kingdom. **Client:** private. **Completion:** 2007. **Building type:** residential. **Gross floor area:** 250 m².
Original building: architect unknown. **Client:** unknown. **Completion:** 1850. **Building type:** warehouse. **Gross floor area:** 160 m².

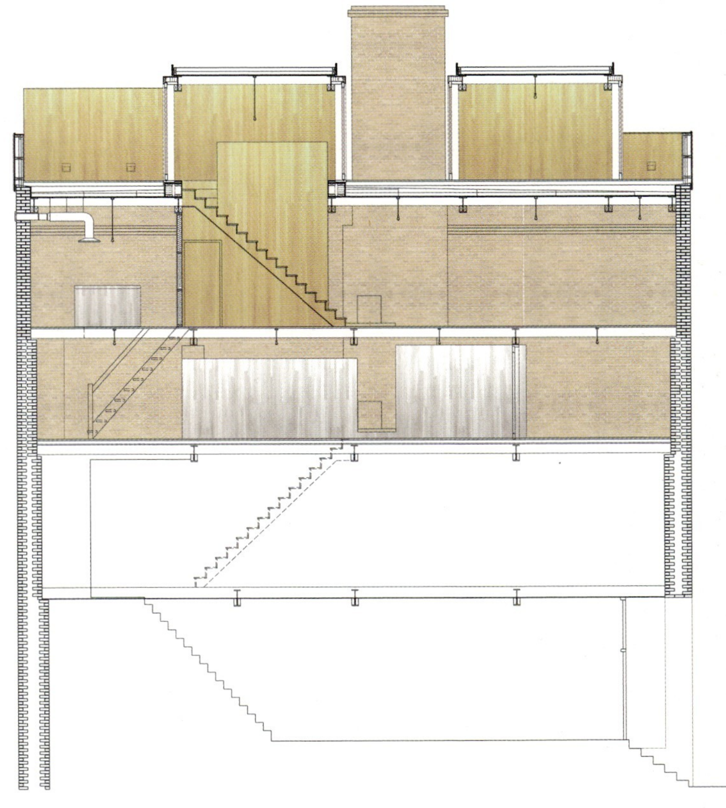

↑ | Exterior
↓ | Kitchen

↑ | Section
↓ | Bathroom

↑ | **Exterior**
→ | **Living room**

New River Bank Barn

Leesburg

Located on the banks of the Potomac River in Virginia, this renovated historic bank barn is host to receptions, parties, and festivities for a family and their guests. Originally built in the late 1800s, Blackburn Architects preserved much of the structure but re-clad it in SIPs panels and new board-and-batten skin. The existing corncrib was converted into a sundeck with views of the owners' horse farm to the west. The north-east façade was replaced with floor-to-ceiling glass, showcasing panoramic views of the Potomac from the main floor and loft. The Bank Barn is a recipient of an AIA Merit Award in Historic Resources and a Southern Living Magazine Home Award in Historic Restoration.

PROJECT FACTS

Address: Leesburg, Virginia, USA. **Client:** confidential. **Completion:** 2006. **Building type:** living. **Gross floor area:** 820 m².

Original building: architect unknown. **Client:** unknown. **Completion:** late 1800s. **Building type:** barn. **Gross floor area:** unknown.

↑ | Façade

← | Section

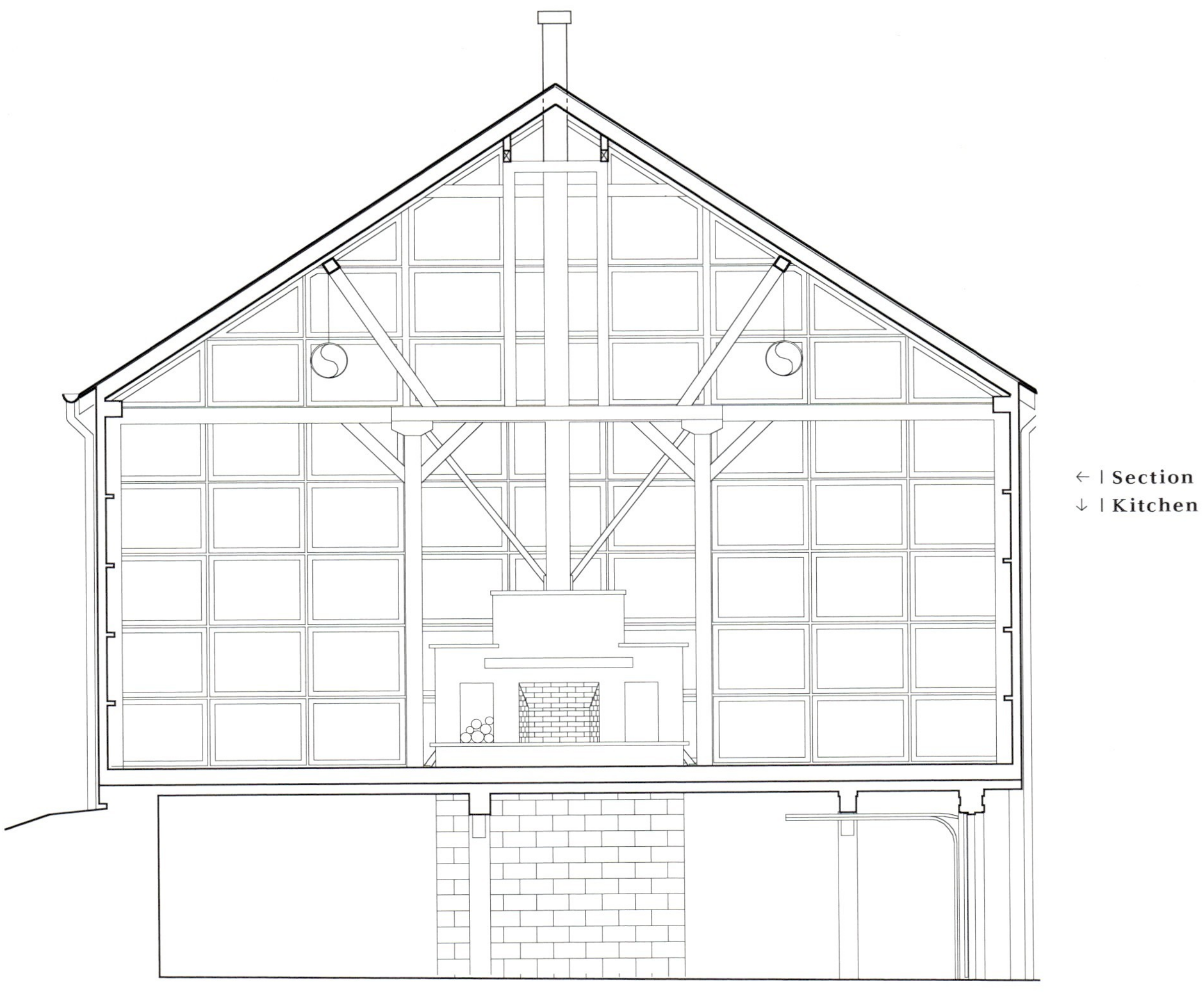

← | Section
↓ | Kitchen

MANIFOLD.Architecture Studio / Kit von Dalwig, Philipp von Dalwig

↑ | Interior
↗ | View from inside the bedroom
→ | View from outside into bedroom

Hirschkron / Camacho apartment

New York City

By removing undesirable, angled built-ins, relocating the master bathroom to the top floor and subtly shifting functions to the perimeter, the architects enhanced the clarity of the space. In combination with glass rails and walls, the three levels of living are continuously connected. The addition of an all-glass façade and sliding door system also created an indoor-outdoor connection between the master bathroom, bedroom and terrace. Low VOC paints and finishes were used throughout the space. Upgrading the insulative qualities using low-e, double-paned glass and planting a perimeter of greenery while also upgrading to a more energy-efficient HVAC system is another key to the design.

PROJECT FACTS

Address: 242 East 7th street 5, New York City, NY 10009. **Client:** Hirschkron / Camacho. **Completion:** 2008. **Building type:** triplex-apartment / penthouse. **Gross floor area:** 130 m².
Original building: architect unknown. **Client:** unknown. **Completion:** 1908. **Building type:** synagogue. **Gross floor area:** unknown.

↖ | Main entrance
↑ | Section
← | Bathroom

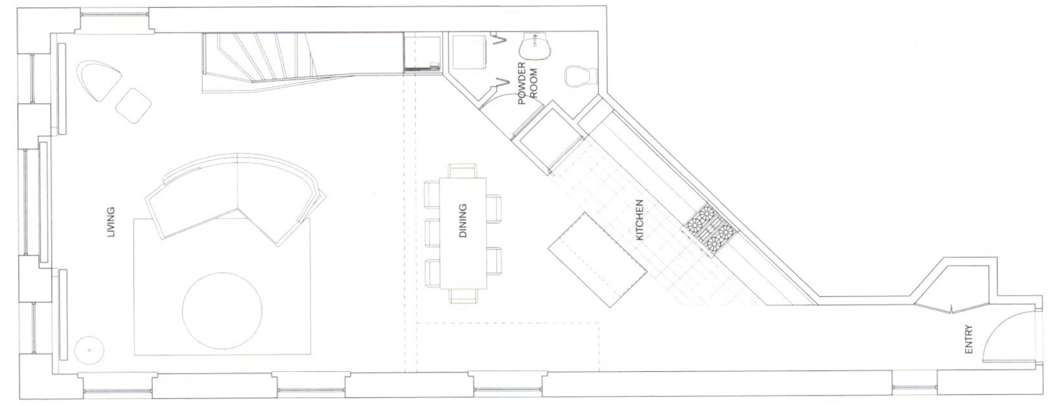

← | Ground floor plan
↓ | Gallery

Swaney Draper Architects

↑ | Kiln house in its surrounding
↗ | Deck
→ | View into the bedroom

Kiln House

Victoria

The building is a simple series of new and existing rural forms linked together in a loose but ordered way to make a house. The idea emerged from the client's request to design a retreat house making use of redundant tobacco kilns located amongst a cluster of sheds on their property. The strategy adopted in converting these kilns to a residential use was to position them together but apart, linking them via a linear strip of service spaces symbolically reinterpreting the verandah and the lean-to. Each kiln becomes a living space of lofty tower-like spaces into which one steps. They become ceremonial or contemplative spaces from which to view the mountains. Between them is a deck, the outdoor room, which allows an interlocking of inside and out.

PROJECT FACTS

Address: Bright, Victoria, Australia. **Furniture and interior Design :** Russell Grainger Design. **Client:** Delany. **Completion:** 2007. **Building type:** residental. **Gross floor area:** 200 m^2.
Original building: architect unknown. **Client:** unknown. **Completion:** unknown. **Building type:** tobacco kilns. **Gross floor area:** unknown.

↖ | View of outside deck
↑ | Side view
← | Floor plan

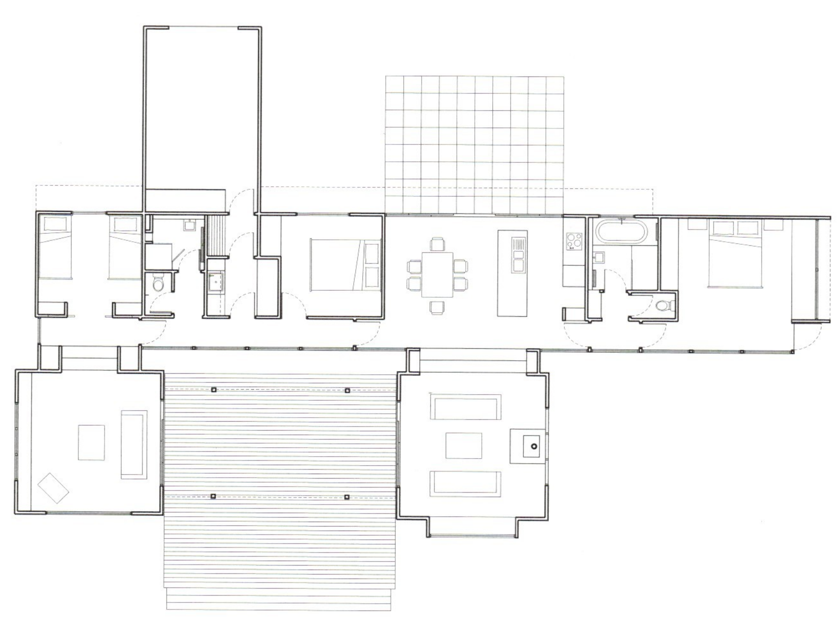

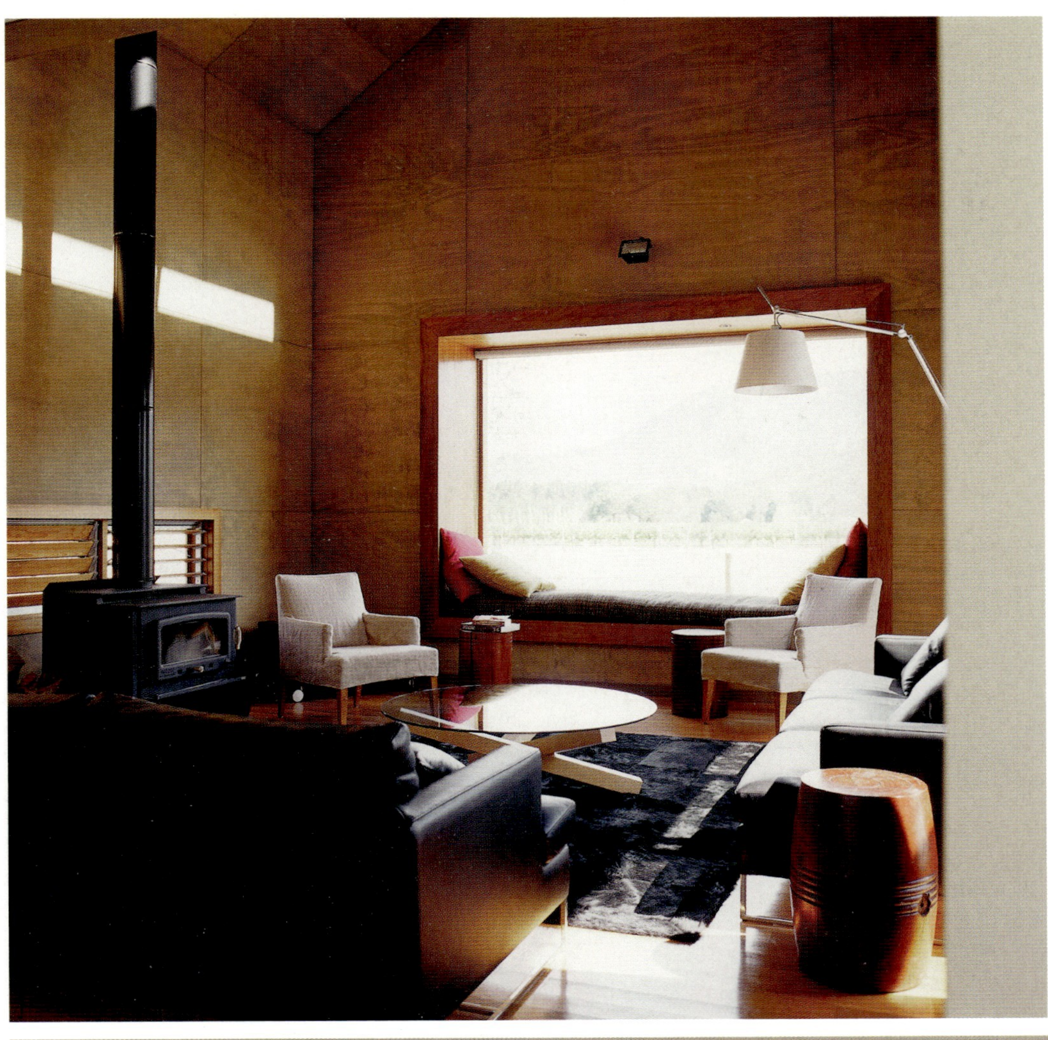

← | Living room
↓ | Kitchen and living room

Werkgemeinschaft
Quasten + Berger

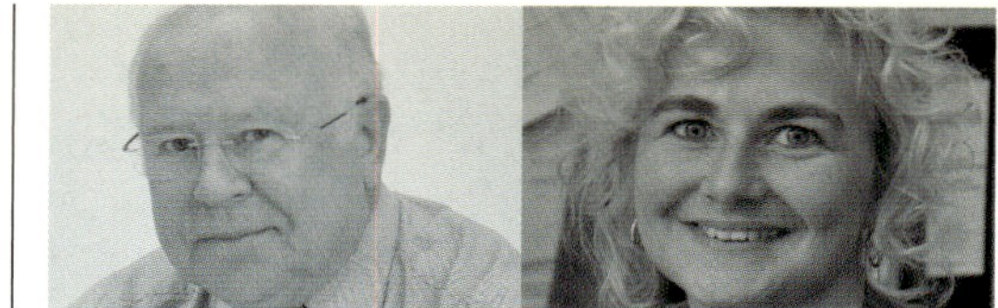

↑ | Main entrance

↓ | Original church building

Retirement Home 'Matthäushof'

Grevenbroich

The architects suggested a residential use for unassisted and assisted living for senior citizens in the former Matthäus Church and the community center of Grevenbroich-Südstadt. Construction elements and symbols typical for sacred architecture were removed or fundamentally redesigned, so that the high section of the sacral chamber was replaced by a residential space, while the lower part of the bell tower was used for the sign announcing the „Matthäushof". Two new structures, which strongly recall the design of the church building, fill up the lot with 32 residential units. A generous community center in the church building and specially designed open areas were also created for elderly citizens from the community.

PROJECT FACTS

Address: Von Bodelschwingh-Straße, 41515 Grevenbroich, Germany. **Client:** Bauverein Grevenbroich eG. **Completion:** 2008. **Building type:** retirement home. **Gross floor area:** 4,391 m^2.
Original building: Joerg Springer, Neuss. **Client:** Evangelische Kirchengemeinde Grevenbroich. **Completion:** 1976. **Building type:** church. **Gross floor area:** 4,391 m^2.

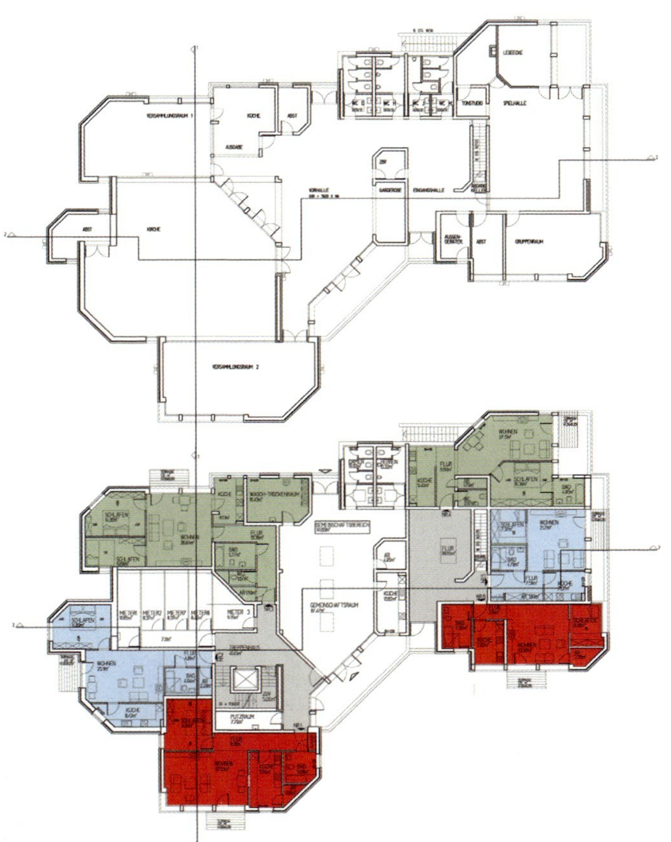

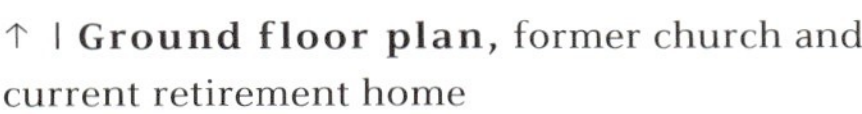

↑ | **Ground floor plan,** former church and current retirement home

↓ | **View from the street**

↑ | **Exterior**

Architektur Büro Jäcklein / Reinhold Jäcklein

↑ | **Interior,** staircase
↓ | **Original building**

Living and work in a former bank house

Volkach

After a long period of vacancy the former bank building from the 1960s was revitalized by converting and refurbishing it. The rear annex was partially removed, making room for a patio. The broad attic sheathing and brick slip cladding was also removed. The uniform window formats, with the subdued color of the plaster façade, and the almost flush gutters contribute to the restrained, quiet look of the building. A shell limestone wall stands between the building and the street and forms a regional link by the selection of the local material. The existing entryway porch was included in the overall concept. An open stairway connects the office spaces on the ground floor and the upper floor.

PROJECT FACTS

Address: Spitalstraße 23, 97332 Volkach, Germany. **Client:** Klaus und Dorothea Hart. **Completion:** 2005. **Building type:** living and commercial house. **Gross floor area:** 450 m².
Original building: architect unknown. **Client:** Sparkasse Volkach. **Completion:** 1972. **Building type:** bank building. **Gross floor area:** 300 m².

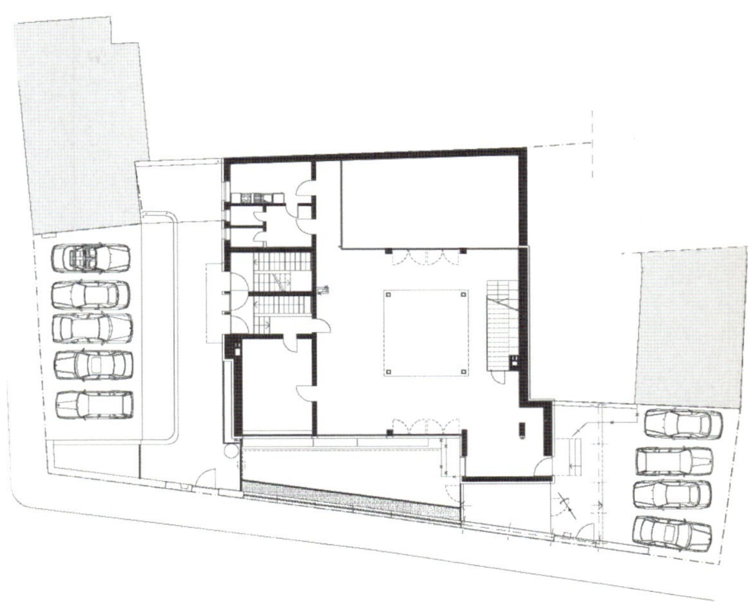

↑ | **Façade**
↓ | **Exterior view from the street**

↑ | **Ground floor plan**

David Archer

↑ | **Front elevation**
→ | **An elegant timber** and glass structure on the rear elevation

The Coach House

Midford

A timber and glass structure on the rear elevation replaces an unsightly neo-victorian-conservatory added to the house in the 1980s. On the ground level this creates a reception room and office area, which benefit from uninterrupted panoramic views of the surrounding countryside. The full height glazing is supported by a series of sections of solid oak cantilevered off the amended floor slab. At the front of the house, one of the twin en removed to provide space for a white calacatta limestone kitchen, which ated from the first floor. The removal of the garage door on the north façade ning in the entrance elevation masonry, which has been glazed to function indow.

PROJECT FACTS

Address: Court Essington, Midford, United Kingdom. **Client:** confidential. **Completion:** 2006. **Building type:** residential. **Gross floor area:** unknown.
Original building: architect unknown. **Client:** unknown. **Completion:** approx 1900. **Building type:** Arts and Crafts coach house. **Gross floor area:** unknown.

↖ | **Kitchen**
↑ | **Corridor,** entrance to the bathroom
← | **Exterior view,** huge glass windows in the kitchen

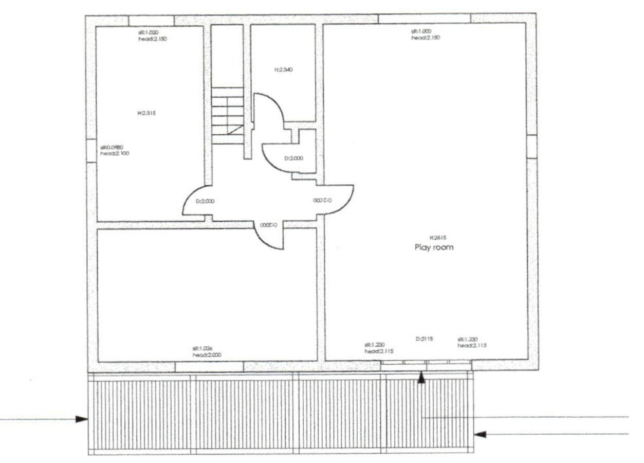

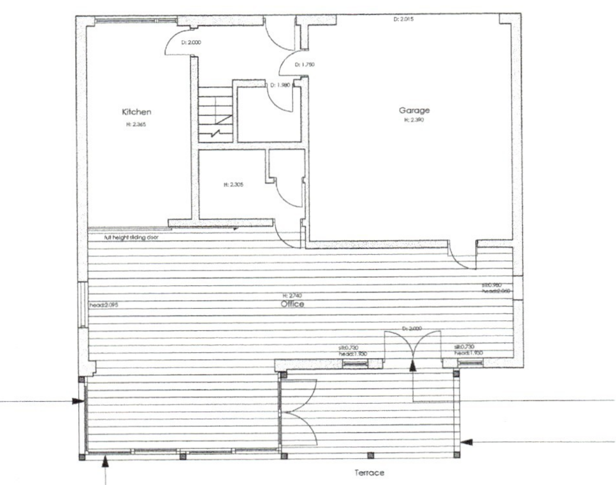

↖ | **First floor plan**

← | **Ground floor plan**

↓ | **View** through the winter garden

van den Valentyn Architektur / Thomas van den Valentyn, Johannes van Linn

↑ | Elevation
→ | Roof terrace

Rosellenturm

Neuss

The former grain silo is a simple utilitarian structure which forms a small building ensemble along with several warehouses. The basic idea behind the conversion of the 20 meter high tower was an „aerie“. The silo has a surface area of 9.01 x 12.24 meters and consists of a 36.5 centimeter thick masonry wall, held together by four reinforced concrete ring beams. The existing interior wood constructions and the roof were completely removed. Three new, reinforced concrete ceilings in the upper third of the tower constitute the new living areas and a rooftop terrace. Access from the ground floor to the roof top terrace is provided by a new exposed concrete pit with a newel stair and elevator.

PROJECT FACTS

Address: Raiffeisenstraße 4, 41470 Neuss, Germany. **Client:** Dr. Stefanie Clemen and Wolfang Hübner. **Completion:** 2006. **Building type:** apartment. **Gross floor area:** 330 m^2.
Original building: architect unknown. **Client:** unknown. **Completion:** 1963. **Building type:** grain silo. **Gross floor area:** unknown.

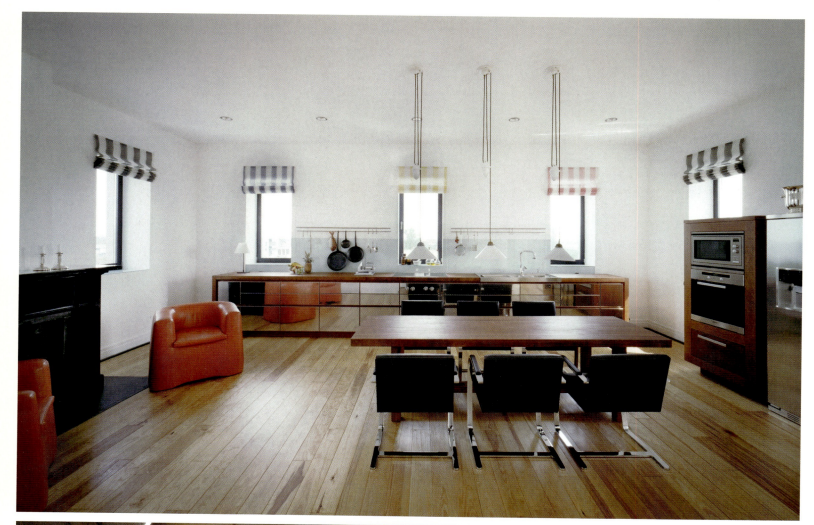

↑ | **Kitchen** and dining area with fireplace
← | **Stairs**
↓ | **Second floor plan**
↓↓ | **First floor plan**

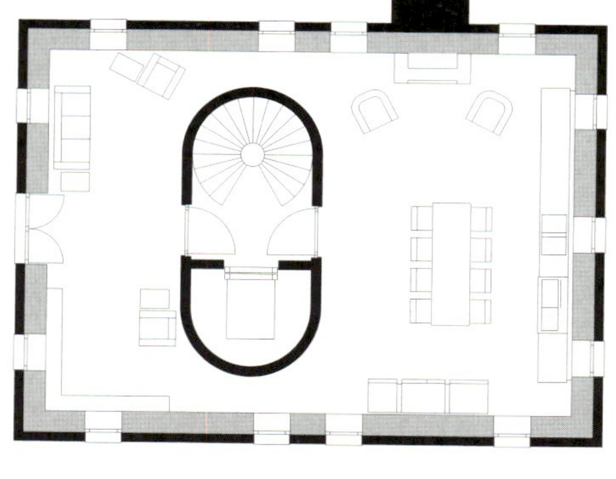

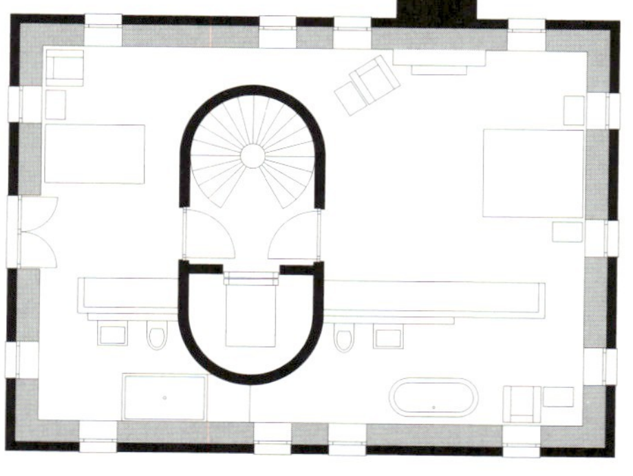

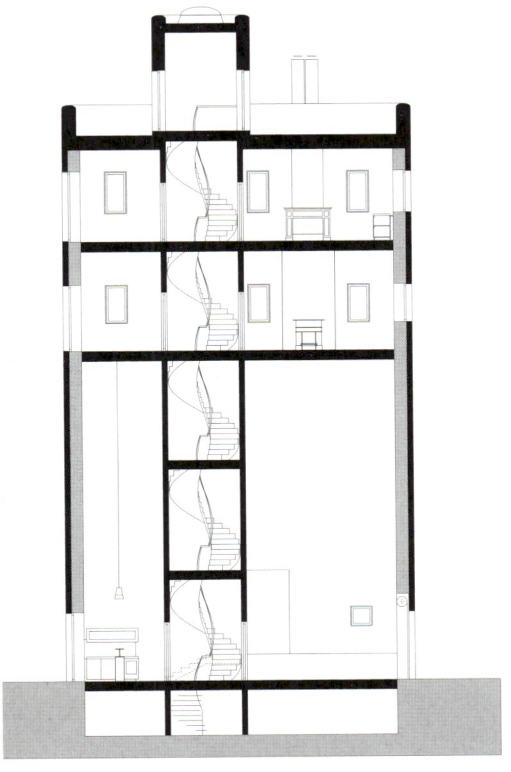

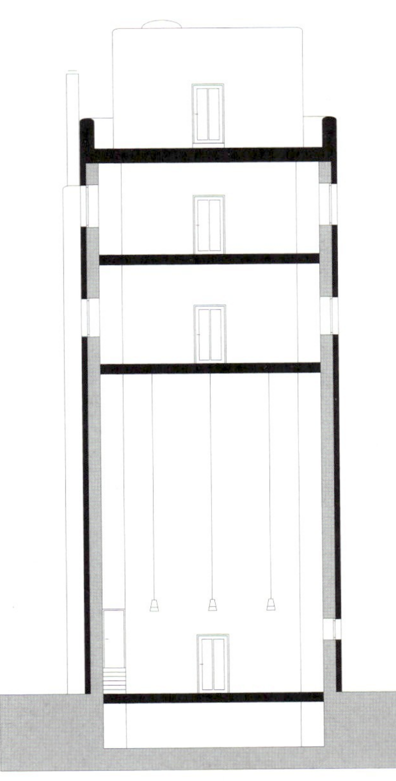

← | **Sections**
↙ | **Entrance hall**
↓ | **Exterior view,** entrance

binnberg design /
Uwe Binnberg

Art in the Bunker – Living in the Tower

Munich

↑ | Exterior view
↗ | Bedroom
→ | Living room
↓ | Original bunker building

This above ground bunker in Munich was built during World War II. It was converted into a residential tower in 2005, with six apartments. Two floors were added to the octagonal, free-standing formerly windowless building which was fitted with a ceiling high window opening at each of the eight corners. In addition, one meter of the existing 2.40 meter thick walls was cut away from the inside. The two new floors were then glazed on all sides with the exterior sun protection continuing the shell of the existing building. In order to disassociate the building from its previous history and introduce the new use, several events with the motto "Art in the Bunker – Living in the Tower" took place during the months leading up to the beginning of construction.

PROJECT FACTS

Address: Claude-Lorrain-Straße 26, 81543 Munich, Germany. **Client:** Uwe Binnberg. **Completion:** 2005. **Building type:** apartments. **Gross floor area:** 690 m^2.
Original building: architect unknown. **Client:** unknown. **Completion:** 1941. **Building type:** bunker. **Gross floor area:** unknown.

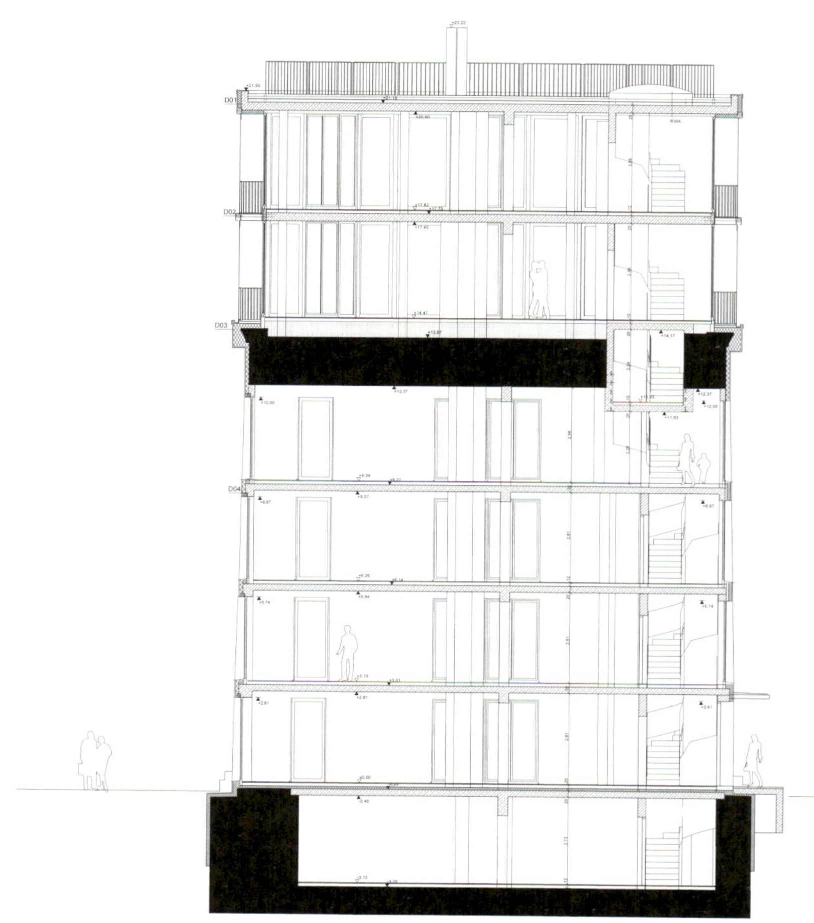

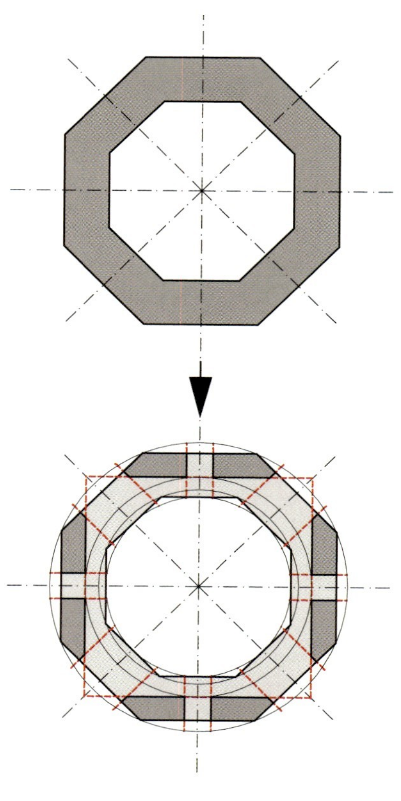

↖ | **Section**
↑ | **Concept of the renovation**
← | **Staircase,** original wall of the bunker

← | **Bathroom**
↙ | **Floor plan,** first to third floor
↓ | **Floor plan,** fourth floor

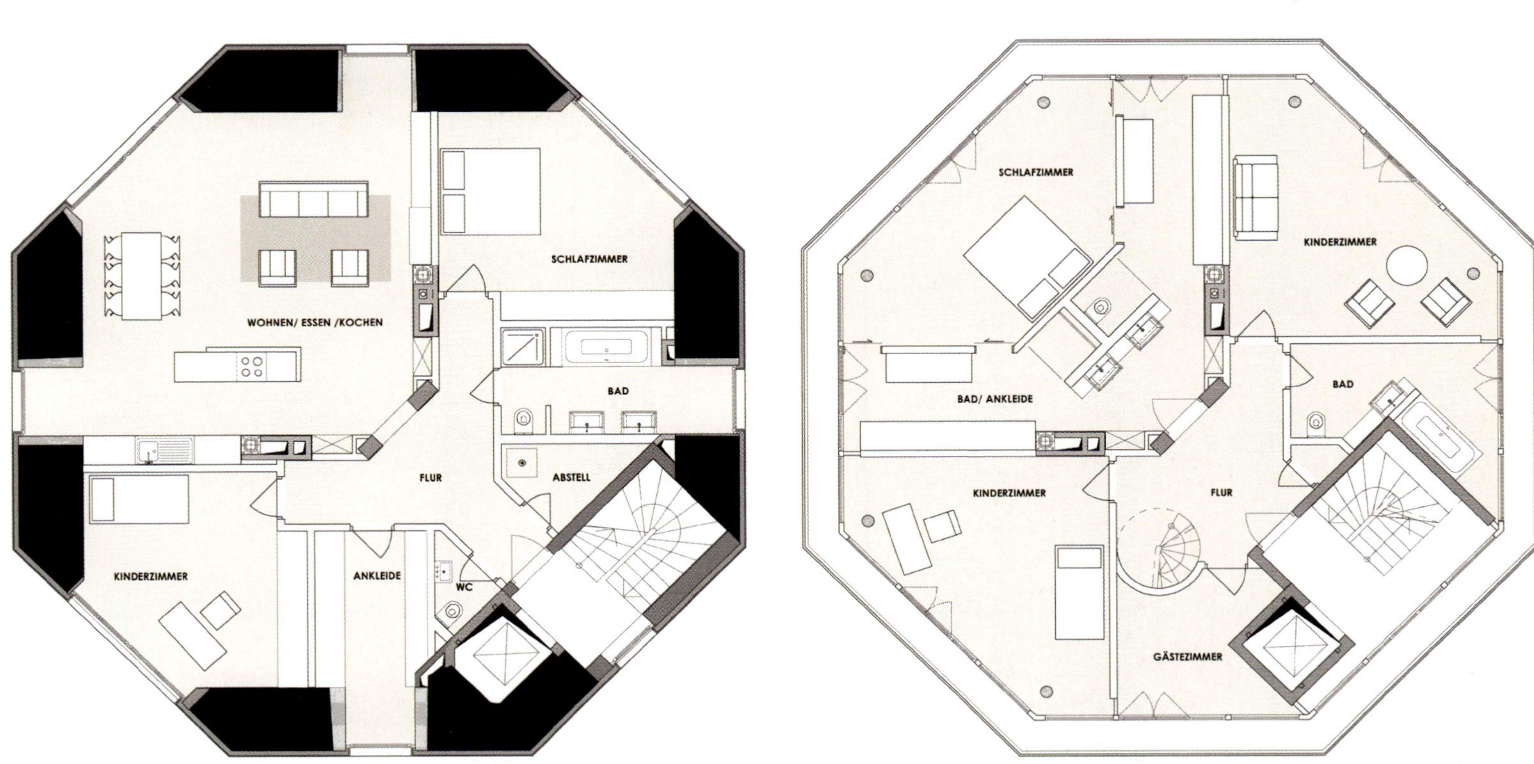

Halle 58 Architekten GmbH
with smarch Architekten

↑ | Ground floor

1800 am Gerzensee

Gerzensee

The long uninhabited farm house lies in an unusual location with a fabulous view of the Bern Alps. The stables of the intact, simple and voluminous building were gutted in order to realize a spatially multilayered living situation. The two story, central living room lives from the tension in form between the unaltered former living quarters with the great old fireplace and the space creating, exposed concrete elements. Differentiated interventions in the façades make way for the insertion of new, restrained glazing and the installation of windows with heritage listing compatible windows. The sightlines reflect the dialogue between the interior and the conservation area surroundings.

PROJECT FACTS

Address: Räschmatt am See, Dorfstrasse 37, 3115 Gerzensee, Switzerland. **Client:** David and Matthias Baumann. **Completion:** 2002. **Building type:** living. **Gross floor area:** unknown.
Original building: unknown. **Client:** unknown. **Completion:** 1800. **Building type:** farm house. **Gross floor area:** unknown.

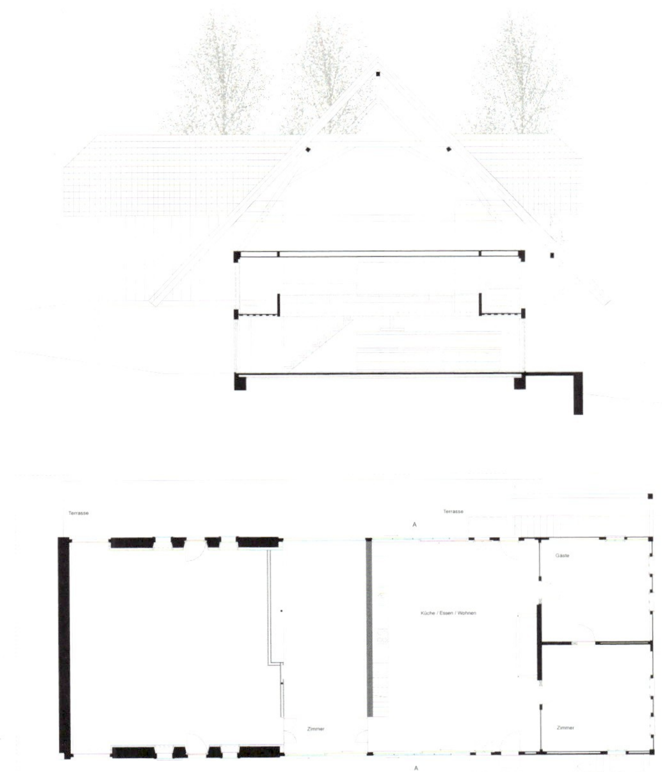

↑ | **Section and ground floor plan**

↑ | **Exterior**
↓ | **Gallery on first floor**

Charlotte Skene Catling

↑ | **Bath house**
→ | **View into passageway,** by day and night

The Dairy House

Somerset

The space was pragmatically re-planned for the conversion to a five-bedroom house with a small pool. Lean-to sheds were removed and an extension added. During the design process the requirements changed from a rental property to those of a week-end house for the client. The intervention was to appear as a natural extension of the existing structure, with an "un-designed" design to combine privacy and seclusion with openness to the wider landscape. The inspiration was both local, in the stacked timber in the yard opposite, and literary, in the 18th century "La Petite Maison – An Architectural Seduction", architectural treatise and erotic novella by Jean-Francois de Bastide.

PROJECT FACTS

Address: The Hadspen Estate, Castle Cary, Somerset, United Kingdom. **Client:** Niall Hobhouse. **Completion:** 2008. **Building type:** residence. **Gross floor area:** 250 m^2.
Original building: architect unknown. **Client:** unknown. **Completion:** unknown. **Building type:** dairy. **Gross floor area:** 190 m^2.

↖ | Interior
↑ | Staircase
← | Sections

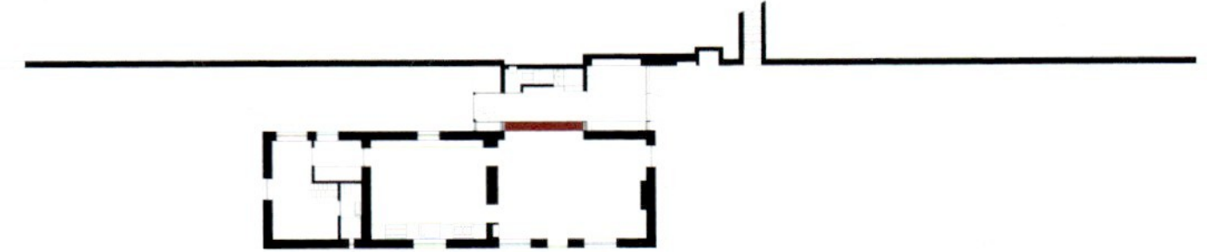

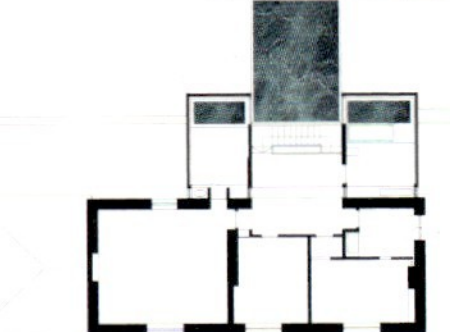

↖ | Ground floor plan
← | First floor plan
↓ | Living room

baurmann.dürr architekten /
Prof. Henning Baurmann

↑ | View from the street
↗ | North-west view by night
→ | South-east view by night
↓ | Original building

Märchenring Residence

Karlsruhe

Since this structure as a whole could not be completely removed without being compelled by the building code to relinquish the greater part of the constructed surface, the ground floor was only partly removed and the rest of the rather conventional one family house was transformed into a striking villa. The newly added floor changes the character of the building, while maintaining the solid foundation. The ground floor, was also completely rebuilt and furnished with, among other things, a guest apartment. The garden with its old stock of trees and pool was liberated from the annexes. The clear style displays a seduded appearence from th street, but offers a high degree of transparency and openness to the garden.

PROJECT FACTS

Address: Hauffstraße 6, Märchenring, 76199 Karlsruhe-Rüppurr, Germany. **Client:** confidential. **Completion:** 2009. **Building type:** residential. **Gross floor area:** 710 m^2.

Original building: architect unknown. **Client:** private. **Completion:** 1962. **Building type:** housing. **Gross floor area:** 600 m^2.

↑ | Living room

← | Entrance area with staircase

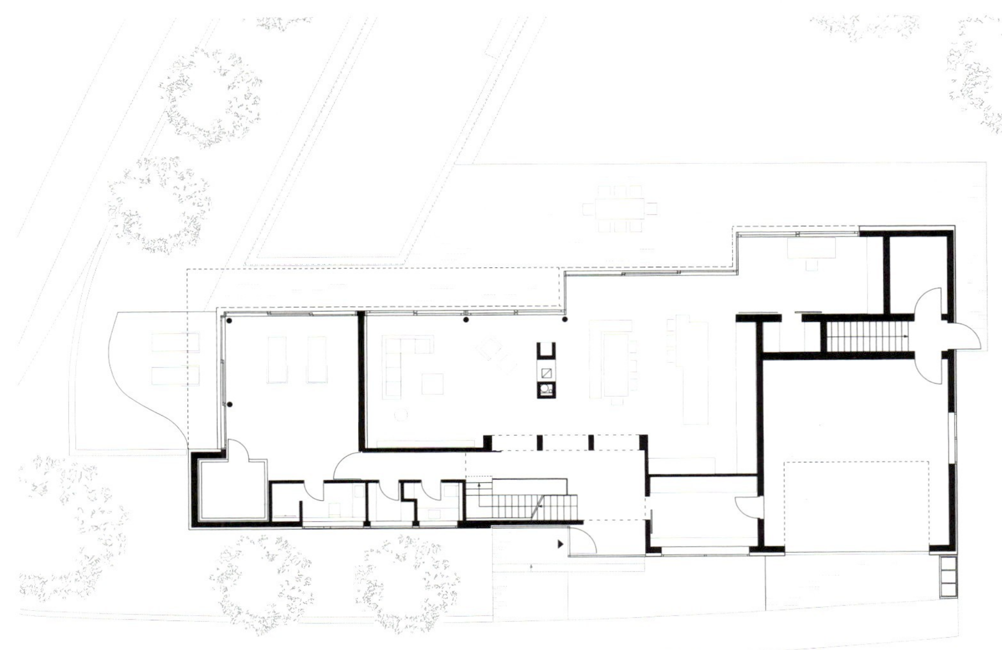

← | Ground floor plan
↓ | Dining area

Sergei Tchoban Architekt
BDA nps tchoban voss
A. M. Prasch, S. Tchoban,
E. Voss / Axel Binder

↑ | **Exterior view**
↓ | **3D visualization,** entire complex

↗ | **Living type,** modern design
→ | **Living type,** classic design

Monroe Park

Berlin

Originally built as a Telefunken electrical appliance factory in the south-west of Berlin in the 1930s, the complex looks back on an eventful history. Serving as an American barracks until the end of the Four-Power status, the extensive buildings are now being converted into high quality residential space, including an overall design concept for the grounds. The new structuring of the access road and interior access areas thereby support the lavish gesture of the complex. Axes of view and symmetry have been consciously adopted. The newly added elements like balconies and stairways lend the prim architecture a residential touch.

PROJECT FACTS

Address: Platz des 4. Juli, 14167 Berlin, Germany. **Architect in charge:** Axel Binder. **Client:** S+P GmbH. **Completion:** 2009. **Building type:** housing. **Gross floor area:** 25,000 m^2.
Original building: Hans Hertlein. **Client:** S + P GmbH. **Completion:** 1930s. **Building type:** industrial. **Gross floor area:** 25,000 m^2.

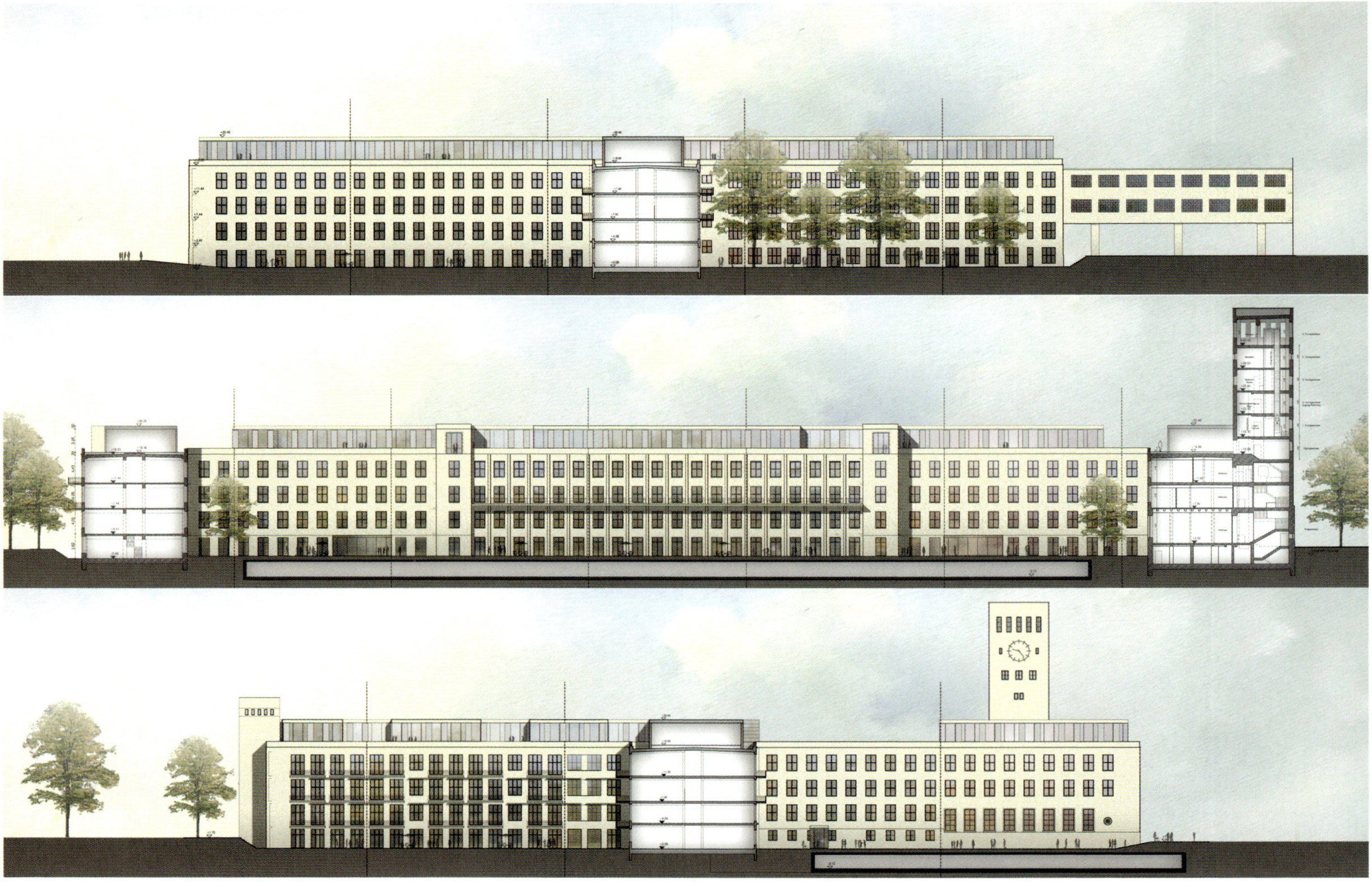

↑ | **Elevations,** north, east, south

↙ | **Site plan**

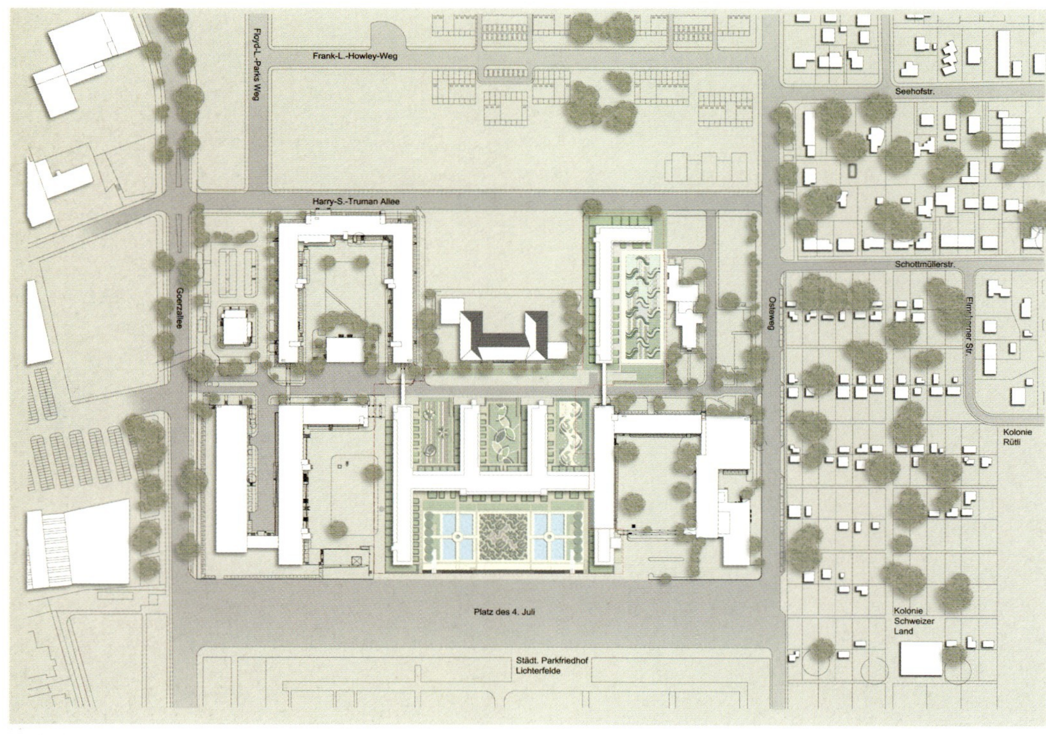

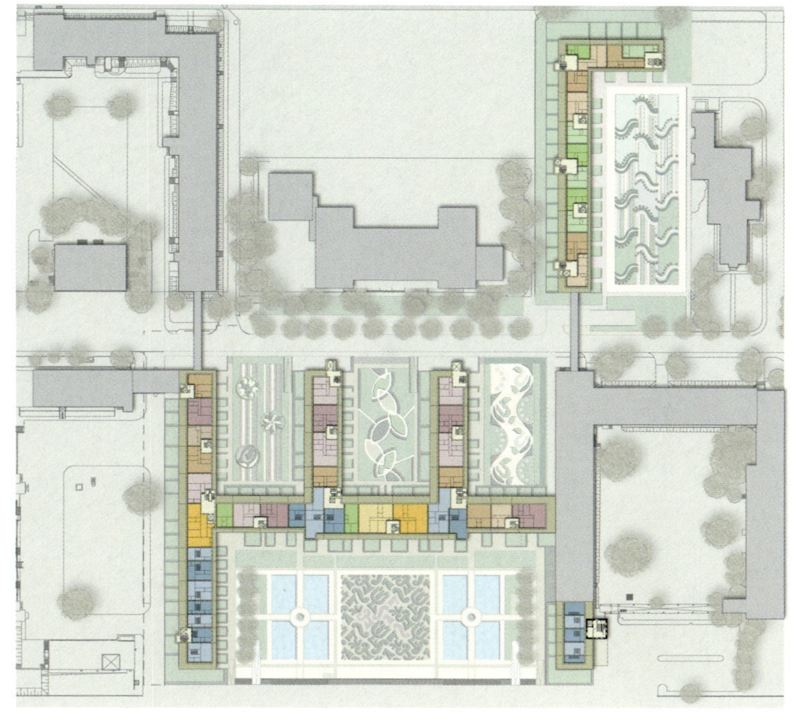

← | Plan

↓ | Billy-Wilder-Mall

C. F. Møller Architects with Christian Carlsen Arkitektfirma

↑ | Side elevation
→ | Exterior view

Siloetten / The Sil(o)houette

Skødstrup

The new apartments are a mix of single story flats and maisonettes, so that the lower levels enjoy a full view and no two flats are the same. The silo contains staircases and lifts, and serves the base of a common roof terrace. Around the tower, the apartments are built up on a steel structure in eye-catching forms, which protrude out into the light and the landscape. This unusual structure of protrusions and displacements provides all of the apartments with generous outdoor spaces. The nature of the silo's "rural high-rise" is unique and – since it is a conversion – no other building in the area can be built to the same height, guaranteeing its status as a free-standing landmark.

PROJECT FACTS

Address: Løgten Bytorv, Løgten, 8541 Skødstrup, Denmark. **Client:** Løgten Midt A/S. **Completion:** 2010. **Building type:** residential. **Gross floor area:** 3,000 m^2.

Original building: architect unknown. **Client:** unknown. **Completion:** 1950s. **Building type:** industrial silos. **Gross floor area:** 150 m^2.

↑ | **Living area,** dining area and kitchen
← | **Two-story apartment**
↓ | **Floor plan**

← | Sections
↙ | Elevation
↓ | Exterior view

rooijakkers + tomesen architecten

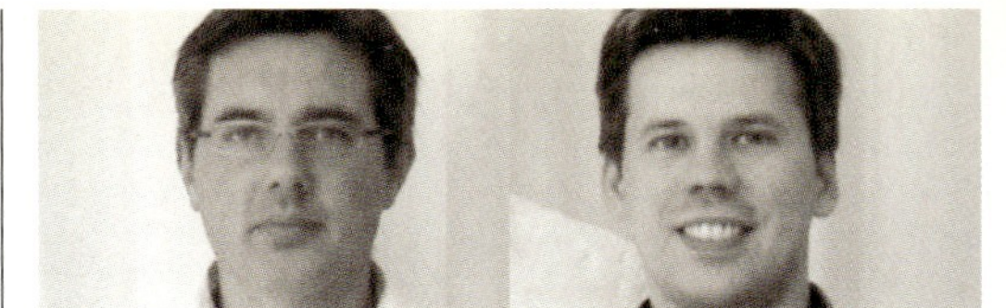

↑ | **Bird's-eye view,** context of sewage tank with DJ's Garden on top
→ | **View from the pond**

DJ's Garden

Amsterdam

In a former sewage treatment plant that was converted into a residential building with seven apartments in 1999 by De Architectengroep, a penthouse has recently been extended by an extraordinary roof terrace – including a pavilion – called DJ's Garden. By utilizing the entire roof area, the living space has been doubled. The pavilion has the character of a full-fledged room with garden view and can be used in many different ways, from its vantage point in the middle of a "green roof" with plants, mosses, sedums and a pond. Thereby the necessity of the gravel roof of DJ's Garden has been turned into a delightful roof garden with a flexible and sheltered outdoor area.

PROJECT FACTS

Address: Tretjakovlaan 16, 1064 PR, Amsterdam, The Netherlands. **Client:** Wim Verbakel, Marion Heres. **Completion:** 2009. **Building type:** apartment building. **Gross floor area:** 144 m^2.
Original building: architect unknown. **Client:** Amsterdam local government. **Completion:** 1930. **Building type:** sewage tanks. **Gross floor area:** 314 m^2.

↑ | **View from the park**
↙ | **Plan,** garden details

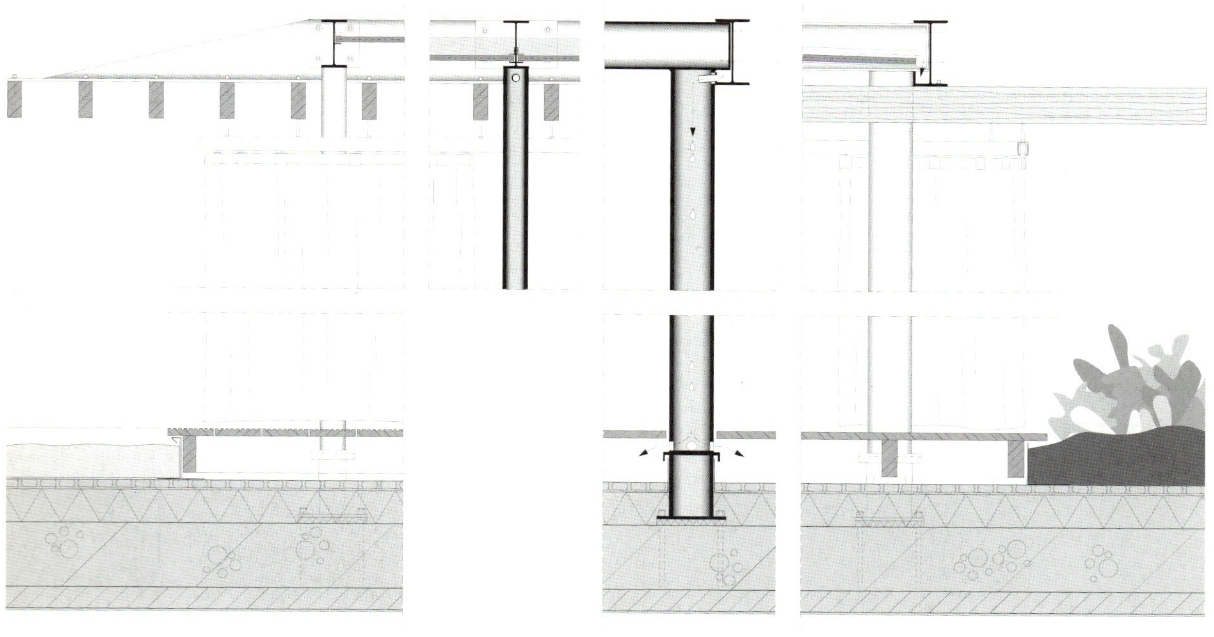

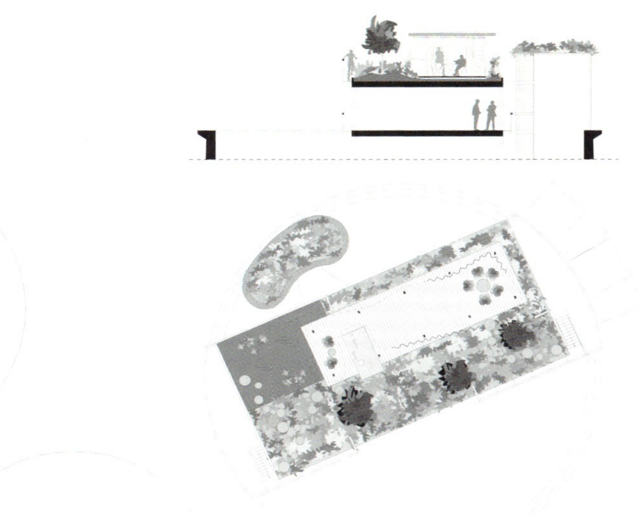

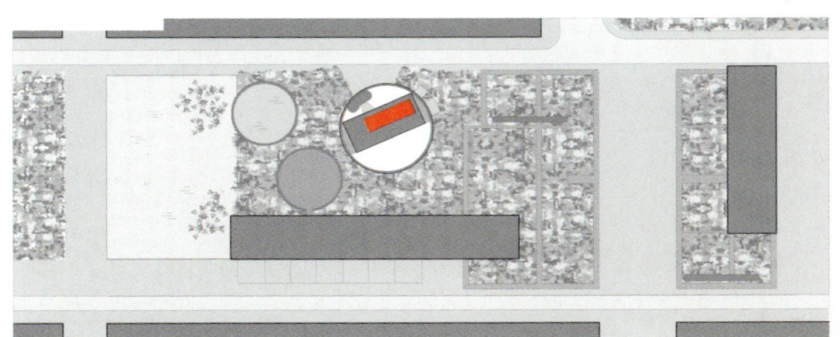

← | **Plans,** section, roof floor plan and situation plan
↓ | **Entering** the roofgarden

Hacin + Associates, Inc. / David J. Hacin, Scott Thomson

↑ | Detail of the façade

Lafayette Lofts

Boston

This renovated five story, 19th century mercantile building within Boston's historic "Textile District" houses 42 loft apartments with a new three story addition. The building massing and elevations conceptually weave the new with the old, recalling the legacy of the textile trade. The new elements harmonize with key alignments and proportions of the original building while clearly remaining contemporary. On the main Kingston Street façade, the massing is broken into twin volumes reinforcing the symmetry of the new entry and principal façade, while lightening the impact of the addition. An illuminated fleur-de-lis symbolizes the fleur-de-lis symbols in the original building.

PROJECT FACTS

Address: 88 Kingston Street, Boston, MA 02111, USA. **Client:** Insight Partners, LLC. **Completion:** 2005. **Building type:** Residential loft condominiums. **Gross floor area:** 5,481 m².
Original building: Winslow & Wetherell. **Client:** Sarah Lawrence Trust. **Completion:** 1893. **Building type:** textile factory. **Gross floor area:** 3,437 m².

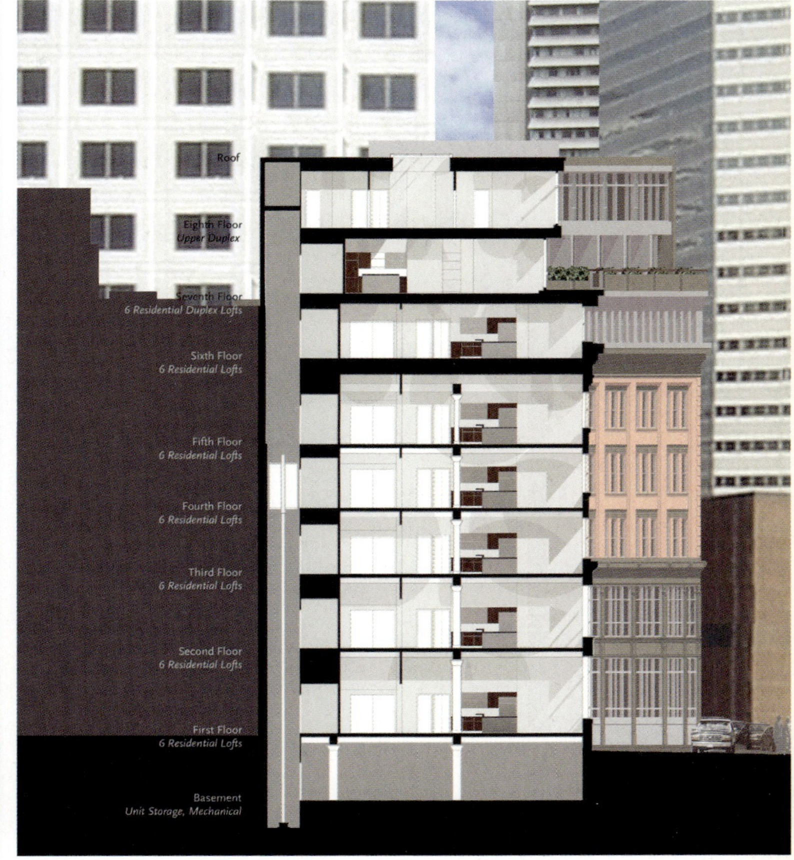

↑ | **Exterior view**
↓ | **Typical loft**
↓↓ | **Penthouse loft**

↑ | **Section**
↓ | **First floor plan**

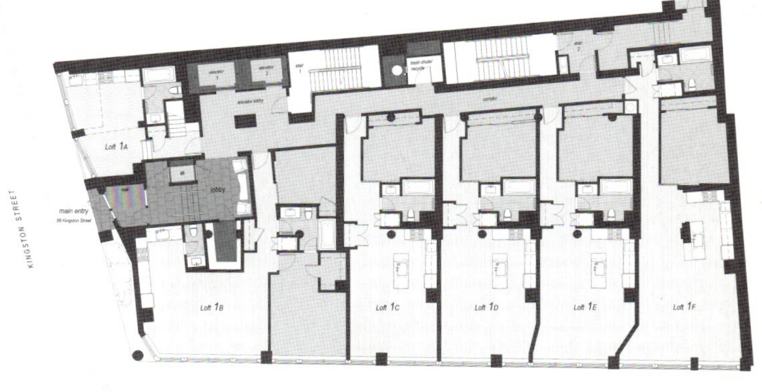

John Ronan Architects

↑ | **New wood flooring and custom kitchens**
→ | **Annex,** inserted steel stair and bridge
↓ | **The historic building,** laundry facility

Yale Steam Laundry Condominiums

Washington DC

The project is the sum of two parallel realities: the existing structure with its acquired character, and the new programmatic interventions inserted into it like furniture. Where new elements meet existing structure, the distinction is minimal, legible and discrete: steel plate insertions in the lobby stand in distinction to the glazed white brick to form bridges and stairs. In the living units, cores clad in birch plywood are inserted into the existing shell to minimally convert the building to its new use; in public areas, insertions of cold-rolled steel plate and glass form bridges and stairs. Laminated glass floor panels in the ceiling above borrow light from the skylights on the second floor roof.

PROJECT FACTS

Address: 437 New York Ave., Washington DC 20001, USA. **Client:** IBG Partners / Greenfield Partners. **Completion:** 2008. **Building type:** condominiums. **Gross floor area:** 3,530 m^2.
Original building: architect unknown. **Client:** Yale Steam Laundry. **Completion:** unknown. **Building type:** commercial laundry. **Gross floor area:** 3,530 m^2.

↖ | **Exterior,** by night
↑ | **View into the lobby from the entrance**
← | **Lobby**

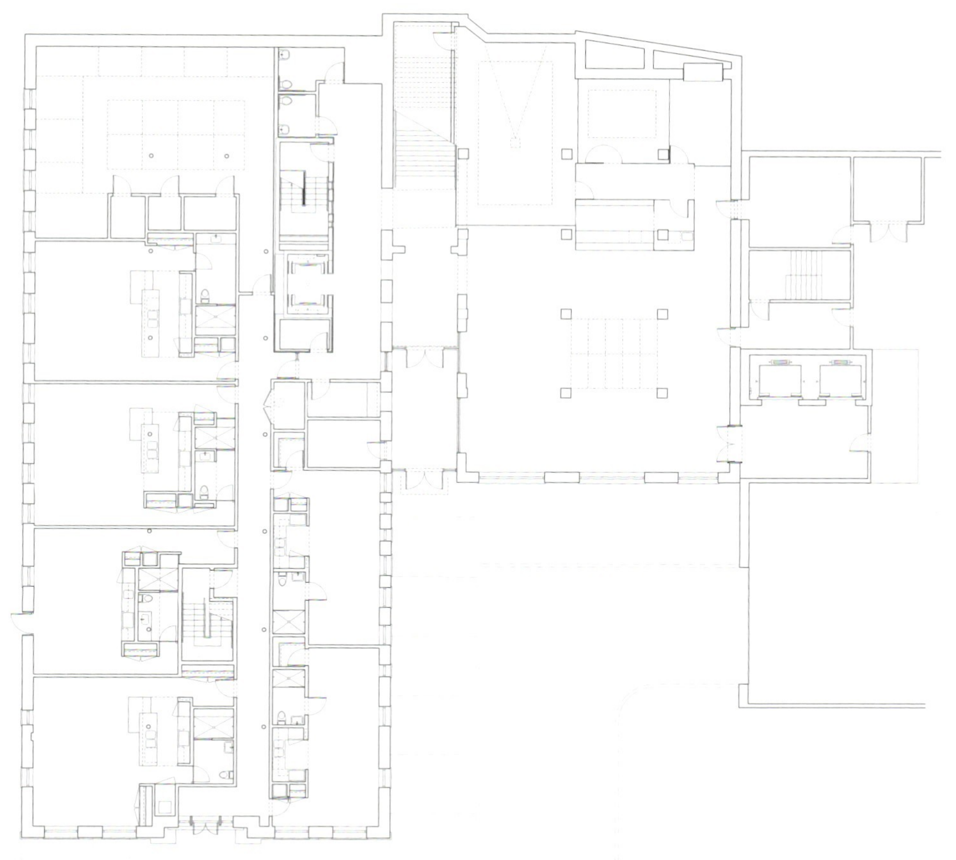

← | Ground floor plan
↙ | View into the glass lined bridge
↓ | Fitness room

Luczak Architekten

↑ | **Exterior view,** garden elevation
→ | **Kitchen** and dining area with gallery
↓ | **Before conversion**

Living in the Above Ground Bunker

Cologne

By adding a penthouse and a new building, this above ground bunker was transformed into 17 apartments in an urban, protected ensemble. The lofts received two story atriums, several levels with open spaces and as galleries, by making 1.10 meter incisions in the concrete walls. Living, working or flexible use spaces flow into each other, with wide openings connecting gardens and terraces. Using a gloomy above ground bunker in an economically profitable way for innovative spatial ideas shows how a piece of urban wasteland can be transformed. The advantage of the row house is combined with that of dense urban construction.

PROJECT FACTS

Address: Werkstattstraße 9, 50733 Cologne, Germany. **Client:** Hohr Immobilien GmbH. **Completion:** 2004. **Building type:** owner-occupied houses. **Gross floor area:** 2,675 m².
Original building: architect unknown. **Client:** unknown. **Completion:** 1942. **Building type:** bunker. **Gross floor area:** unknown.

↑ | **Roof,** bedroom
← | **Bunker wall** with piano
↓ | **Sketch**

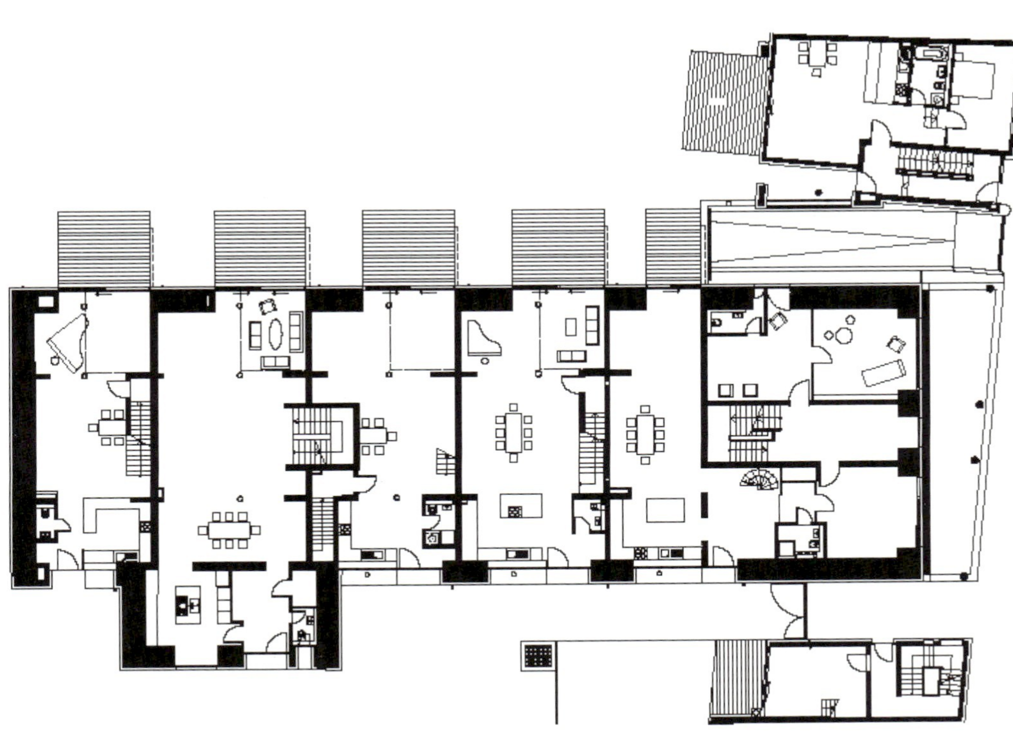

← | Ground floor plan
↓ | Bathroom

Atelier PRO architekten

↑ | **Façade** in morning light
↗ | **Converted church entrance** with former church bell in the background
→ | **Renewed church** threshold with dwellings in the background
↓ | **Former church**

Ludgerhof

Lichtenvoorde

Atelier PRO was alarmed by the prospect of the demolition of this beautiful building set about designing a housing complex for it. The interior of the church became the enclosed court of a residential block. The apartments extended along the former façade and outwards. The materials of the church façade were turned to face inwards, reversing the inside and outside. The roof was removed and the sacristy is now a play area on the plaza, with the church floor becoming the surface of the plaza. The apartments are unusual, beeing narrow and deep, separated from one another by a greenhouse, four meters wide. The perimeter wall can be seen through the greenhouses and the footprint of the church can still be seen.

PROJECT FACTS

Address: Ludgerhof 1–16, 7131 EG Lichtenvoorde, The Netherlands. **Client:** Stichting Heelweg / WBC projecten. **Completion:** 2005. **Building type:** apartments. **Gross floor area:** 2,970 m^2.
Original building: Gerard Schouten. **Client:** Parish administration Ludgerkerk. **Completion:** 1970. **Building type:** church. **Gross floor area:** 904.5 m^2.

↑ | **Courtyard detail** with former baptismal font
↓ | **Ground floor plan**

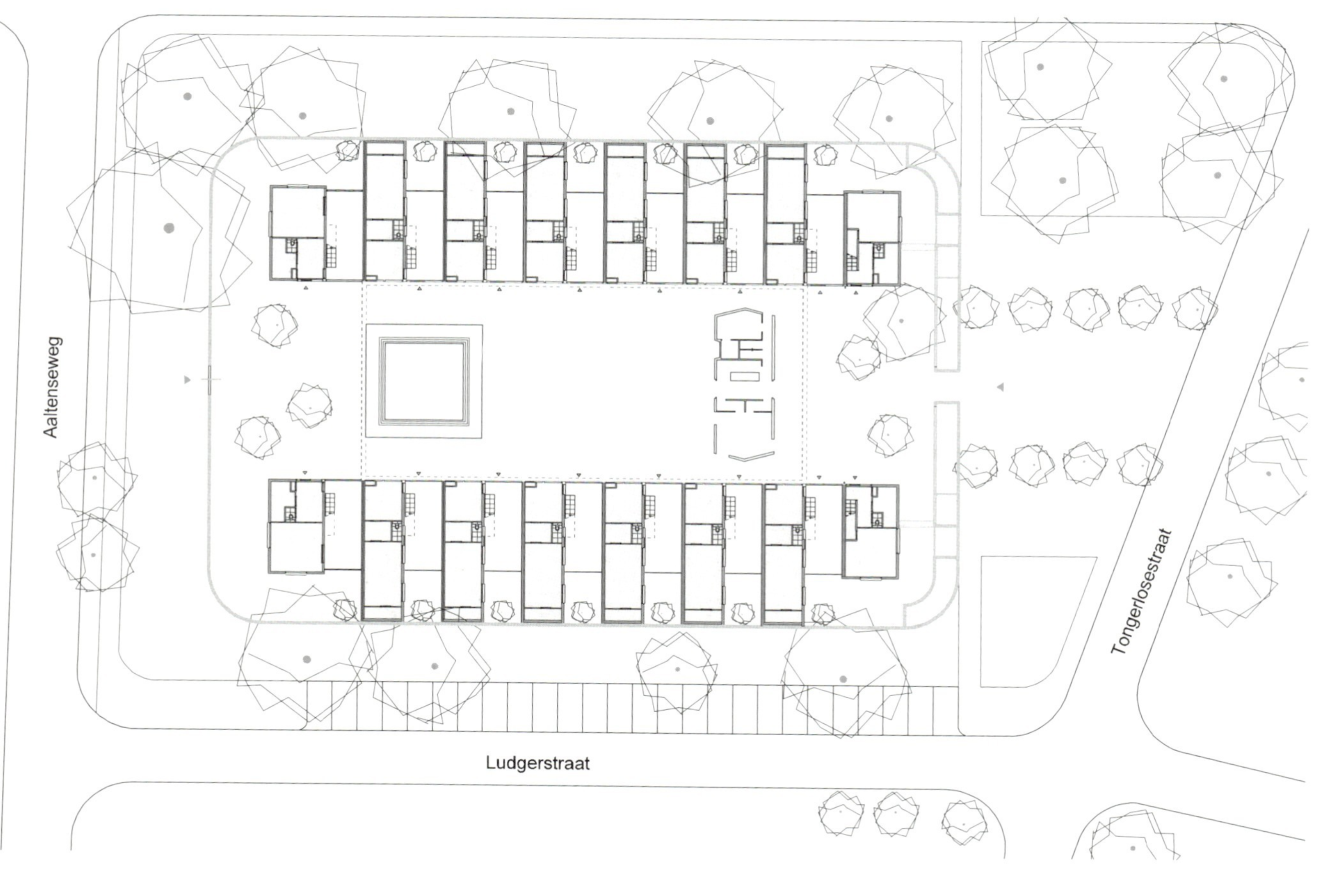

← | **Plans,** housing types
↓ | **Former church alter,** within the courtyard

Franke Rössel Rieger Architekten / Heinz Franke, Thomas Rössel, Heike Rieger

↑ | **View southwest,** former chapel

Living in the former Jesuit monastery

Munich

The historically listed complex was converted into 14 apartments, with the total area expanded by one fourth. The entire hexagonally arranged facility is built on the principle of the equilateral triangle, creating room layouts with either acute or obtuse angles. The dramatic effect of the steeply ascending chapel and library towers is emphasized by the low roof of the adjoining building. Golden sheet metal cladding on the extensions to the original building provides a contrast to the extensive restoration of the exposed concrete surfaces. The library tower was outfitted with large windows, providing the over 500 square meter large apartment with an expansive view and much daylight.

PROJECT FACTS

Address: Zuccalistraße 16–20, 80639 Munich Nymphenburg, Germany. **Client:** Mattusch Wohnbaugesellschaft mbH. **Completion:** 2009. **Building type:** housing. **Gross floor area:** 3,500 m². **Original building:** Paul Schneider von Esleben. **Client:** Oberdeutsche Provinz des Jesuiten-Ordens. **Completion:** 1965. **Building type:** order, editorial house of Jesuits. **Gross floor area:** 2,500 m².

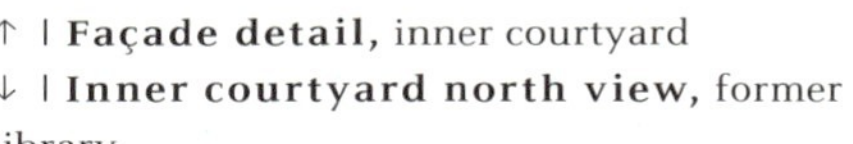

↑ | **Façade detail,** inner courtyard
↓ | **Inner courtyard north view,** former library

↑↑ | **Sketch inner courtyard,** excistence and new building
↑ | **Sketch,** room

Szymon Rozwałka (C+HO_aR), Tomas Pejpek

↑ | Apartment in its sorrounding
↘ | Building process

Apartment on the Top of a Grain silo

Olomouc

The project involved the transformation of a grain silo into a residential house. As the original building was never intended as a place of residences, the renovation necessitated some structural changes to the original structure. Using the lift that broke the perspective, the architects proposed a functional design of a house consisting of separate spaces which are connected in a "non-perspective" fashion with a separation of the relationship between time and space. The passage from one space to another is limited by the lift to opening and closing the same lift door. Each of the spaces (entrance space, garden, residential space and private space) are designed differently and the differences between them are more important than the characteristics of these spaces per se.

PROJECT FACTS

Address: Polska ulice, Olomouc, Czech Republic. **Client:** Barbora Kralik and Radim Kralik. **Completion:** 2007. **Building type:** apartment. **Gross floor area:** 423 m².
Original building: Jan Tymich. **Client:** Hanácké Mlýny a.s. **Completion:** 1941. **Building type:** grain silo. **Gross floor area:** unknown.

↑ | Exterior
↓ | View from inside in the top

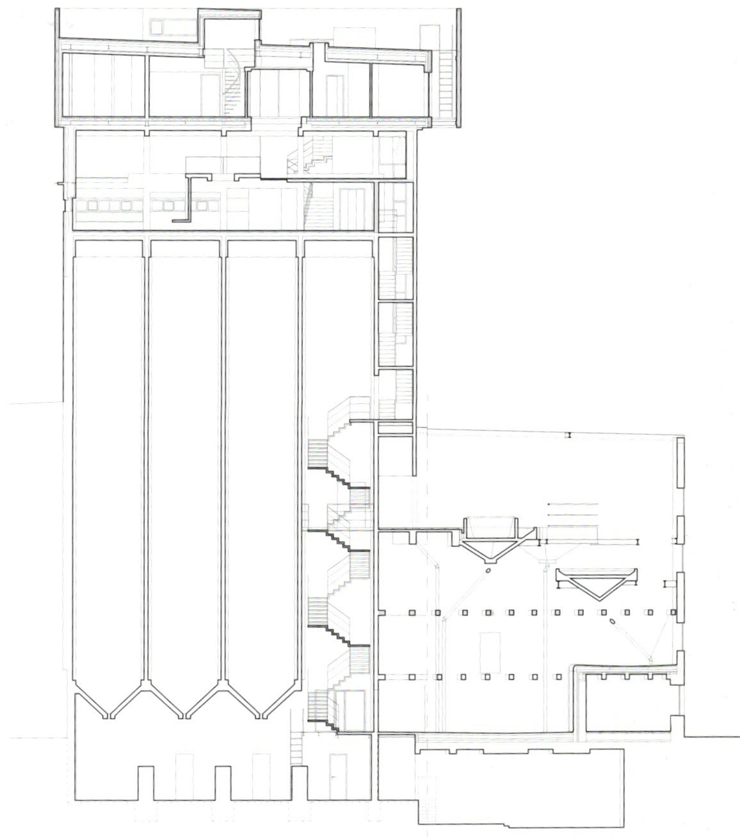

↑ | Section

Davidsson Tarkela Architects / Hannele Storgårds, Jaana Tarkela, Aki Davidsson

↑ | **Street elevation**, façade
↓ | **Before conversion**

Tikkurila Silk Mill

Vantaa

The industrial milieu of the Silk Mill in Tikkurila is one of the listed environments in the City of Vantaa. The mill was built in stages between 1934 and 1964. Production in the mill ended in 1977 and since then the buildings have been occupied by various businesses and organizations. Renor Oy, the owner of the mill's premises is now converting the property into loft-type apartments developed around the shell and core principle. The residents themselves are left the possibility to organize their own living spaces according to their needs and wishes. Some of the original buildings have to be replaced. The new development will be carried out according to the same loft model, adapting the new buildings into the old factory milieu.

PROJECT FACTS

Address: Tikkurilantie 44, 01300, Vantaa, Finland. **Client:** Renor Oy. **Completion:** ongoing. **Building type:** residental. **Gross floor area:** 18,000 m².
Original building: Herman Küs. **Client:** Tikkurilan Silkki Oy. **Completion:** 1934, 1964. **Building type:** industrial. **Gross floor area:** 14,500 m².

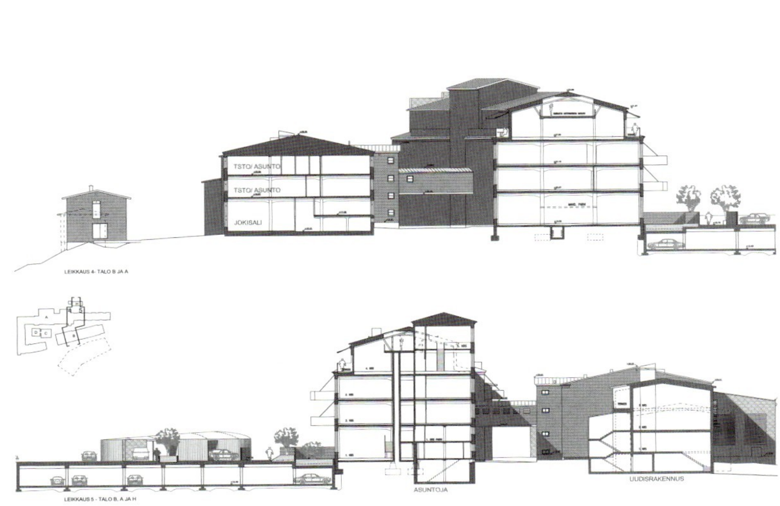

↑ | **Sections**
↓ | **Interior view,** living area

↑ | **Interior view,** apartment example

Tonkin Zulaikha Greer

↑ | **Exterior view,** street elevation
↓ | **Historical view**
→ | **The silos building,** seen from the railway

Silos Apartments

Newtown

The Crago Mill concrete silos and complex of tall timber storage bins were originally used for the storage of grain. This project converts these structures into residential apartments, with associated open space, while retaining the industrial qualities, scale and aesthetics of the existing complex. The existing ground-level bases of the historic silos and bins have architecturally impressive timber and concrete structural forms, and have been designed as the two main foyers. As the top of the silos, a new three-story metal-clad 'crown' provides space for a penthouse. The Silos Apartments take advantage of the circular plan forms to create unusual but rational room shapes, reconciling southern views with northern sunlight access.

PROJECT FACTS

Address: 1 Gladstone Street, Newtown, NSW 2042, Australia. **Heritage Architect:** Goddan Mackay Logan. **Landscape Architect:** 360 degrees. **Client:** Angus Developments and Grant Samuels. **Completion:** 2005. **Building type:** multi residential (apartments). **Gross floor area:** 7,000 m^2.

Original building: Thomas Robinson & Son, Nixon and Allen Architects. **Completion:** 1930 (concrete silos), 1898 (complex of timber storage bins). **Building type:** flour mill.

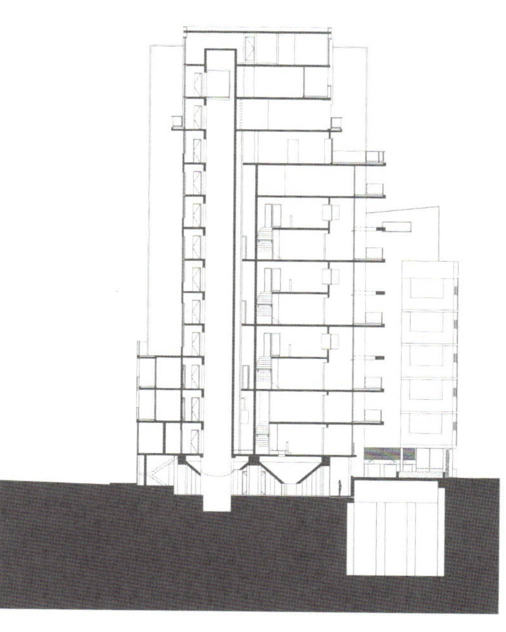

↖ | **Interior view,** living room
↑ | **Section**
← | **Interior view,** showing the textured wall surfaces that remind us of the building's past

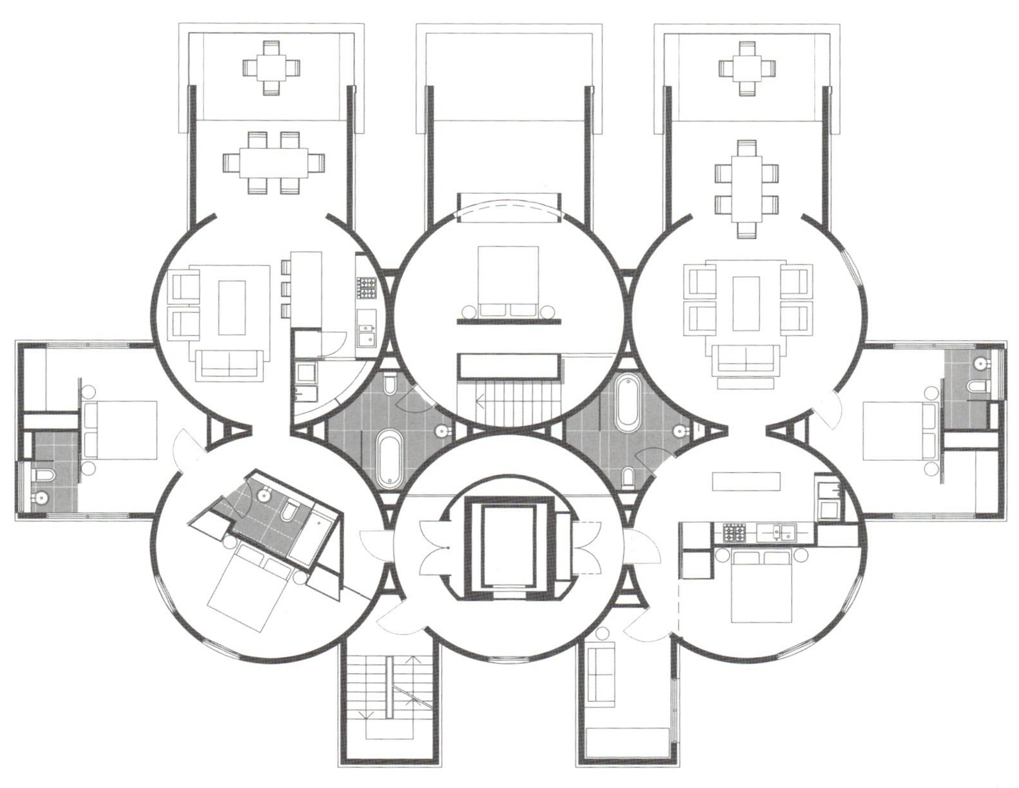

← | **9th floor plan**
↓ | **The concrete wheat hoppers** at ground level are retained as a feature in the foyer space

Aleks Istanbullu Architects / Corinna Gebert, Aleks Istanbullu

↑ | **West façade**
↗ | **Rooftop patios**
→ | **View from Industrial Street**
↓ | **Elevation original building**

Biscuit Company Lofts

Los Angeles

Nearly all the original floor finishes, including bathroom terrazzo, concrete vaults and one-inch-thick maple floors, were preserved and restored. Additional materials such as steel-clad columns, exposed brick interior walls and bronze windows retain vital esthetic attributes of the lofts. On the exterior, the original gas sconces were restored as elegant sentinels alongside the three historic entrances. The three street-facing loading docks with brick paving provide a dramatic setting for the restaurant and bar. Seven annex loading docks were transformed into three-story townhouse style lofts with ground level patios overlooking a newly created urban pocket park.

Address: 1850 Industrial Street, Los Angeles, CA 90021, USA. **Executive Architect:** Don Barany Architects. **Client:** Linear City, LLC. **Completion:** 2006. **Building type:** live and work lofts. **Gross floor area:** 13,411 m².

Original building: Eckel & Aldrich Architects. **Client:** National Biscuit Company (Nabisco). **Completion:** 1925. **Building type:** biscuit factory. **Gross floor area:** 11,929 m².

↑ | **Interior,** unit 712 in prior rooftop lightwell

← | **Interior,** rooftop unit

← | **Typical floor plan**
↓ | **Interior,** furnished

Paulus van Vliet architects with Blok Kats van Veen architects

↑ | **Exterior view,** existing building + new extra space on top
↓ | **Existing building**

Carré at Dolderse Hille

Den Dolder

The exclusive residential area of Dolders Hille rises from the wooded area of Utrecht Hill, near Den Dolder. This area, still partly in use by Altrecht as a hospital for psychiatric healthcare is surrounded by nature and beautiful, historic buildings. The pavilions were designed by the architects Poggenbeek and Mertens in the early 20th century. The approach chosen for the redevelopment takes into account future development, in line with the historical structure. A careful attitude preserving the historical nature of the site makes it possible to live truly surrounded by nature in the monumental Carré. In addition to the natural surroundings, the nine houses have a beautiful view over the courtyard.

PROJECT FACTS

Address: Dolderseweg 164, 3734BN Den Dolder, The Netherlands. **Client:** nine private houseowners. **Completion:** 2012. **Building type:** dwellings. **Gross floor area:** 1,448 m². **Original building:** H. F. Mertens. **Client:** Altrecht (agency for mental healthcare). **Completion:** 1937. **Building type:** ateliers. **Gross floor area:** 1,080 m².

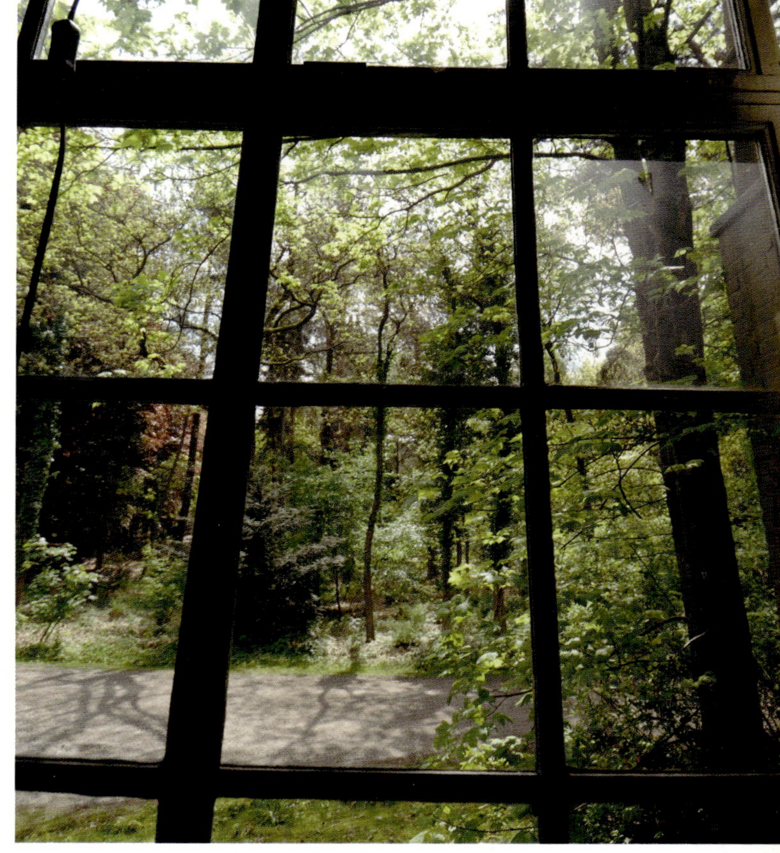

↑ | **Ground floor plan**
↓ | **Existing courtyard**

↑ | **View** from inside to surroundings

Angelis+Partner Architekten

↑ | View from the street
→ | Refurbished natural stone façade

Senior residence Carl-Fried Haus

Cologne

Because of the central location in Cologne and the intact and statically flexible basic building structure the decision was made in favor of a radical conversion of the existing stock to a residence for senior citizens with care units and a parking garage. The original high quality street façades made of natural stone were carefully refurbished. The access and use structure of the four building components was completely rethought so that most of the almost 100 apartments were oriented to the courtyard, with the communicative access hallways serving as a natural shield to the traffic axes. The new use is shown in the play of color of the hallways through the perforated façade of the original building.

PROJECT FACTS

Address: Sachsenring 67, 50677 Cologne, Germany. **Client:** WEKA GmbH. **Completion:** 2008. **Building type:** senior residence. **Gross floor area:** 15,131 m^2.

Original building: Hanns Koerfer, Horst Mathow, Dipl.Ing. Hans Menne. **Client:** Grundstücksverwaltung, Gesellschaft Sachsenring. **Completion:** 1960. **Building type:** commercial. **Gross floor area:** 15,131 m^2.

↑ | Inner courtyard
↙ | Standard floor plan
↗ | Cafeteria
→ | Lobby

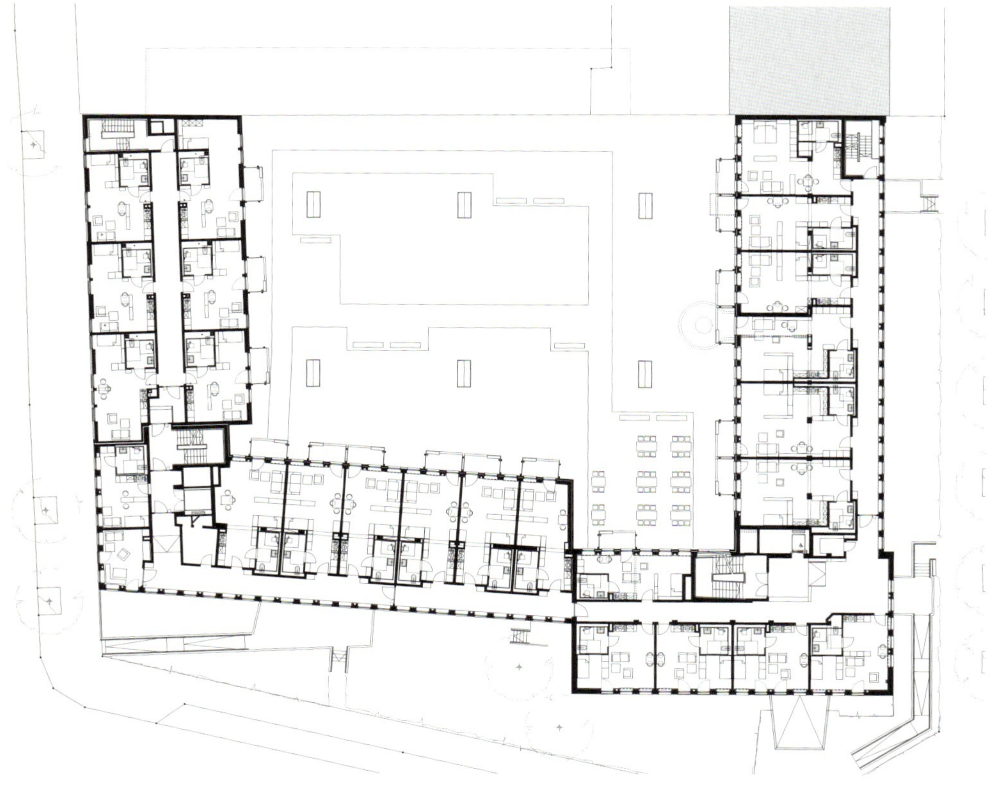

MIXED-USE

studioinges Architektur und Städtebau / Stefan Schwirtz, Thomas Bochmann, Francesca Saetti

↑ | Exterior
→ | Exterior detail by night

experimenta Science Center

Heilbronn

A slender new structure augments the existing building on an island on the Neckar River. The annex is equipped with the same brick shell as the warehouse, underscoring its stand-alone effect. The foyer in the new building is connected with a glazed space between the twin buildings. Along the connecting wall to the old structure greenish yellow aluminum panels provide an artificial contrast to the natural, brown and red bricks. A recessed main stairway turns this wall into as sculpture. Bridges connect it with the permanent exhibition in the warehouse, whose interior rooms retain their impressive reinforced steel skeleton.

PROJECT FACTS

Address: Kranenstraße 14, 74072 Heilbronn, Germany. **Client:** City of Heilbronn. **Completion:** 2009. **Building type:** museum, science center. **Gross floor area:** 8,713 m².
Original building: Architect Hermann Wahl. **Client:** Carl Hagenbucher & Söhne. **Completion:** 1936. **Building type:** silo. **Gross floor area:** 4,517 m².

↑ | **Staircase system**

↙ | **Isometry**

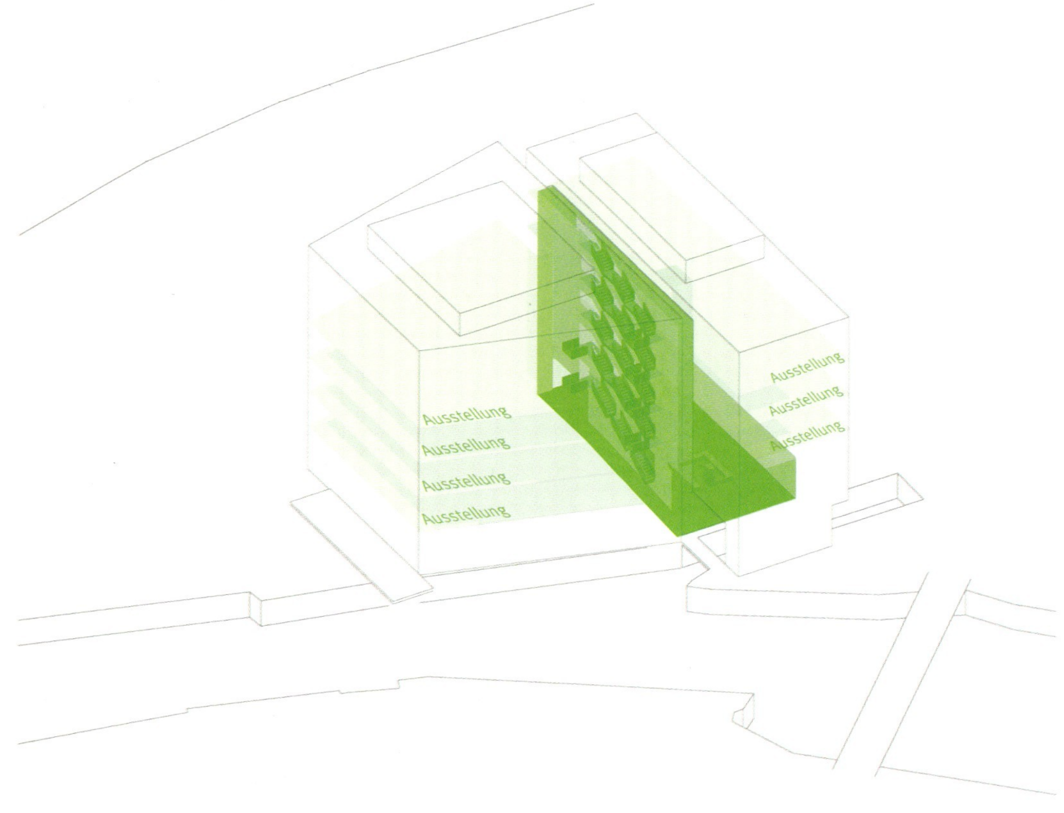

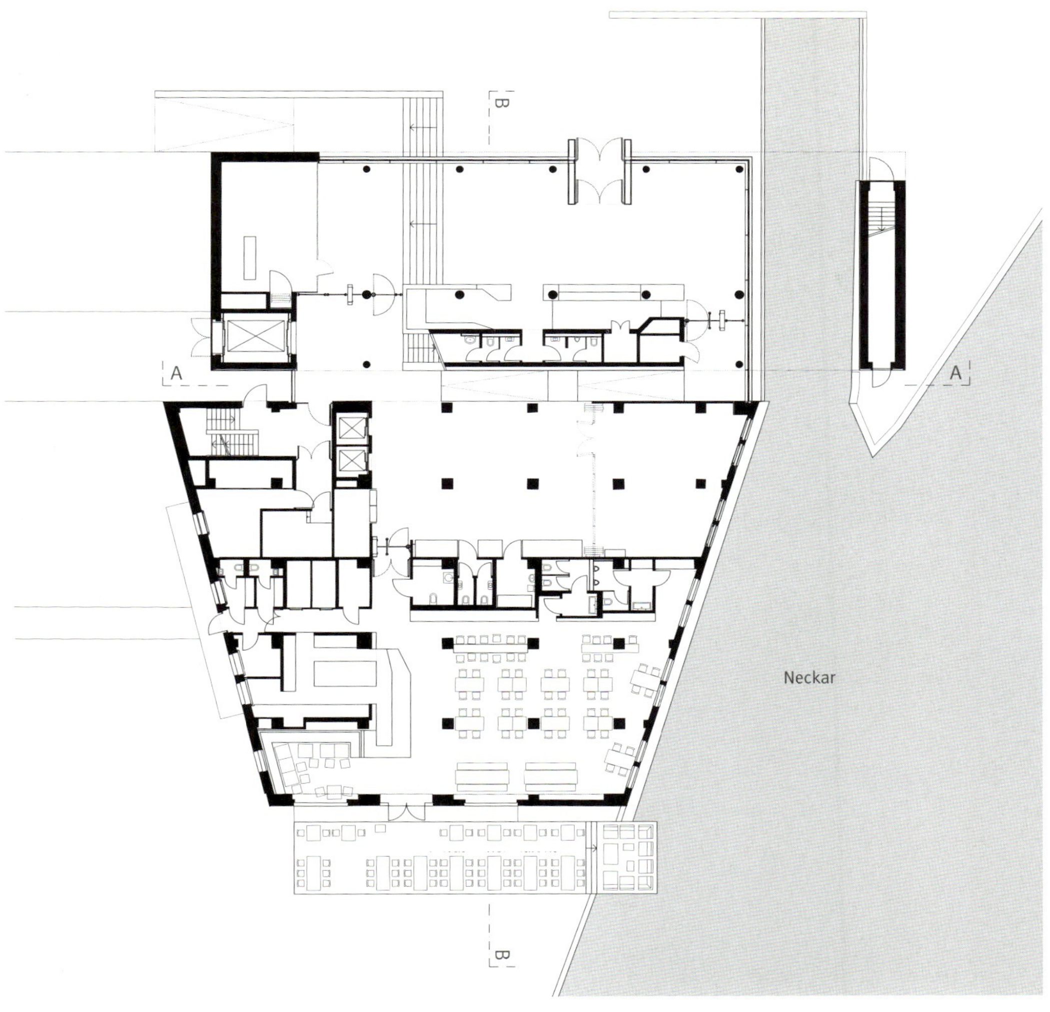

← | **Ground floor plan**
↓ | **Exhibition room,** in the old silo

Thomas Pink | Petzinka Pink Architekten

↑ | **North façade,** main entrance
→ | **Rear elevation,** entrance

Rote Halle

Düsseldorf

Special emphasis was placed maintaining the characteristic atmosphere in the refurbishing of this former industrial hall. The brick façades were restored and the reveals were reconstructed. All constructive elements in the building interior were cleaned entirely, but not plastered, in order to retain the raw industrial character. The loft character was enhanced by an additional light admitting gable. A glass wall installed on the entryway side provides a view of the central greened atrium. The material composition of concrete, stone, brick and glass apportioned with green area produces a virtuoso accord with the established showrooms.

PROJECT FACTS

Address: Rather Straße 49c, 40476 Düsseldorf, Germany. **Interior Architects:** e15. **Client:** Petzinka Wohn- und Gewerbeimmobilien GmbH. **Completion:** 2006. **Building type:** showrooms, offices. **Gross floor area:** 2,051 m².

Original building: architect unknown. **Client:** Rheinmetall AG. **Completion:** 1912. **Building type:** industrial hall. **Gross floor area:** unknown.

↑ | **Showroom,** first floor
← | **Stairs,** mixed materials
↓ | **Plans,** first floor and ground floor

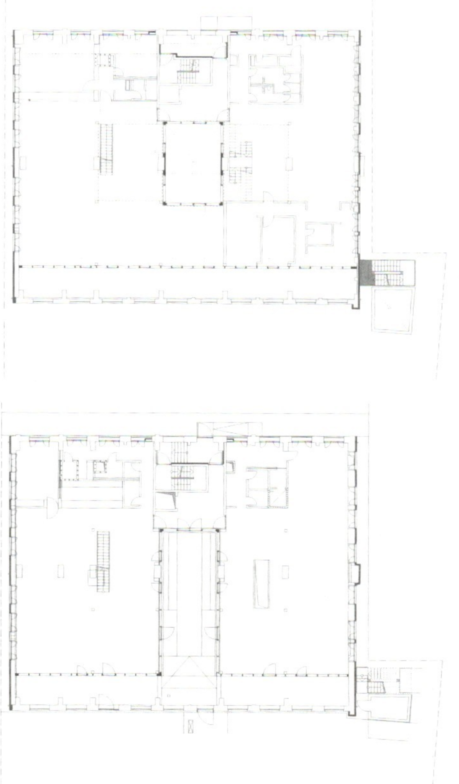

← | **Section**
↓ | **Atrium,** planted with inner glass façade

Thomas Pink | Petzinka Pink Architekten

↑ | **New development,** new office building with "Verheiratetenhaus"

↗ | **Barracks**

→ | **New development**

Ideenbotschaft

Düsseldorf

The refurbishing of the historically listed Wilhelminian Ulanen barracks was conducted in the overall urban developmental context, with the prudent addition of new buildings and annexes. The former soldiers' quarters, the latrine and the Verheiratetenhaus (quarters for married soldiers) were retained and repaired. On the site of the demolished structure a new five story, mainly brick building was erected, which joins the existing building and the new construction in an ensemble. The green area was protected and like the former drill grounds was resurrected as a public campus. The so-called „embassy of ideas" (Ideenbotschaft) has operated as the new, central location for the international Grey advertising agency since 2008.

PROJECT FACTS

Address: Platz der Ideen 1 + 2 (Rossstraße 133a, b und 135), 40476 Düsseldorf, Germany. **Interior architect:** Cossmann & de Bruyn. **Client:** LEG location- and project development Düsseldorf GmbH. **Completion:** 2008. **Building type:** campus, training rooms, offices, apartments. **Gross floor area:** 20,841 m^2. **Original building:** architect unknown. **Client:** City of Düsseldorf. **Completion:** 1890. **Building type:** barracks. **Gross floor area:** unknown.

↑ | **Barracks,** meeting room
← | **Roof floor barracks,** heightening
↓ | **Section**

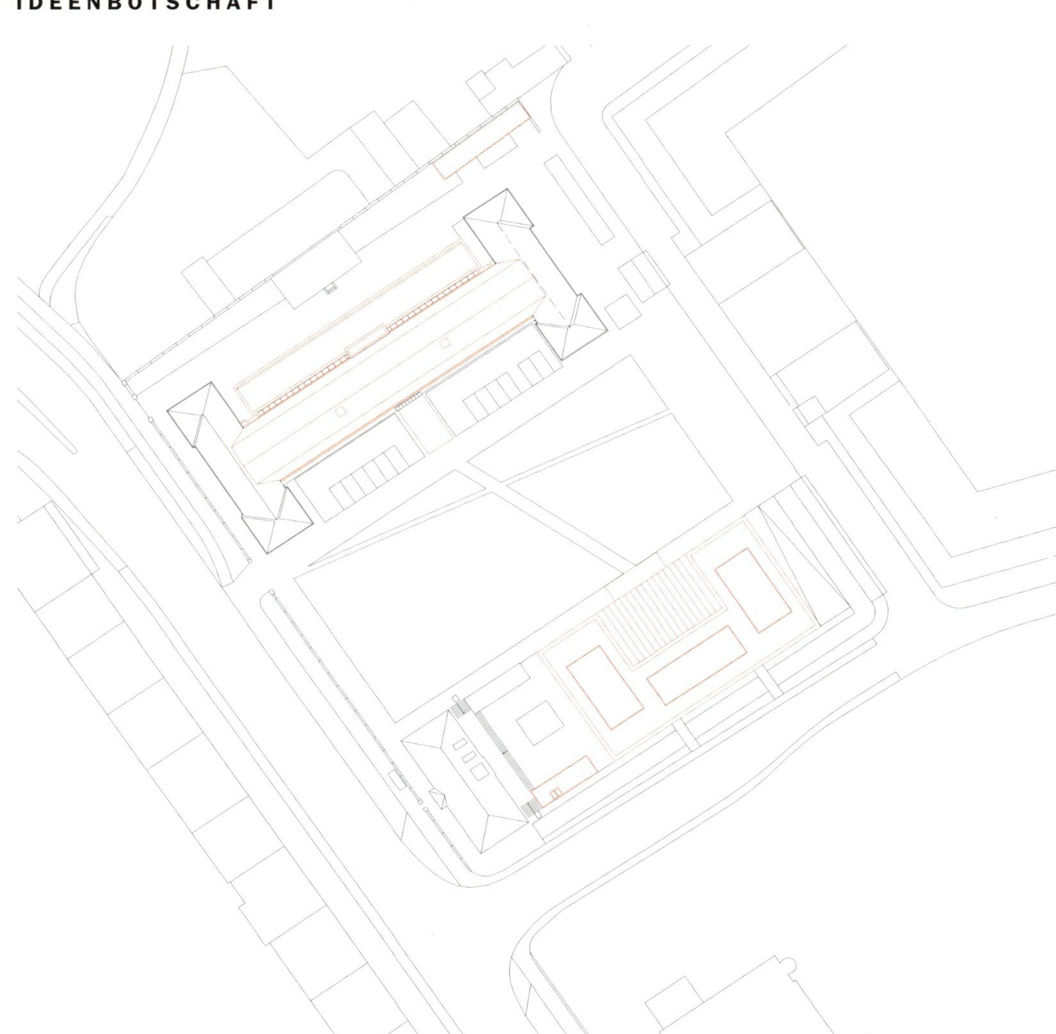

← | **Site plan**
↓ | **Canteen,** former "Verheiratetenhaus"

Dirk Jan Postel
(Kraaijvanger • Urbis)

↑ | **District Office,** Center for Fine Arts in the background
↓ | **Section**

District Office Oost-Watergraafsmeer

Amsterdam

The district offices are located in a building with a stepped gable on the south side that mediates between the different heights of the complex. The new façades are made partly of brick and partly of stone. Four original façades of buildings from the gasworks have been retained on the south side. Two of the original plant buildings have been restored to accommodate the art library. The community school is located in a new building with an entirely different syntax of long, horizontal bands of windows and an arched entrance. The transition between public and private spaces in the complex is seamless. The building encloses two long, semi-public areas, one of which is covered.

PROJECT FACTS

Address: Oranje-Vrijstaatplein 2, 1093 NG Amsterdam, The Netherlands. **Client:** J.P. van Eesteren. **Completion:** 2009. **Building type:** offices, center for fine arts, community school. **Gross floor area:** 17,782 m².

Original building: Isaac Gosschalk. **Client:** The British Imperial Continental Gas Association. **Completion:** 1885. **Building type:** gasworks. **Gross floor area:** unknown.

↑ | **Connection**, new designed and reconstructed façade

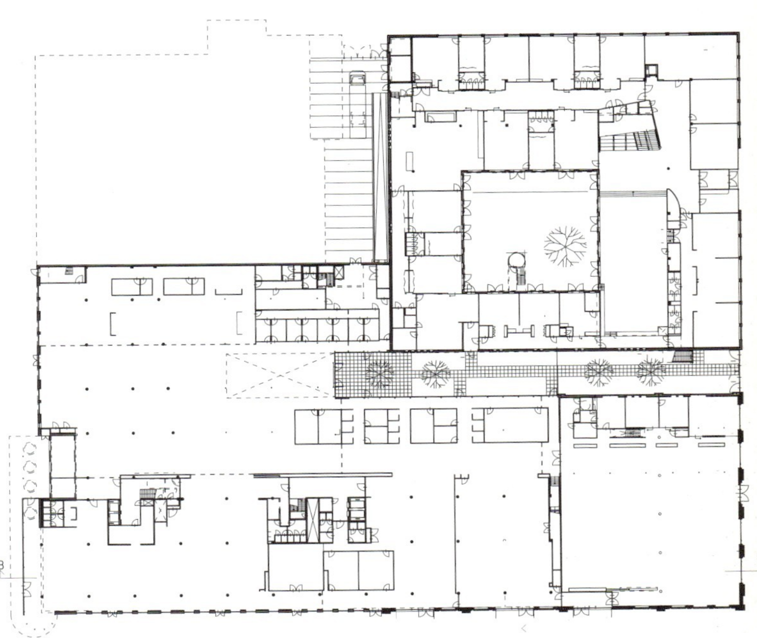

↑ | **Ground floor plan**

↓ | **Interior of the Center for Fine Arts**

Hamonic + Masson

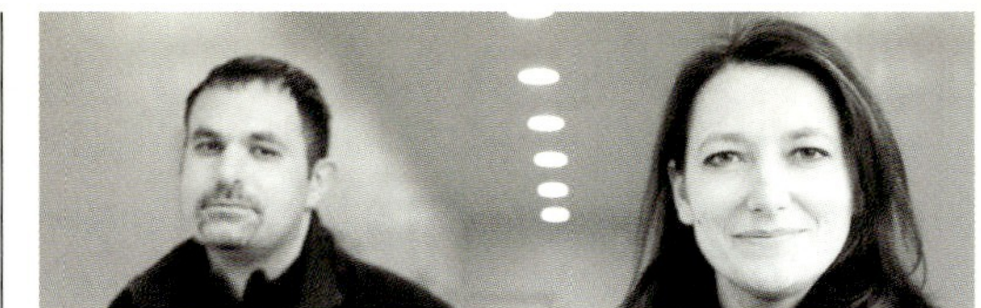

↑ | View from park

The Docks Dombasles

Le Havre

The architects'-mixed-use office and housing building is part of an initiative to preserve and reuse the industrial heritage of the southern quarters of Le Havre. Through its scale, rhythm, shape and materials, the project forms an integral part of a re-envisioned harbor landscape. A 19th century brick warehouse, or alvéole, was conserved and incorporated into the project to house the office space required in the programme. The warehouse's silhouette and scale subsequently inspired the module that was repeated for the housing portion of the project. The use of modules allowed for a prefabricated construction system.

PROJECT FACTS

Address: S16, rue Saint-Nicolas, Docks Dombasles, 76600 Le Havre, France. **Structural engineer:** Peyronnel. **Client:** Investir Immobilier. **Completion:** 2009. **Building type:** apartments and offices. **Gross floor area:** 3,024 m^2.
Original building: Dubret-Debaines. **Client:** unknown. **Completion:** 1854. **Building type:** docks. **Gross floor area:** unknown.

↑ | **Floor plans**
↓ | **View** from river basin

↑ | **View** of the terrace of a duplex

Sergei Tchoban Architekt BDA nps tchoban voss
A. M. Prasch, S. Tchoban, E. Voss / Philipp Bauer

↑ | Main façade
→ | Interior

Ernst-Reuter-Haus

Berlin

Begun in the 1940s, the neo-classical three wing complex was finally completed in 1956 as the seat of the German Association of Cities and Towns. After 50 years full of change the intention was to adapt the building with its natural stone façade and spacious interior rooms for contemporary use by means of individual targeted measures, thereby allowing its atmospheric potential to unfold. With these contemporary interventions the structural forms of the 1940s could be harmonized with the interior decoration of the 1950s. Additional space was gained with extensions on the third floor and the attic as well as the construction of another floor in the rear.

Address: Straße des 17. Juni 110–114, 10623 Berlin, Germany. **Architect in charge:** Philipp Bauer. **Lighting design:** Scott Lightning. **Client:** Cenda Invest AG. **Completion:** 2010. **Building type:** mixed-use. **Gross floor area:** 25,596 m².
Original building: Walter Schlempp. **Client:** Deutscher Gemeindetag (DGT). **Completion:** 1941. **Building type:** governmental building. **Gross floor area:** 24,532 m².

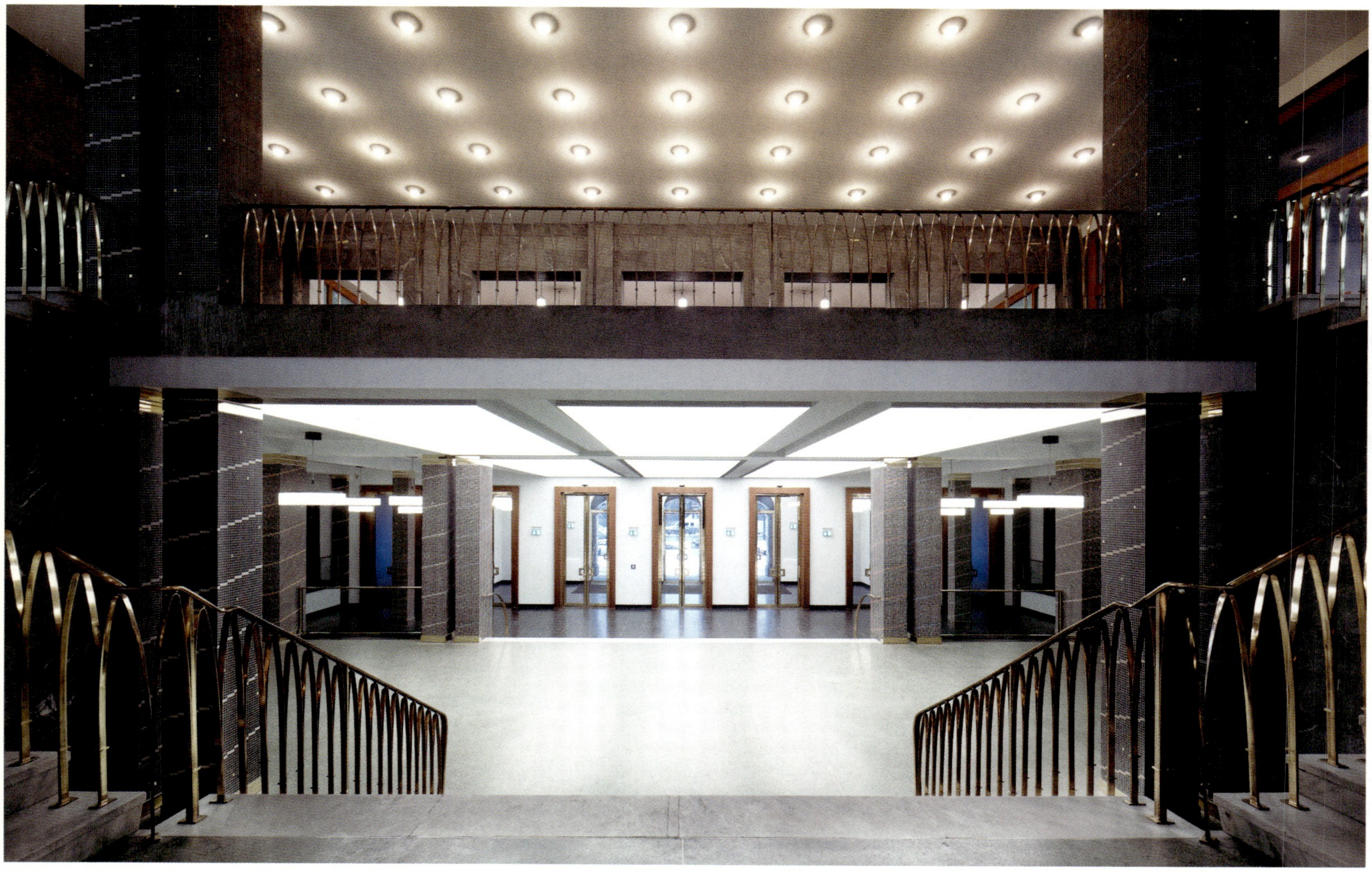

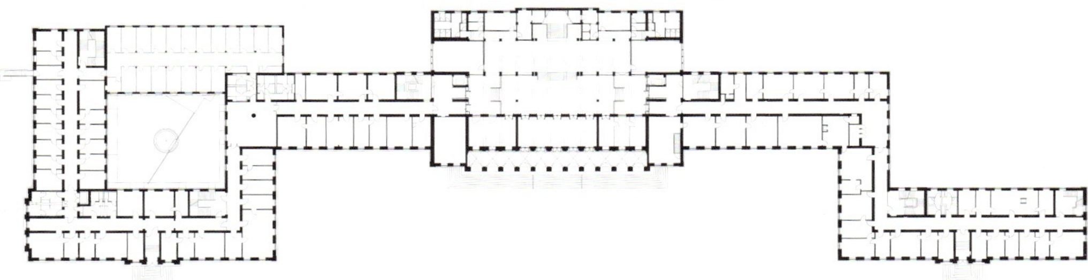

←← | **Staircase**
↙↙ | **Staircase,** view into the lobby
← | **Ground floor plan**
↙ | **Arcades,** by night
↓ | **Detail of the door**

BURO II & ARCHI+I

↑ | Façade
↓ | Before conversion

Picanol Site Reconversion

Ypres

When the city of Ypres acquired the former Picanol factory, it cleared the path for an important new urban development: the revaluation of the canal area and its integration with the city center. The City Council made a strategic decision to assign public services a location in this new district together with private functions. The project recoup the most important factory buildings, concentrates the library and the art and music academy on the industrial site, giving the new single family homes and apartment buildings a strategic location on the site and rethinking the design of the public space. The project functions as generator for a broader development that will be addressed inlater design stages.

PROJECT FACTS

Address: Weverijstraat / Polenlaan, 8900 Ypres, Belgium. **Client:** City of Ypres. **Completion:** 2009. **Building type:** public. **Gross floor area:** 10,510 m² (public); 17,463 m² (private).
Original building: Le Marchand and Ribaucourt. **Client:** Alfred Valcke. **Completion:** 1921. **Building type:** weaving factory. **Gross floor area:** unknown.

↑ | **Overview**

↑ | **Library,** reading room
↓ | **Exterior view**

RE-ACT NOW Studio / arch.
Mario Kuibus & the team

↑ | Exterior view

→ | Entrance
↓ | Longitudinal and cross sections

Renovation of Rahova Commodities Exchange

Bucharest

The new functions the house needed were based on great flexibility and a general transparency. The architects therefore chose to restore the valuable part of the building and to rebuild the rest with a completely new concept, in stark contrast with the existing situation – exactly the kind of approach that is lacking in Bucharest. This former goods exchange building was the most prominent part of the Customs – Goods Exchange – Warehouses ensemble. The architects restored the long vacant building to its nostalgic charm, framing it with a modern environment, using the candid and simple beauty of technology.

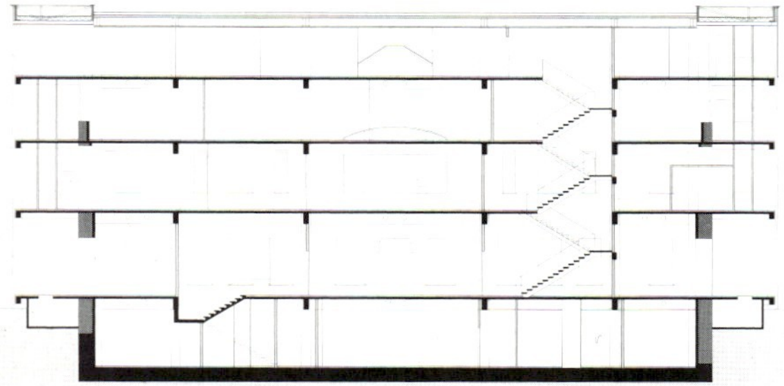

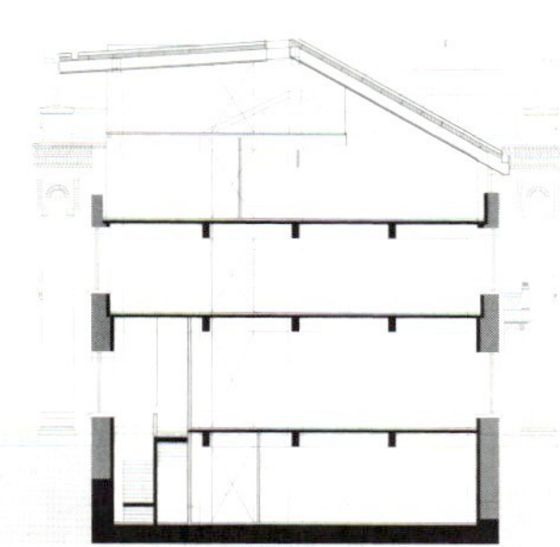

PROJECT FACTS

Address: Rahova Street no 196A, Bucharest, Romania. **Client:** The ark. **Completion:** 2008. **Building type:** mixed-use. **Gross floor area:** 3,000 m².
Original building: Giulio Magni. **Client:** Rahova Commodities Exchange. **Completion:** 1898. **Building type:** office. **Gross floor area:** 2,300 m².

↑ | **Office area,** upper level
← | **Office area,** second floor

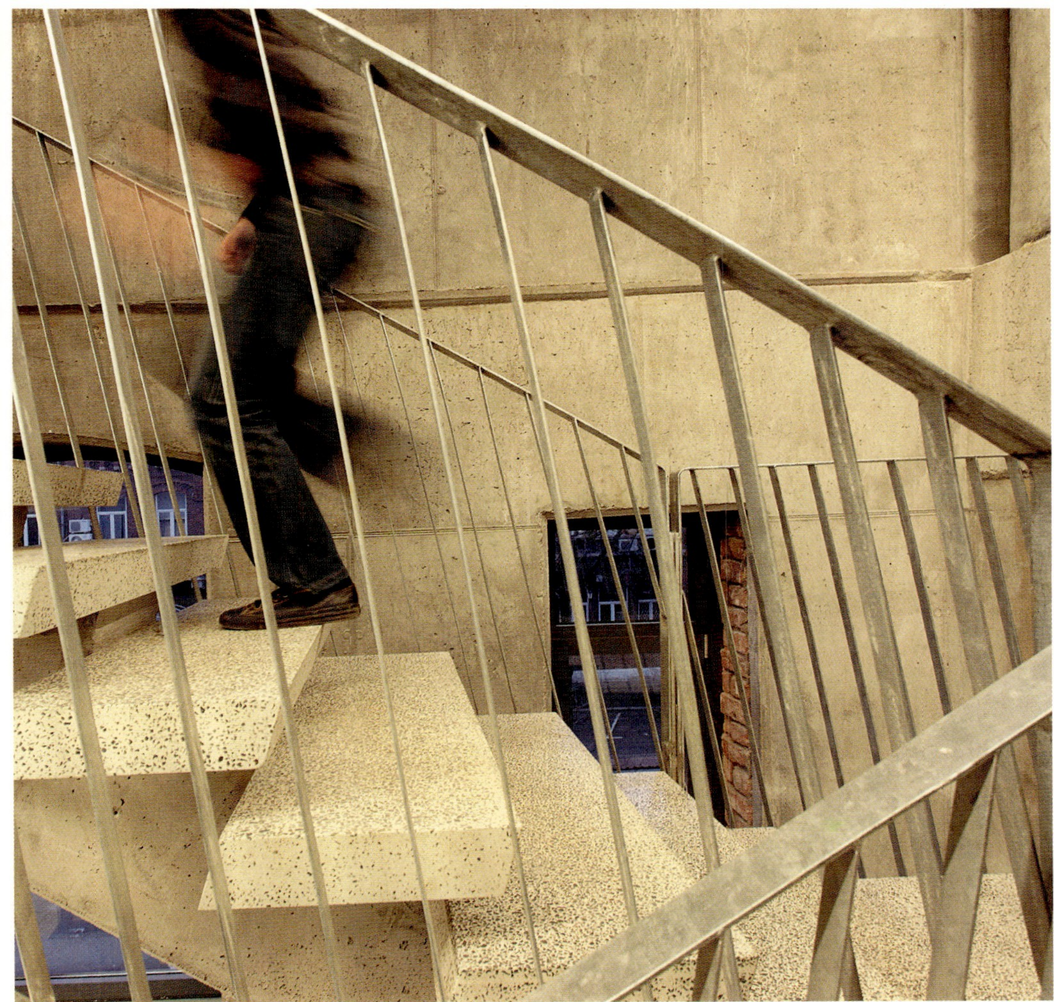

← | Stairway
↓ | Second floor plan

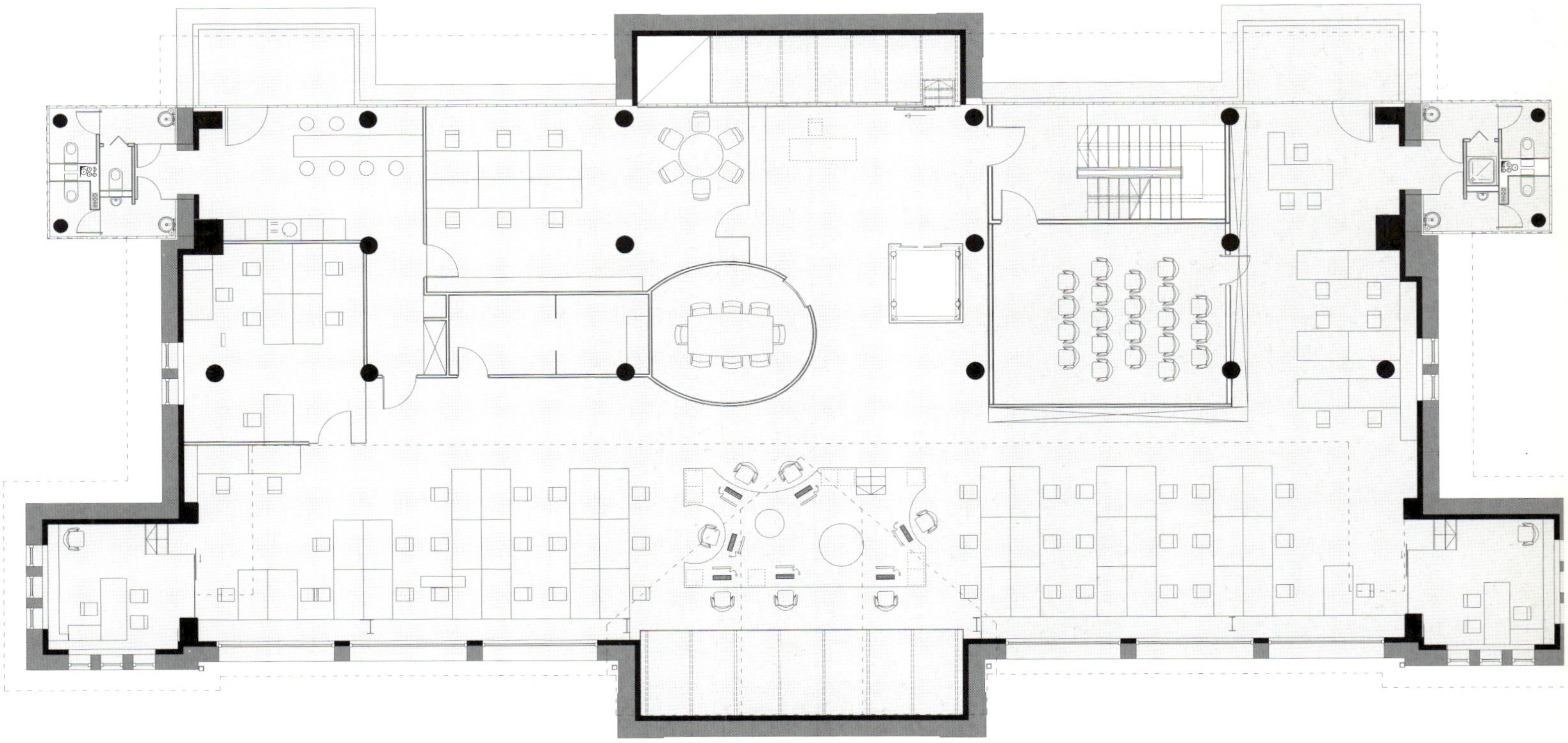

diederendirrix / Bert Dirrix

↑ | **Exterior view,** on the left side the sports hall, on the right side the school
→ | **Playground,** on the roof

The Hangar

Eindhoven

Two volumes which were slid into the building were added to the characteristic airplane hangar. A large part of the hangar has been kept empty which allows space for a covered square, that also functions as the entrance to the complex. A central corridor, also covered by the hangar, connects the square to a playground that opens towards the ecological green zone. The corridor is enclosed on one side by a colorful, transparent volume that houses a community center with library. A volume situated partially in the ground lies on the other side, with a playground on the roof. It houses a sports center and a gathering space. The buildings are connected by way of an underground volume.

PROJECT FACTS

Address: Meerbos 2–18, 5658 LA Eindhoven, The Netherlands. **Client:** Woonveste Vastgoed BV. **Completion:** 2009. **Building type:** multifaceted community. **Gross floor area:** 8,600 m². **Original building:** BABOV (Bureau Aanleg, Beheer en Onderhoud Vliegvelden). **Client:** Koninklijke Luchtmacht. **Completion:** 1952. **Building type:** airplane hangar. **Gross floor area:** 2,000 m².

↑ | **Auditorium** with indoor playgrounds
↙ | **Sections,** longitudinal and cross section

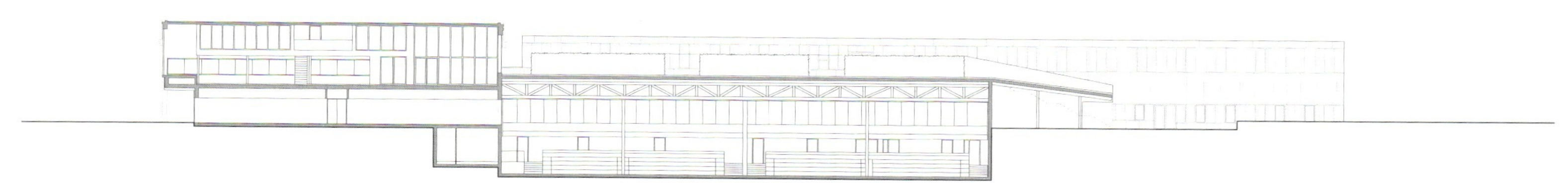

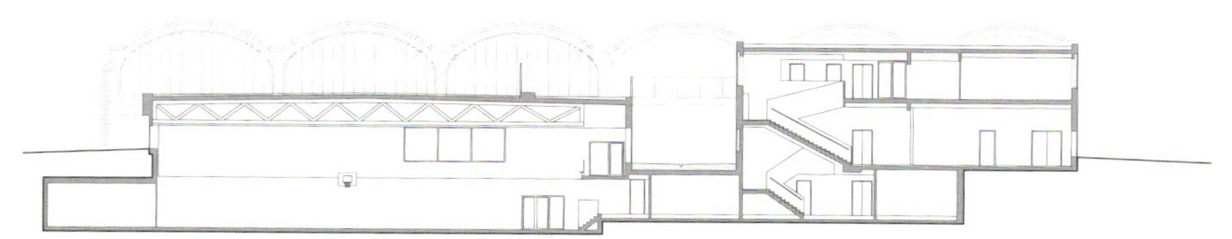

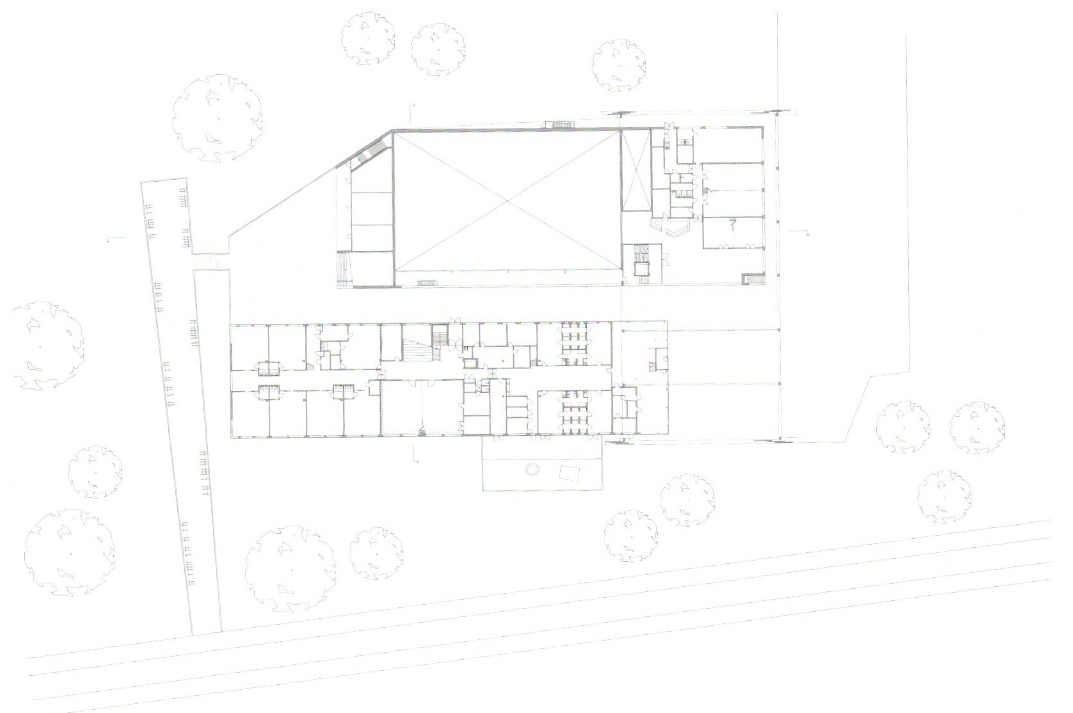

← | **Ground floor plan**
↓ | **Interior view,** sports hall

51N4E / Johan Anrys, Freek Persyn, Peter Swinnen

↑ | Night view
→ | View from Beethovenstraat

Lamot

Mechelen

The Lamot brewery has been subject to a continuous process of extension and demolition, a process where redundant parts are torn down without emotion and the required infrastructures are simply added. During the process the architects eagerly learned from this logic, re-employing it for the future development of Lamot, a mixture of congress facilities and cultural amenities. Converting this awkward giant into a public building brought to the fore new standards of accessibility, orientation, light and views. It entails a surgical operation on an urban scale. Slitting open the building's first floor is a calculated implosion, leaving no doubt as to the future ambition of Lamot.

PROJECT FACTS

Address: Van Beethovenstraat 8/10, 2800 Mechelen, Belgium. **Execution design:** Architectencooperatief. **Client:** City of Mechelen. **Completion:** 2005. **Building type:** congress and heritage center. **Gross floor area:** 6,600 m².

Original building: architect unknown. **Client:** Lamot. **Completion:** 1922. **Building type:** brewery. **Gross floor area:** 4,950 m².

↑ | **Interior**

← | **First floor plan**

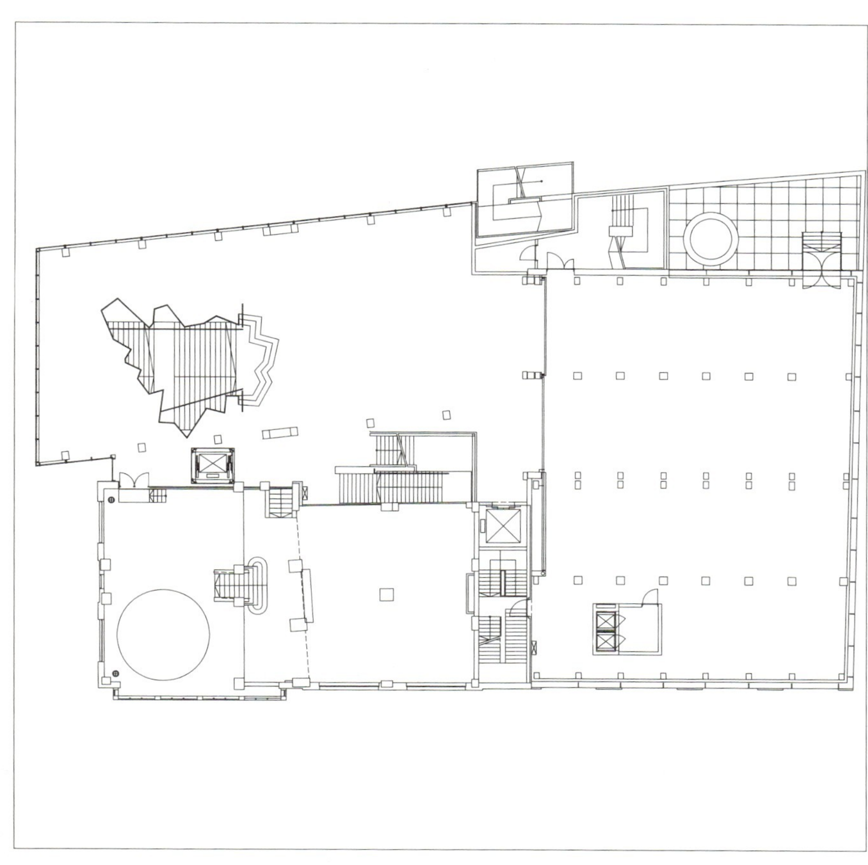

← | View from canal
↑ | Model
↓ | Façade

Hacin + Associates, Inc. / Mathew Manke, Scott Thomson, David J. Hacin

↑ | View of completed project
→ | Exterior
↓ | Original building

FP3

Boston

FP3 is the adaptive reuse of two historic structures, a new rooftop addition and an infill building in the historic Fort Point Channel district. Prompted by the desire to preserve the original structures, a careful search for architectural cues and rhythms resulted in a new structural steel structure woven through the original heavy timber structure to support the new three story rooftop addition. By retaining most of the heavy timber structure, less new material was required to construct the project, less waste was generated and the original buildings are more truly preserved to continue as vital, purposeful pieces of the urban fabric. The timbers that were removed were re-milled and used as cladding in the new lobby space.

PROJECT FACTS

Address: 346, 348, 354 Congress Street, Boston, MA 02210, USA. **Client:** Berkeley Investments. **Completion:** 2008. **Building type:** mixed-use. **Gross floor area:** 13,471 m².
Original building: Morton D. Safford. **Client:** Boston Wharf Co. **Completion:** 1894 (348 Congress), 1899 (354 Congress). **Building type:** textile storage and manufacturing. **Gross floor area:** 8,361 m².

↑ | **View of lobby and gallery space**
← | **Plan,** basement

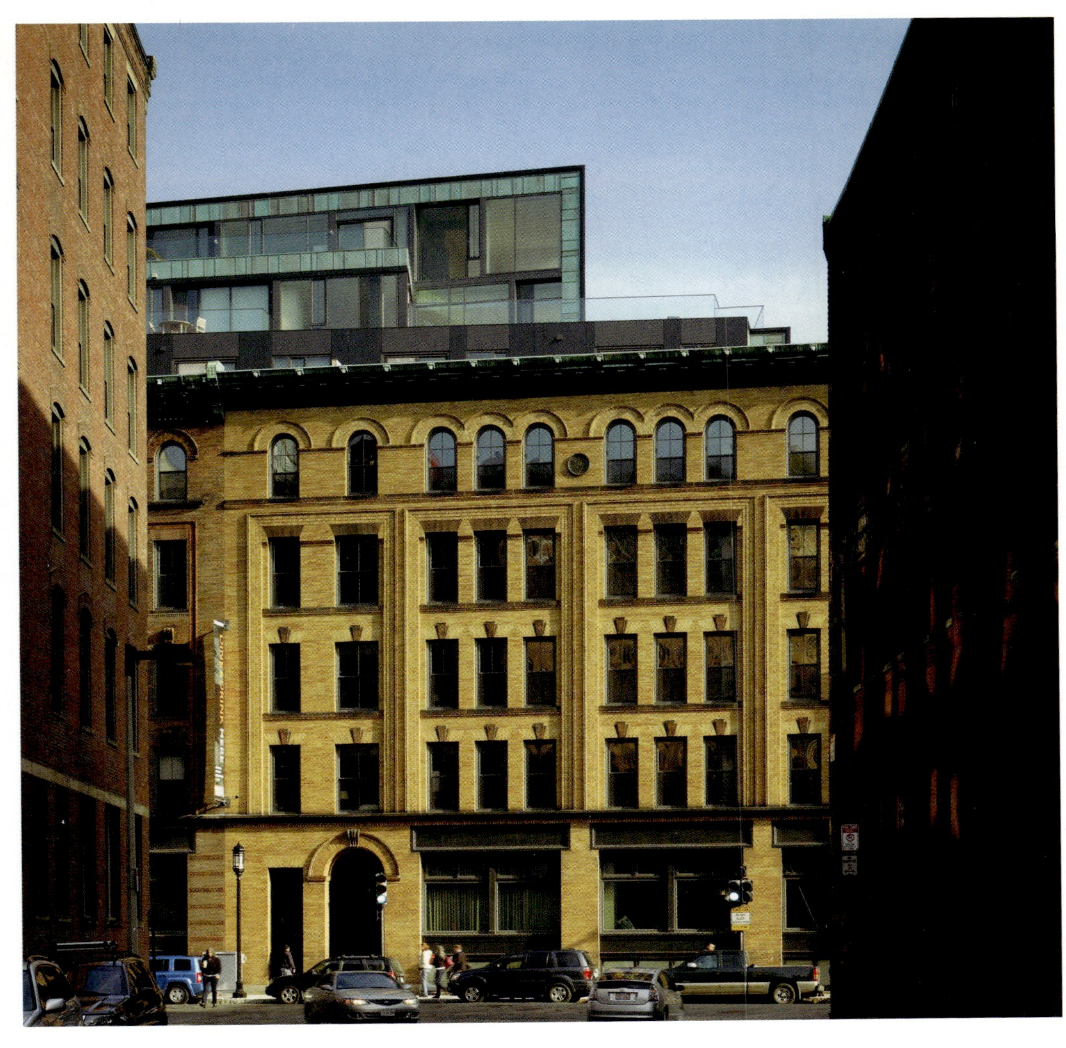

← | Façade
↓ | 3D visualization of folded plane addition

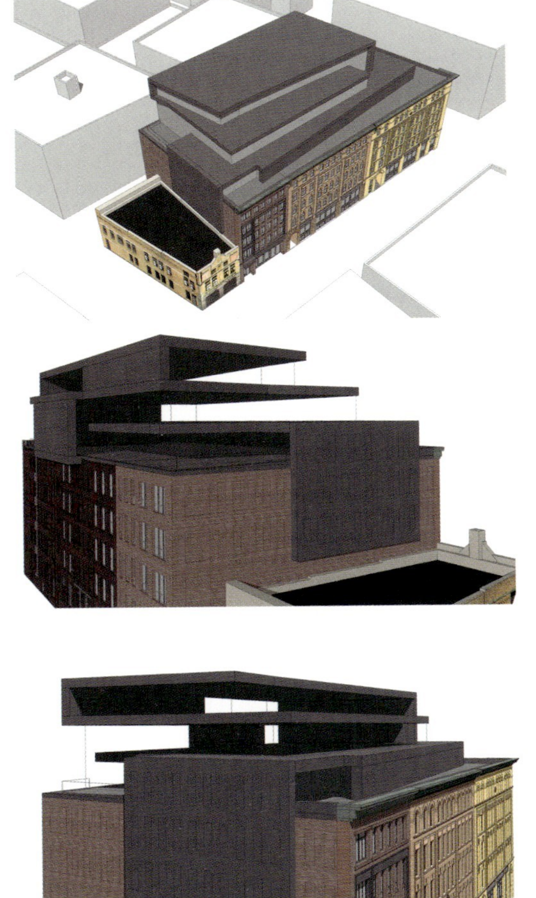

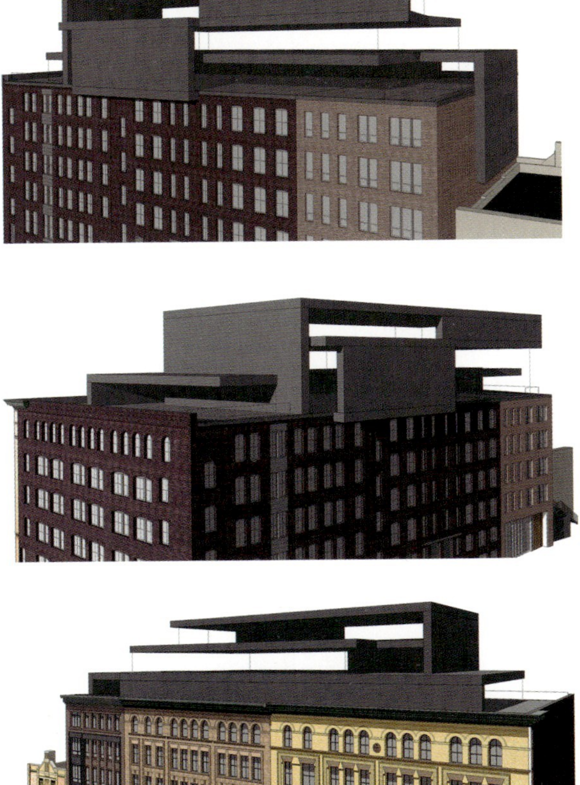

Inbo

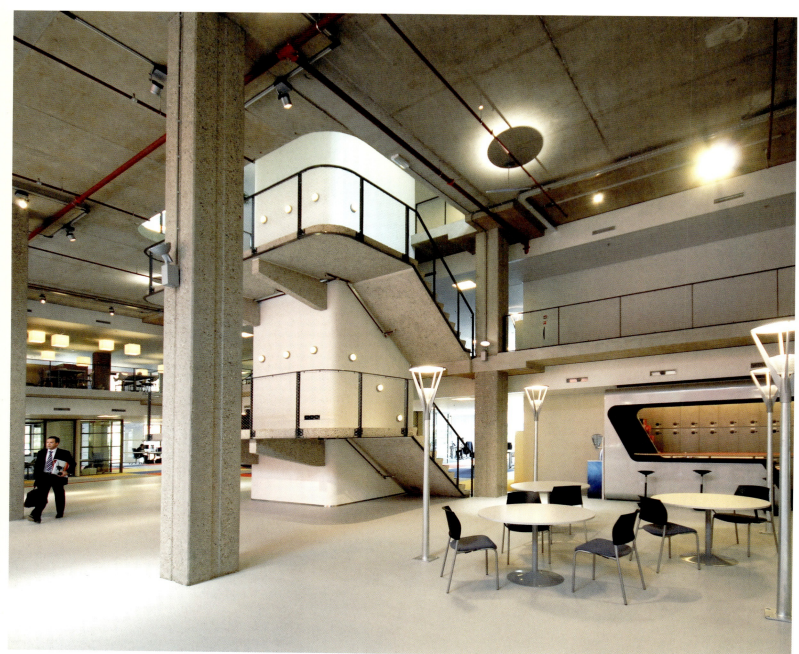

↑ | **Interior view,** heart of the office building

The Village Office

Houten

The Samas European headquarters completed in 2006 is an unusual conversion of an unmarketable concrete complex into a modern office building. The typical 1980s style concrete structure underwent an astounding metamorphosis by means of targeted interventions into the statics. The formerly dark showroom was transformed in just one year into an airy, friendly and open working environment. In spite of the fact that the existing structure was for the most part maintained, the building gained in coherence by emphasizing spatial quality. The newly added central patio is a fulcrum of this reorganization. New, large roof openings, relatively few partitions and new vantage points create a new impression of spatial transparency.

PROJECT FACTS

Address: Elzenkade, 1, 3992 AD, Houten, The Netherlands. **Client:** SAMAS Nederland. **Completion:** 2006. **Building type:** showroom and office. **Gross floor area:** 8,650 m².
Original building: architect unknown. **Client:** SAMAS Nederland. **Completion:** 1982. **Building type:** office. **Gross floor area:** 8,800 m².

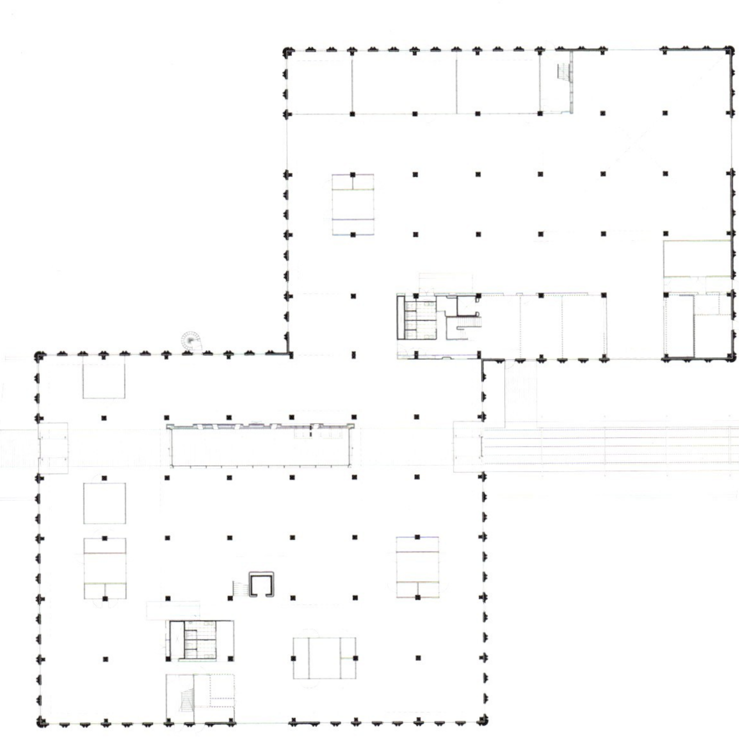

↑ | **Ground floor plan**
↓ | **Exterior view,** renovated façade

↑ | **Interior view,** view into the patio

XTEN Architecture

↑ | Exterior view
→ | Main entrance

Ford Ching

Los Angeles

Ford Ching was built as a vaudeville theater in the 1920s, was then used as a Chinese language cinema in the 1940s, and has now been converted into 1,200 square meter lofts and neighborhood retail spaces serving the emergent art scene in Chinatown. The leasable space along North Figueroa Road was enlarged while preserving the integrity of the local landmark. The remodeled theater has been used for two lofts lit by a new interior courtyard. The new layer alternates with the previous uses and forms, keeping the old layers as background. The exterior with its neon marquee has been restored while the art gallery and fashion gallery reuses on North Figueroa bring new life to the complex.

PROJECT FACTS

Address: 720 Figueroa Street, Los Angeles, CA 90012, USA. **Client:** Kimsing International. **Completion:** 2008. **Building type:** mixed-use gallery, residential, fashion. **Gross floor area:** 1,200 m^2.
Original building: architect unknown. **Client:** unknown. **Completion:** 1920s. **Building type:** vaudeville theater and shops. **Gross floor area:** 950 m^2.

↑ | Living room
← | Doors under the projecting roof

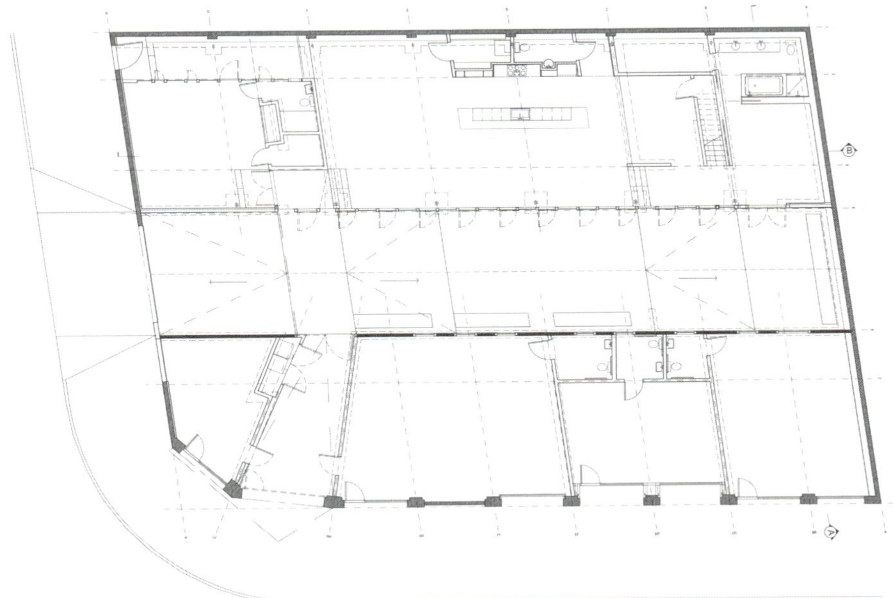

← | Ground floor plan
↓ | Interior

Pugh + Scarpa Architects / Gwynne Pugh, Angela Brooks, Lawrence Scarpa

↑ | **East elevation,** full view from parking deck
→ | **Intersection,** light-gauge steel volumes atop existing structure

Fuller Lofts

Los Angeles

Consisting of 102 units of affordable and market-rate lofts along with 1,440 square meters of commercial space, the program adds two stories of penthouse lofts above the original four-story structure, as well as a directly adjacent new two-story parking structure. Located conveniently near to a station on a recently constructed light-rail line, the Fuller Lofts was the first transit-oriented development begun in the area, and has spurred the revitalization of Lincoln Heights. The original neo-classical façade is preserved – along with the elegant, formal lobby – and is crowned by a striking steel-clad façade wrapping the addition on the upper floors. Inside, an atrium courtyard was cut into the structure, bringing light and air into the center of the building.

PROJECT FACTS

Address: 200 N. San Fernando Road, Los Angeles, CA 90031, USA. **Client:** Livable Places. **Completion:** 2010. **Building type:** mixed-use commercial residential. **Gross floor area:** 12,271 m^2.
Original building: architect unknown. **Client:** Fuller Paint Co. **Completion:** 1925. **Building type:** warehouse. **Gross floor area:** 9,615 m^2.

200 NORTH

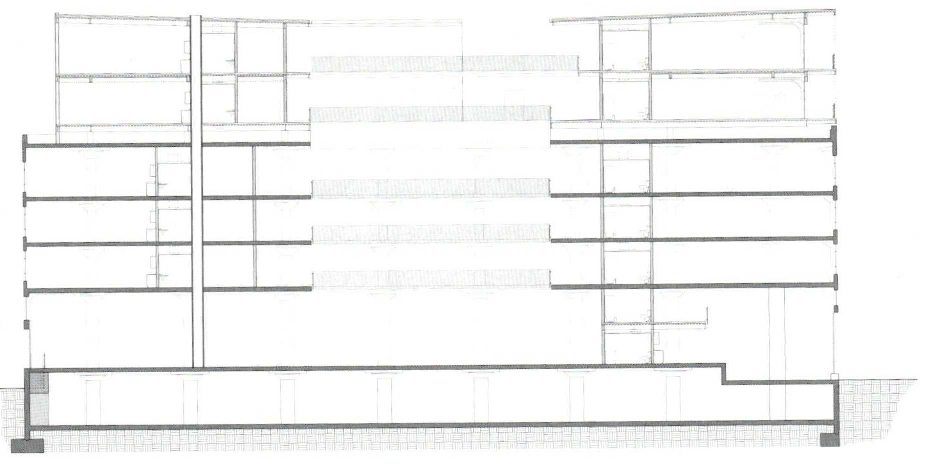

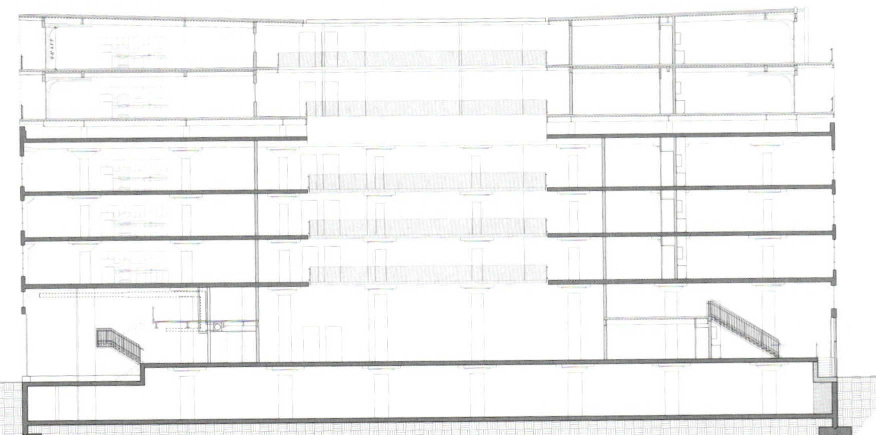

←←| **San Fernando Road elevation,** neoclassical versus industrial-chic

← | **Sections**

↓ | **Interior,** typical loft apartment

Jensen Architects, Jensen & Macy Architects

↑ | **View over plinth and reflecting pool**
↗ | **Exterior,** by day
→ | **Exterior,** in the evening

Walden Studios

Geyserville

A concrete barn in scenic Sonoma County is completely transformed by inserting a new building inside its heavy walls. The new structure uses frameless glass walls to create light-filled interior spaces, while large cuts in the existing walls frame views of the surrounding vineyards. The mixed-use building accommodates work and living units, arts-related offices and other leased spaces. A new plinth, raised above the floodplain of the Russian River, anchors the building and provides panoramic views over the landscape. At the southeast corner of the building a nearly flush reflecting pool dissolves the border between indoors and outdoors, creating a feeling of a seamless plane connecting the interior aluminum flooring and the landscape beyond.

PROJECT FACTS

Address: 275 State Highway 128, Geyserville, CA 95441, USA. **Structural Engineer:** Tipping-Mar + Associates. **Client:** H K Enterprises. **Completion:** 2006. **Building type:** mixed-use. **Gross floor area:** 1,858 m².

Original building: architect unknown. **Client:** Sunsweet Growers Inc.. **Completion:** 1920s. **Building type:** barn. **Gross floor area:** 817.55 m².

↑ | View from mezzanine
← | Illuminated shower in mezzanine

← | Breezeway detail
↓ | Plans

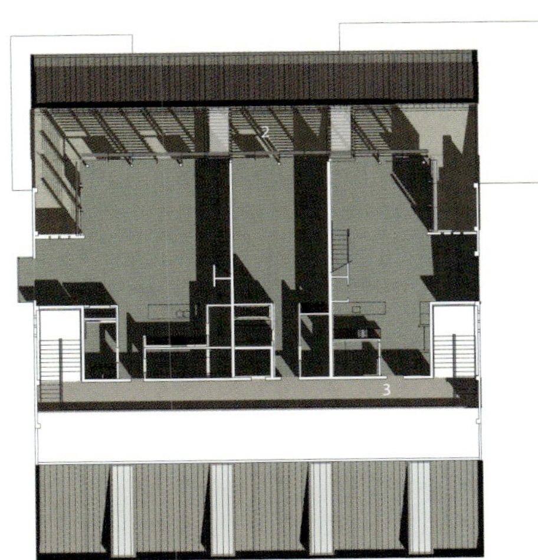

form, environment, research
(fer) studio LLP

↑ | **The renovated old masonry structure**
↓ | **Plans,** first and second floor
→ | **Exterior,** at night

The Green Building

Louisville

The project resuscitates the structural masonry shell of the old store and implants a modern core, including a twelf meter high lobby. The building's original mortar joint façade remained intact while the 1980s storefront was replaced by an angled, recessed wood and aluminum façade that steps back visually, drawing in visitors towards the entryway. Though the space is long and narrow, natural light and outdoor views flood the interior through an ascending glass spine that bridges all three floors and breaks the roof into three planes. The spine cascades down the backside of the space, providing views to the green roof below. Today, the four story structure houses a street side cafe, The Green Building Gallery, and an event and office space.

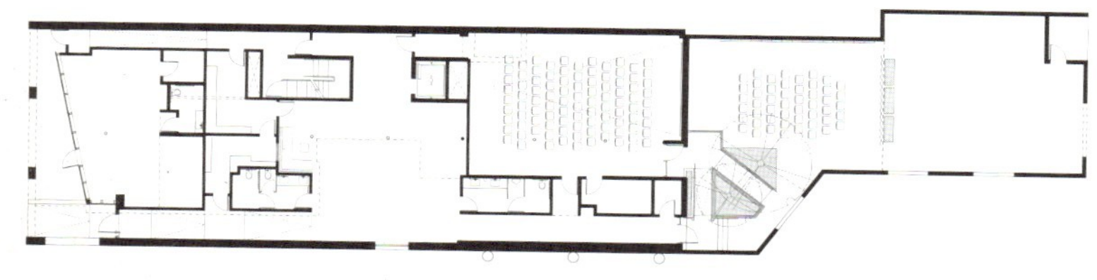

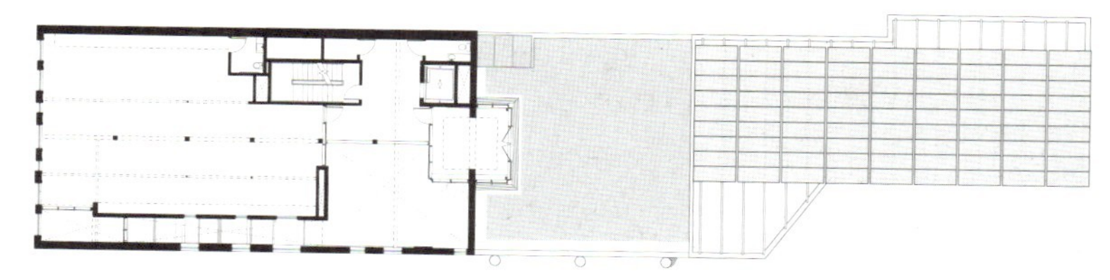

PROJECT FACTS

Address: 732 East Market Street, Louisville, KY 40202, USA. **Client:** Gill & Augusta Holland. **Completion:** 2008. **Building type:** mixed-use commercial. **Gross floor area:** 1,244.5 m^2.
Original building: architect unknown. **Client:** unknown. **Completion:** 1895. **Building type:** commercial retail. **Gross floor area:** 712.5 m^2.

← | Twelf meter high lobby
↓ | Corn-blasted exposure of original old growth wood members

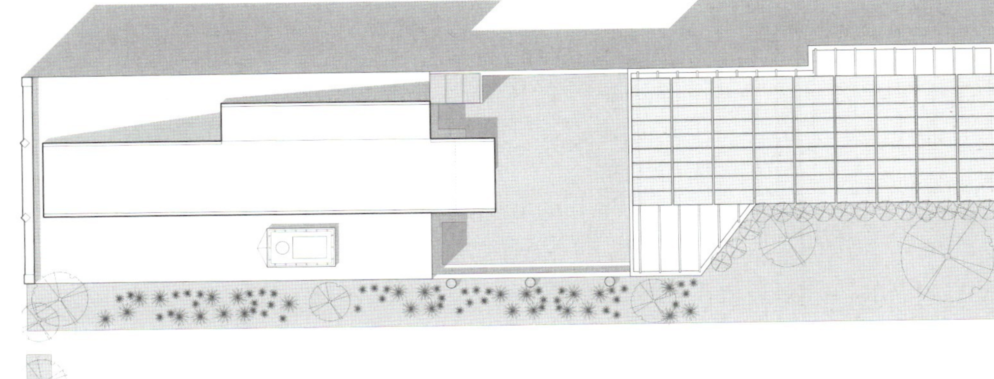

← | **Roof plan**
↓ | **Office area,** with old growth lumber

OFFICE

Pi de Bruijn,
de Architekten Cie.

↑ | **Entrance area**
→ | **Glass-roofed atrium** to serve as a foyer

Redevelopment headquarters Essent

Den Bosch

This typical example of traditional Delft School architecture was designed by the architect C.H. de Bever. With its sloping roofs, turrets and clock towers, the building resembles an abstract castle. It was decided to weave the original component and the extension into a single complex, slotting the old building logically into the whole. A special feature is the meeting room suite with restaurant housed in the old building. Its inner court is transformed into a glass-roofed atrium to serve as a foyer for the surrounding meeting rooms. The result is a supremely compact and harmonious whole under one roof, with no distinction between old and new, between the meeting rooms and the office floors.

Address: Vlijmenseweg 4, 5211 AK Den Bosch, The Netherlands. **Client:** Essent. **Completion:** 2007. **Building type:** office. **Gross floor area:** 39,000 m^2.
Original building: Cornelis Hubertus de Bever. **Client:** P.N.E.M. **Completion:** 1956. **Building type:** mixed-use. **Gross floor area:** 12,000 m^2.

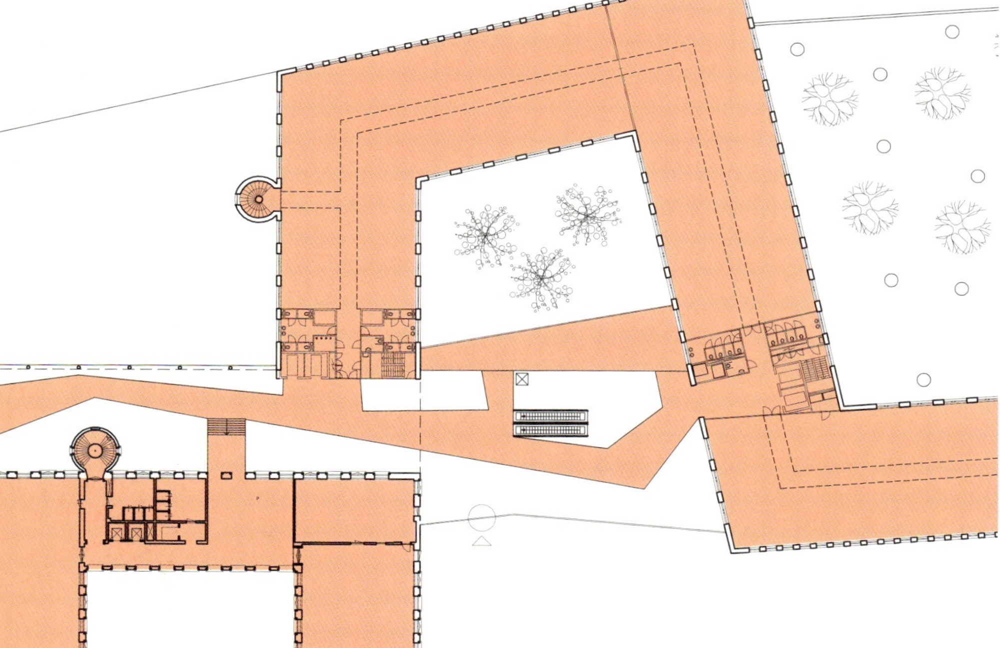

↖ | **Atrium,** entrance to basement floor
↑ | **Office floors**
← | **First floor plan**

← | **Cross section through atrium,** "mainstreet" and garden

↓ | **Cafeteria** with view to the inner courtyard

Architekturbüro [lu:p] /
Renee Lorenz

↑ | Exterior view east
→ | Exterior view south

Architekturbüro [lu:p]

Grub am Forst

This residential house has been renovated and converted into an architectural office. A concrete strip combining various functions is the striking architectural element. Starting out as company label it evolves into a red carpet for all visitors before folding into the stair entrance and finally serving as canopy. Both façade and roof are clad in larch wood, giving the building a uniform appearance. The rearrangement of some windows allows unusual, specific views of the surroundings. Various recesses within the white plastered walls expose the original plaster almost like wall paintings. By the innovative use of traditional materials and detail solutions a 50-year-old house has been turned into a modern architectural office.

PROJECT FACTS

Address: Ringstraße 21, 96271 Grub am Forst, Germany. **Client:** Renee Lorenz. **Completion:** 2007. **Building type:** office. **Gross floor area:** 165 m².
Original building: architect unknown. **Client:** Margarete and Otto Lorenz. **Completion:** 1956. **Building type:** residential house. **Gross floor area:** 165 m².

↑ | Façade detail
↙ | Cross section
↓ | Original building

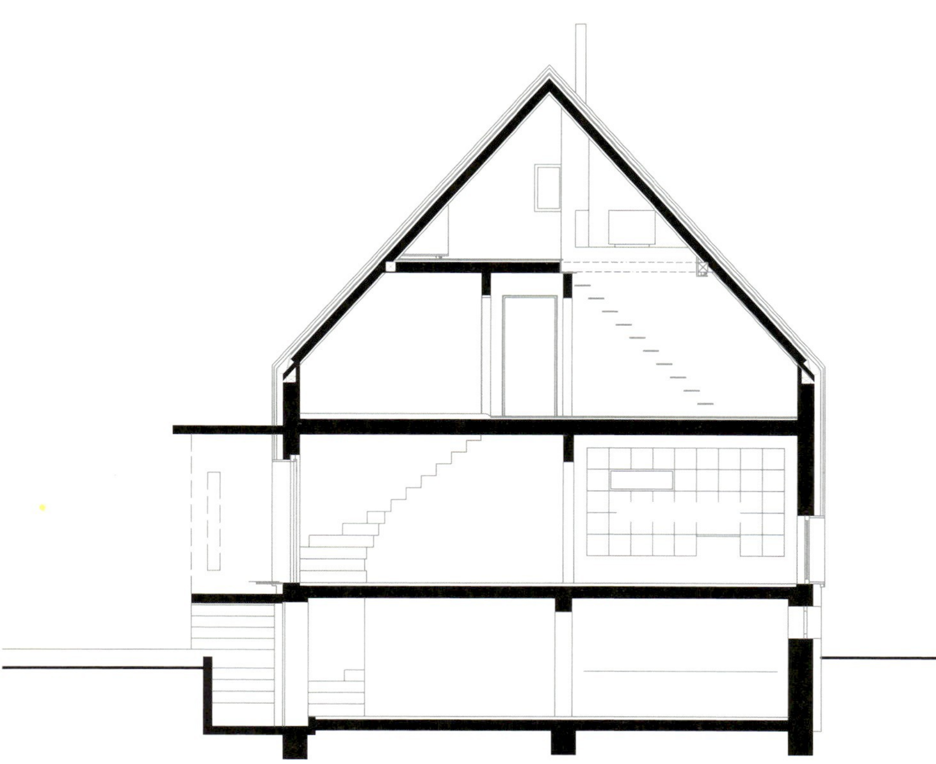

↑ | **Meeting room**
↗ | **Staircase**
↓ | **Floor plans,** ground floor, first floor, attic

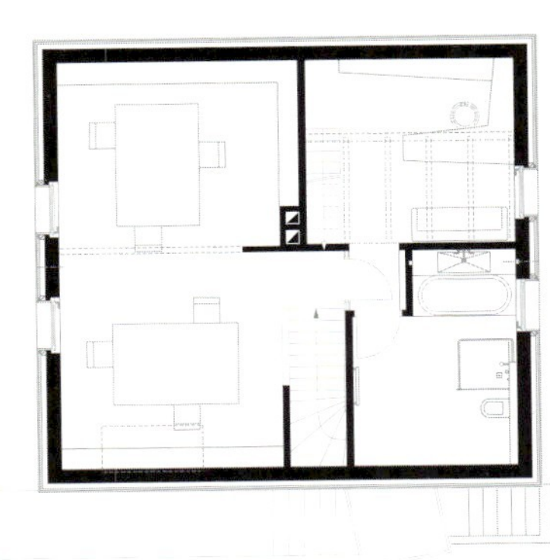

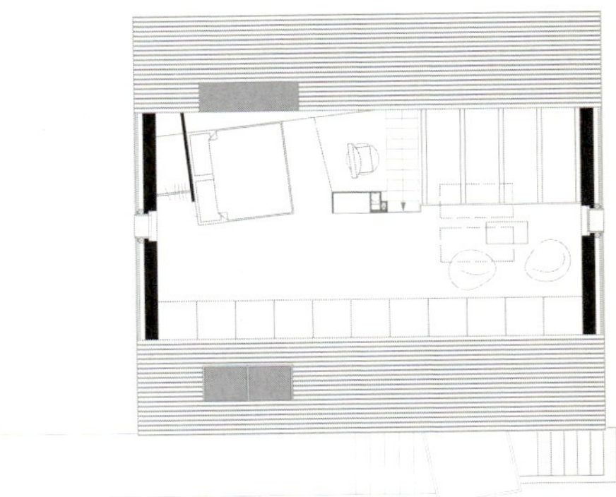

oliv architekten

↑ | Exterior
→ | Office area

Werbeagentur Djermester / Lindner

Wasserburg

This former printing facility offered the advertising agency the deep and narrow lots running to the street that are typical of the Wasserburg area. A virtue was wrested from necessity by locating the unlit photo studio and cutting more space into in the deep parts of the building. The rest of the space provides room for 12–14 work places, two separate offices for the managers, a conference room and the obligatory small kitchen and sanitary facilities. The windows were retained in the context of the heritage-listed old town area. High ceilings, glazed partitions, curtains and sliding panels as well as dark flooring without thresholds ensure that the impression of spatial expanse is maintained.

PROJECT FACTS

Address: Ledererzeile 43, 83512 Wasserburg, Germany. **Client:** Djermester & Lindner GmbH. **Completion:** 2004. **Building type:** design agency. **Gross floor area:** 350 m².
Original building: architect unknown. **Client:** unknown. **Completion:** unknown. **Building type:** print shop. **Gross floor area:** 350 m².

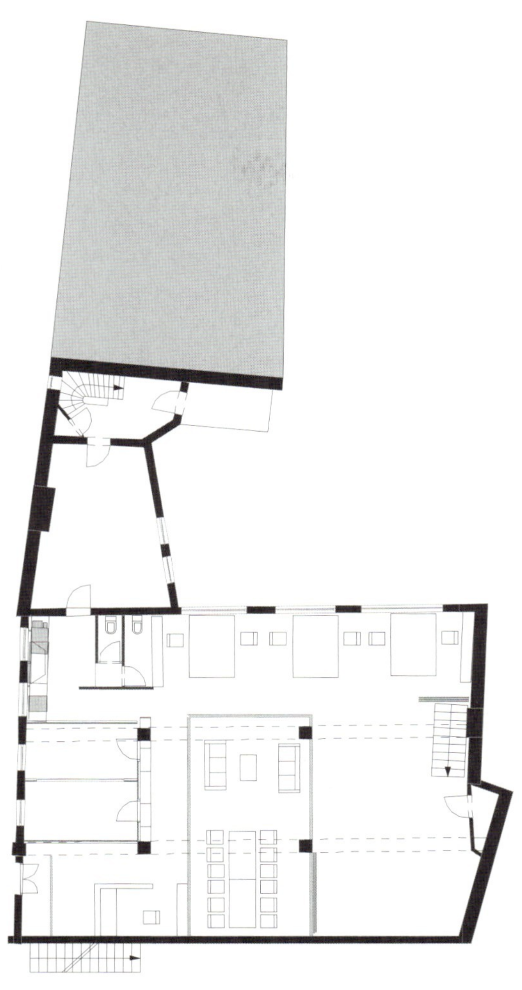

←←| Photographic studio
↙ | Glass fitting
← | First floor plan
↓ | Office area

Sergei Tchoban Architekt BDA nps tchoban voss
A. M. Prasch, S. Tchoban, E. Voss

↑ | **Façade,** view from the street

House Benois

St. Petersburg

A dilapidated factory building once stood at the former location of the house of the Russian artist Aleksandr Benois, on the boundary between the garden of the Kuschelev-Besborodko mansion and the Piskarevski-Prospekt today. This building was converted into a multi-purpose business center. The design of the new building is devoted to Benois' stage designs, which made Russian art and theater known internationally. The digital copies on the glass panels of the front façade are based on Benois' theater costume sketches. The panels are mounted in an aluminum mullion transom construction, which covers the entire façade as a substructure.

PROJECT FACTS

Address: 44 Swerdlowskaja Naberezhnaya, 190000 St. Petersburg, Russia. **Architect in charge:** Paul Olufs. **Client:** Project Company Teorema. **Completion:** 2007. **Building type:** office. **Gross floor area:** 30,400 m^2.

Original building: KPI Institute. **Client:** Rossiya electrical equipment combine. **Completion:** about 1970. **Building type:** industry building. **Gross floor area:** 10,052 m^2.

↑ | **Façade,** detail from the street

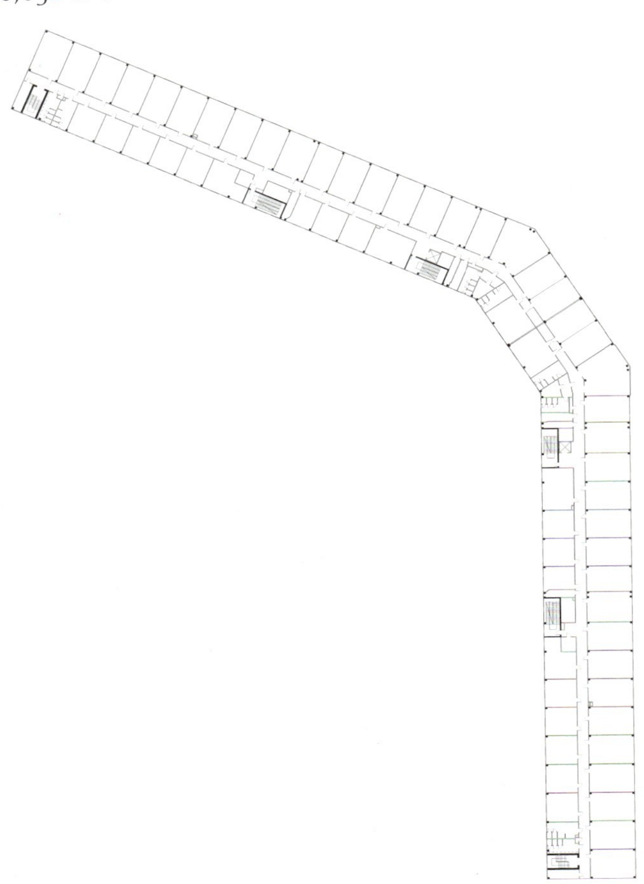

↑ | **Floor plan**

↓ | **Façade,** detail from the courtyard

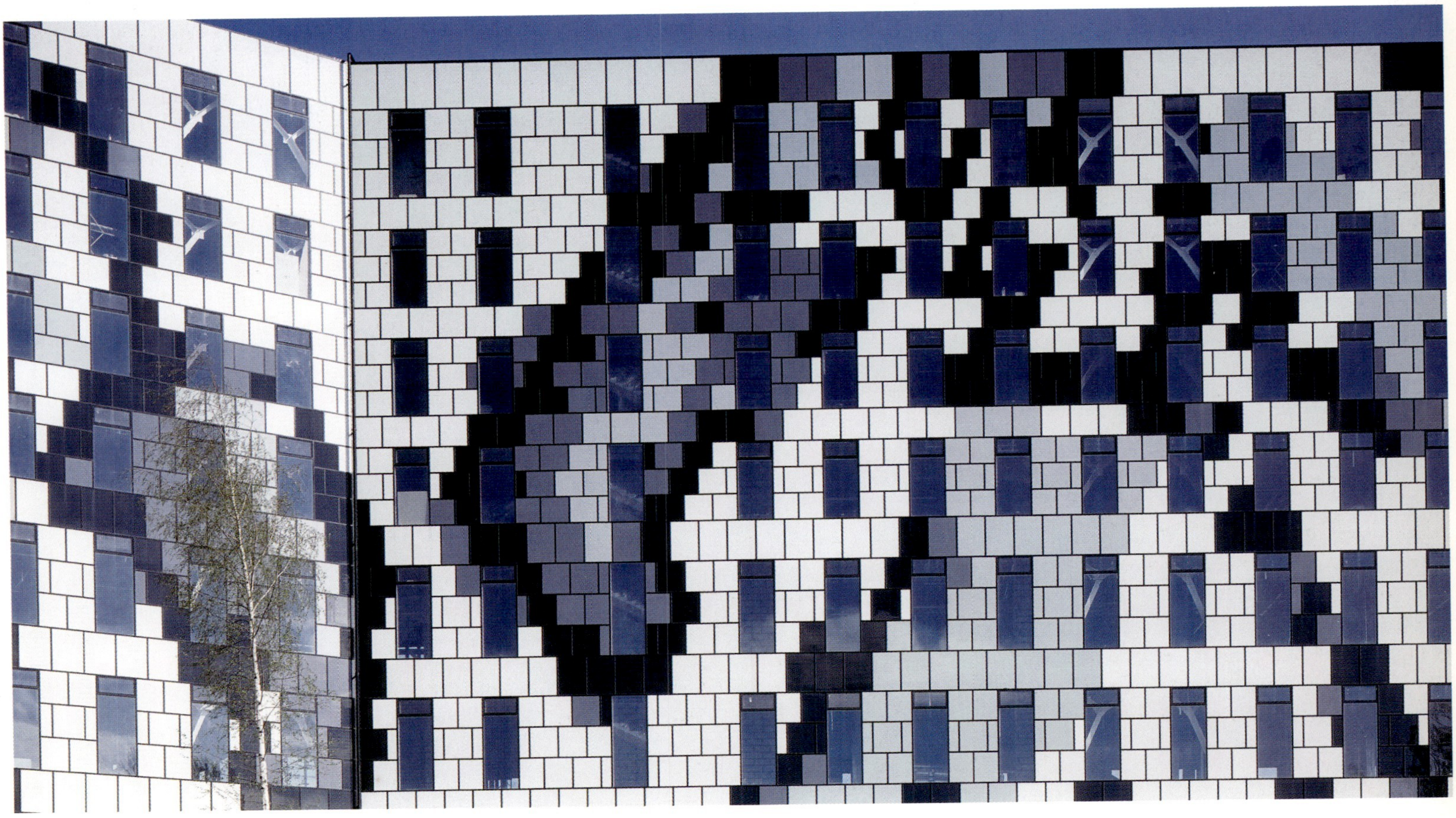

Christoph Kalb Architekt ARB
DipArc BSc

↑ | Interior
→ | Exterior

Water Tower Office

Dornbirn

After removing the pipelines the raw exterior of the water tower was covered inside with insulation and a cladding of girder plaster tiles, thus retaining the characteristic raw concrete façade. The solid concrete girders and supports support a gallery freely hung in the space. Due to this suspended construction the proportions of the space of 10 x 12 meters and a room height of 5.5 meters are unaffected. The gallery is surrounded by the air space, creating a room within a room. Indirect lighting designed especially for this space emphasizes the spatial effect of the construction. A construction of untreated steel provides the outside access to the elevated ground floor level.

PROJECT FACTS

Address: Färbergasse 15, 6850 Dornbirn, Austria. **Client:** Christoph Kalb. **Completion:** 2004. **Building type:** office. **Gross floor area:** 150 m².
Original building: Architect unknown. **Client:** Company Franz Martin Rhomberg. **Completion:** 1970. **Building type:** industrial facility. **Gross floor area:** 150 m².

↖↑ | **Interiors**
← | **Site plan**

← | **New entrance,** steel
↙ | **Ground floor plan**
↓ | **Section**

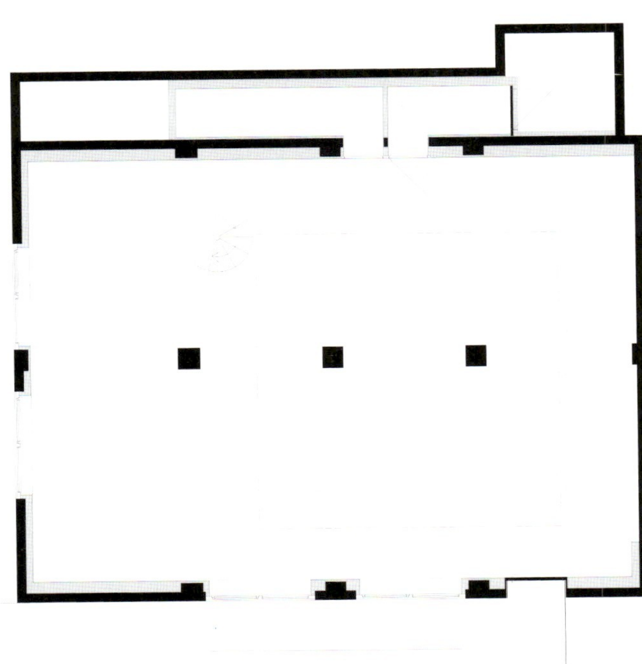

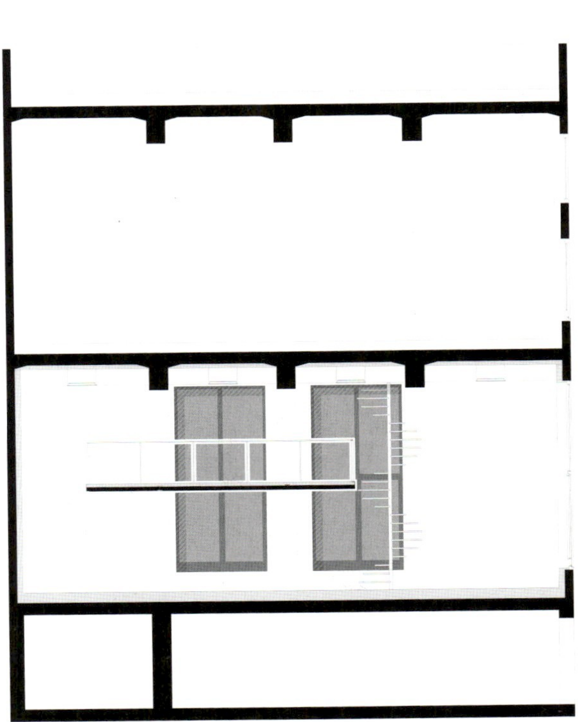

Albert France-Lanord Architects

↑ | Granit cave
→ | Conference room

Pionen – White mountain

Stockholm

"Pionen" is situated in an amazing location 30 meters beneath the granite rock of the Vita Berg Park in Stockholm. The internet provider found in the rock shelters a new home for its server halls and offices. The starting point of the project was to consider the rock as a living organism. The humans try to acclimate themselves to this alien world and extract the "best" elements from earth: light, plants, water and technology. The architects created strong contrasts between rooms where the dominated by rocks, where the human being is a stranger, in contrast to rooms where the human being takes over totally. The main room is not a traditional space, limited by surfaces but instead is defined by the emptiness inside a mass.

PROJECT FACTS

Address: Renstiernas gata 37, Stockholm, Sweden. **Client:** Bahnhof AB. **Completion:** 2008. **Building type:** office building. **Gross floor area:** 1,200 m^2.

Original building: architect unknown. **Client:** Swedish Armed Forces. **Completion:** 1943. **Building type:** nuclear shelter. **Gross floor area:** 1,200 m^2.

↑ | Office space
← | Office floor

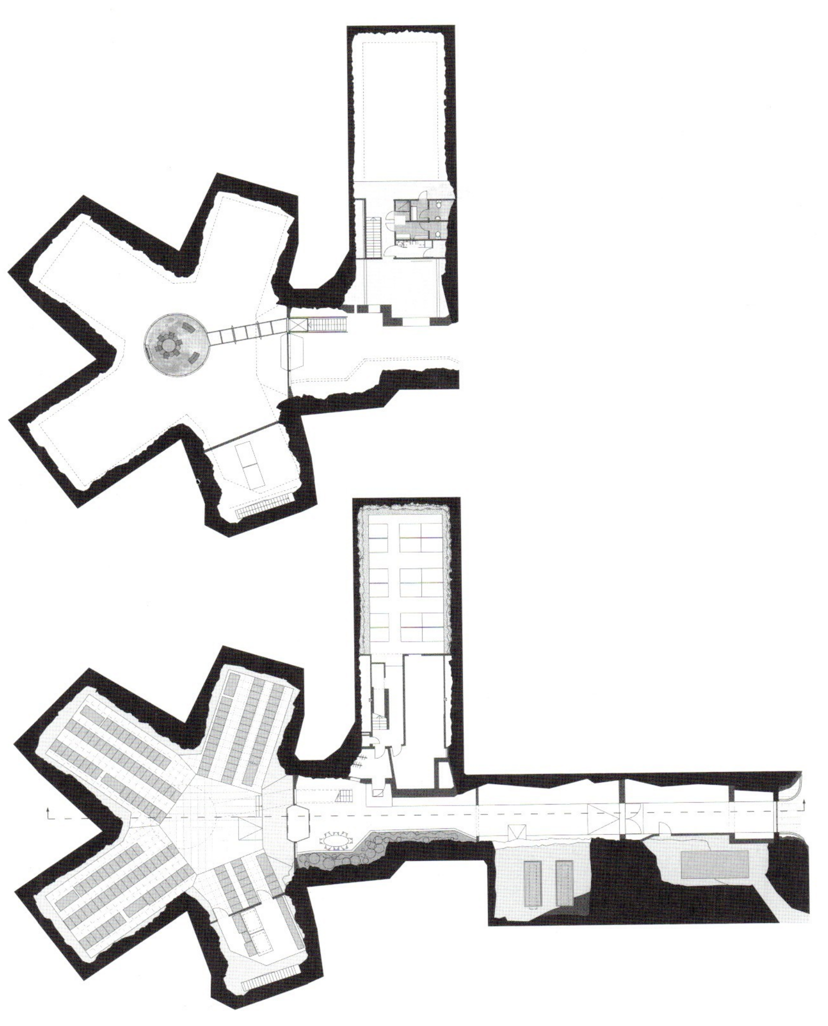

← | Floor plans

↓ | Machine room for power generators

Fung + Blatt Architects, Inc.

↑ | Conference room exterior

3ality Digital

Burbank

This film production facility inhabits two 1940s masonry warehouse bays, separated by a bearing wall that allowed very limited open access between the spaces. The architects' assignment was to design a dynamic work environment with administrative and technical wings that include offices, workshops, editing rooms, equipment cage and long sight lines for camera staging. A circular conference room that becomes the vortex of the environment was also introduced. It straddles the central dividing wall and propels into motion a series of ripples whose trajectories penetrate and diminish the separation while establishing auxiliary spaces for informal gathering.

PROJECT FACTS

Address: 55 E. Orange Grove Avenue, Burbank, CA 91502-1827, USA. **Client:** 3ality Digital. **Completion:** 2007. **Building type:** office. **Gross floor area:** 1,860 m².
Original building: architect unknown. **Client:** unknown. **Completion:** 1940. **Building type:** masonry warehouse bays. **Gross floor area:** unknown.

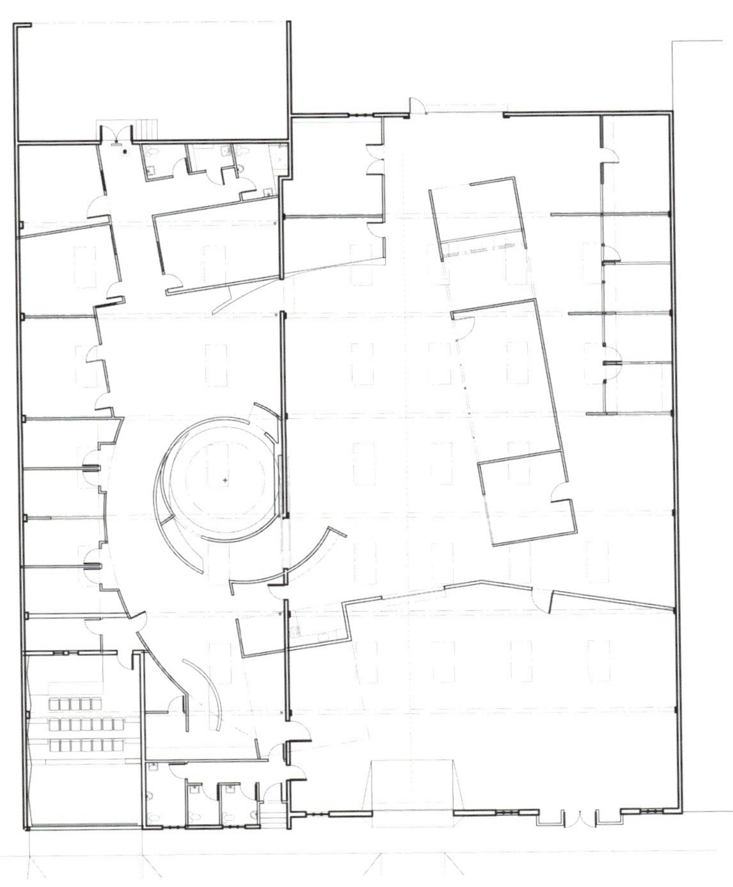

↑ | **Floor plan**
↓ | **Entrance area,** reception

↑ | **Conference room,** entrance

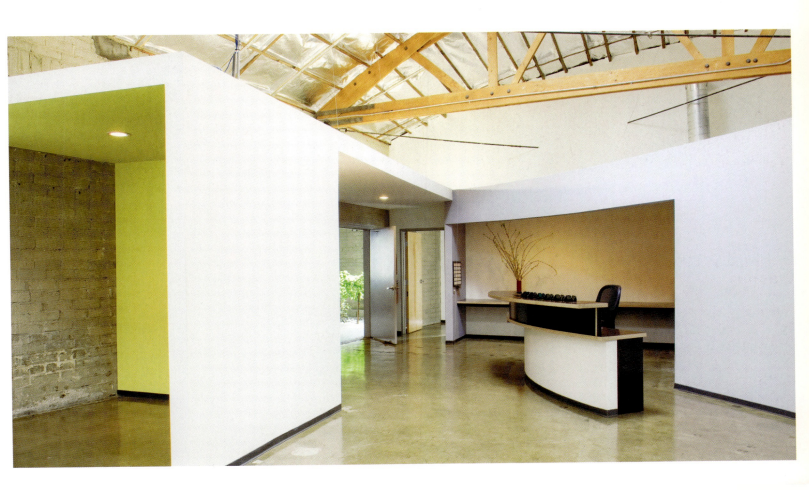

L6 studio /
Adriana Dimitrova,
Ivaylo Zahariev

↑ | **Façade,** office is open

Architecture in a Container

Sofia

The home of the L6 Studio is perhaps in an unexpected location. The small, multi-level space opens out onto the street by means of folding metal doors with wooden slats. When closed, they match the wooden boarding of the building, reminiscent of an industrial container. The interior design is plain, with visitors first encountering a concrete floor. The levels are separated into functional zones: meeting spaces, workplaces and a store. A few features have been placed in this basically white space. The maintenance zone is located separately in the basement.

PROJECT FACTS

Address: Listopad 6, Sofia 1202, Bulgaria. **Client:** L6 studio. **Completion:** 2008. **Building type:** architecture studio. **Gross floor area:** 55 m².

Original building: PANDA Studio. **Client:** confidential. **Completion:** 2000. **Building type:** garage and basement store. **Gross floor area:** 55 m².

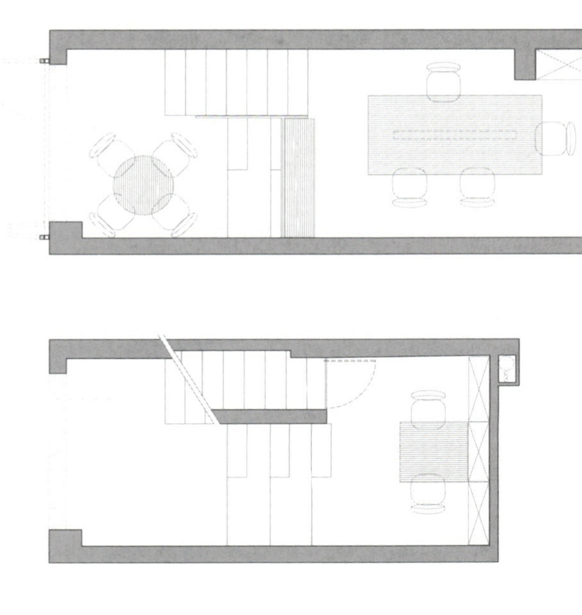

↑ | **Façade,** office is closed

↓ | **Working area**

↑ | **Floor plans**

↓ | **Entrance and meeting area**

Klous + Brandjes Architecten bna / R.W.M. van Baalen, C.J.M. Brandjes

↑ | Corner window of the "diamond"
→ | View from the "Oude Gracht"

Office Van Alckmaer voor Wonen

Alkmaar

The housing organization "Van Alckmaer voor Wonen" occupies a new office in the center of Alkmaar in the former "Stadtstimmerwerf", with a history going back to 1600. In 2003 the office and the organization were transformed , so Klous + Brandjes Architecten used the analysis of the organization and the building history as the basic principle for the design of the office. This resulted in the removal of obscure annexes and the restoration of the U-shaped head structure. The organization needed a larger floor area than the old building could provide, so a new development was required. This resulted in a diamond shaped volume that responds to and contrasts with the environment while imperceptibly connecting the old with the new.

PROJECT FACTS

Address: Keetgracht 1, 1811 AM Alkmaar, The Netherlands. **Client:** Van Alckmaer voor Wonen. **Completion:** 2006. **Building type:** office. **Gross floor area:** 810 m^2.
Original building: architect unknown. **Client:** City of Alkmaar. **Completion:** 17th century. **Building type:** urban carpenter's workshop. **Gross floor area:** 750 m^2.

←←| Reception and lobby
↙ | Front office ground floor
← | Draft sketch
↓ | The "diamond"

OTH, Ontwerpgroep Trude Hooykaas

↑ | **Exterior view,** glass louvers which can be opened per segment
→ | **Entrance** in a portal frame

Kraanspoor

Amsterdam

Kraanspoor is a light-weight transparent office building of three floors built on top of a concrete crane way on the grounds of the former NDSM shipyard, a relic of Amsterdam's shipping industry. This industrial monument has a length of 270 meters, a height of 13.5 meters and a width of 8.7 meters, and was saved from demolition in 1997. The new construction assembled on top of this old concrete base is the same 270 meters long, with a width of 13.8 meters, accentuating the length of Kraanspoor and the expansive view of the river IJ and the old city center of Amsterdam. In acknowledgement of its foundation, the building is lifted by slender steel columns three meters above the original crane way.

PROJECT FACTS

Address: Kraanspoor 12–58, 1033 SE Amsterdam, The Netherlands. **Client:** ING Real Estate Development Netherlands, Den Haag. **Completion:** 2007. **Building type:** office. **Gross floor area:** 12,500 m². **Original building:** J. D. Postma. **Client:** NDSM (Nederlandsche Dok en Scheepsbouw Maatschappij) shipyard. **Completion:** 1952. **Building type:** crane way. **Gross floor area:** 440 m².

↑ | **Meeting room** in the stairwell
↓ | **Floor plans,** ground floor and first floor plan

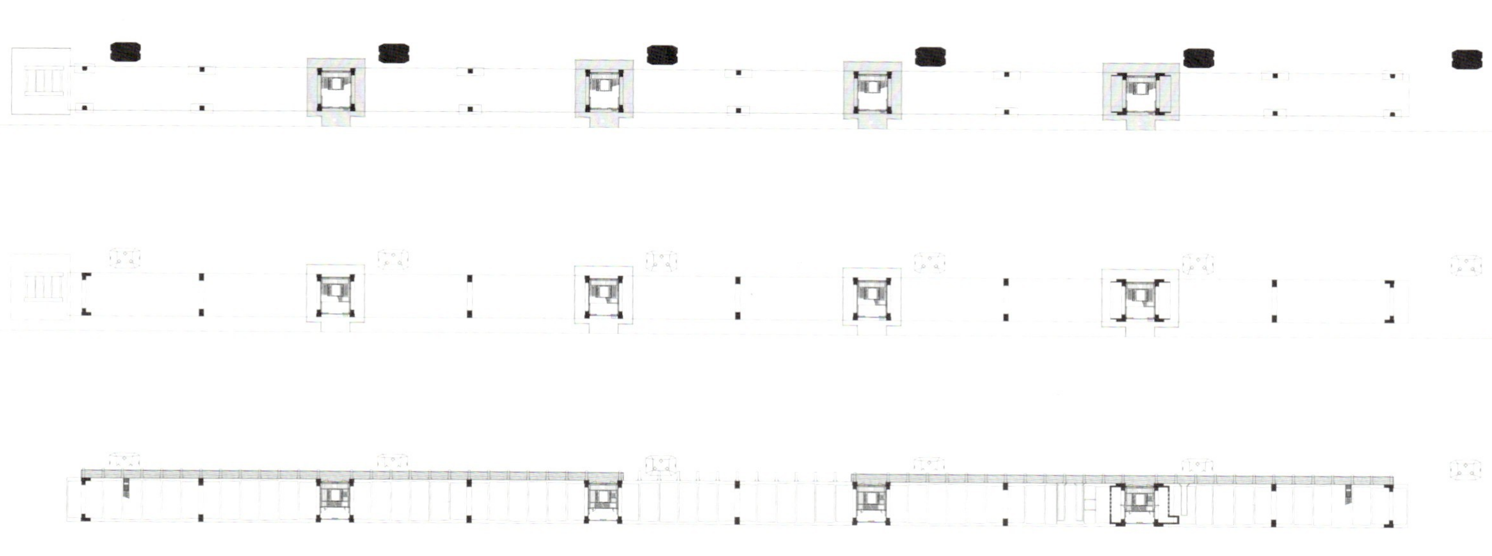

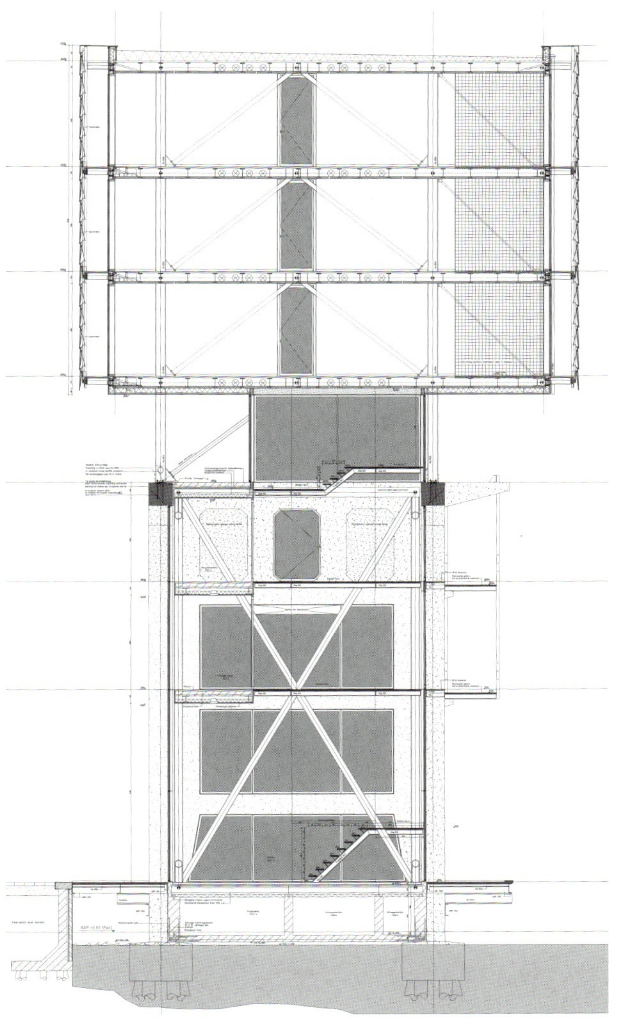

← | **Cross section**

↓ | **Exterior view,** Kraanspoor at night

Davidsson Tarkela Architects / Jaana Tarkela, Aki Davidsson

↑ | **Interior view,** the multi-purpose hall
→ | **New spiral staircase**
↓ | **Before conversion**

VTT Valimo

Espoo

Built in two phases between 1955 and 1961, the former Helsinki University of Technology laboratory is today one of the oldest buildings on the Otaniemi campus and a protected landmark. The building has been renovated as a showcase for the VTT, the Technical Research Center of Finland. The building's main space, housing the test foundry, was transformed into a new multi-purpose hall. It now hosts VTT's PR-events and research demonstration. The first floor and basement comprise the office and training spaces. The steel framed raised floor of the foundry space forms the core of the building's ventilation solution, with reference to the earlier use.

PROJECT FACTS

Address: Metallimiehenkuja 2, 02150, Espoo, Finland. **Client:** Senaatti-kiinteistöt. **Completion:** 2006. **Building type:** office, showroom. **Gross floor area:** 2,090 m^2.

Original building: Alvar Aalto. **Client:** Helsinki University of Technology. **Completion:** 1961. **Building type:** foundry engineering laboratory. **Gross floor area:** 2,090 m^2.

↑ | The main entrance
↓ | Ground floor plan

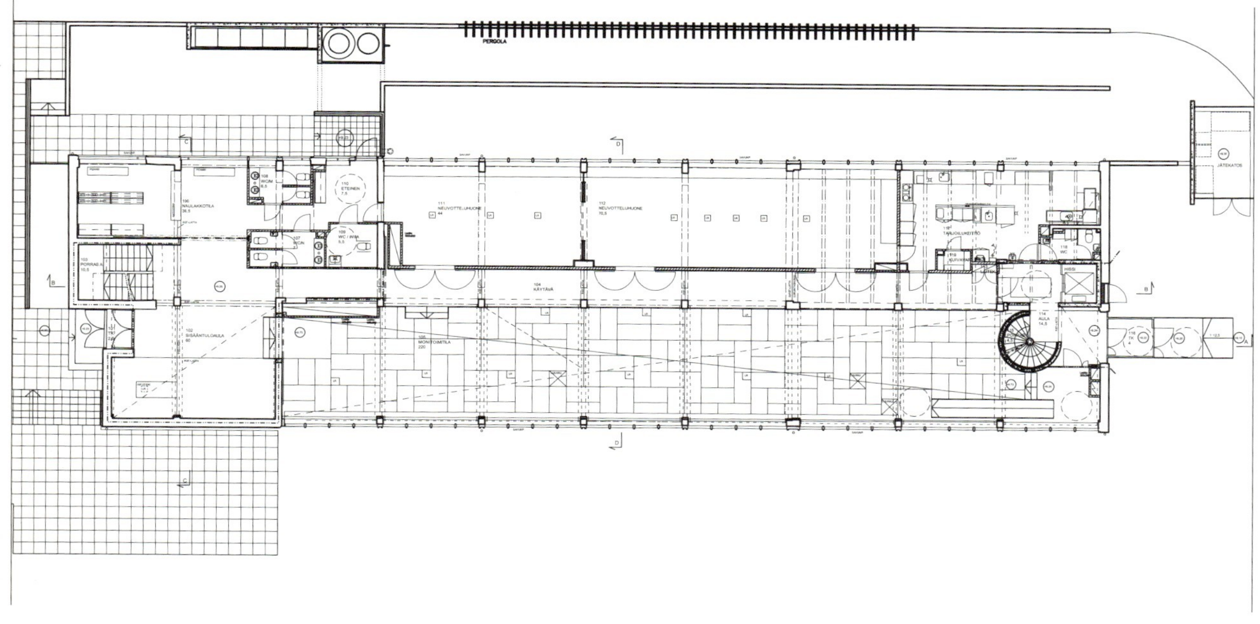

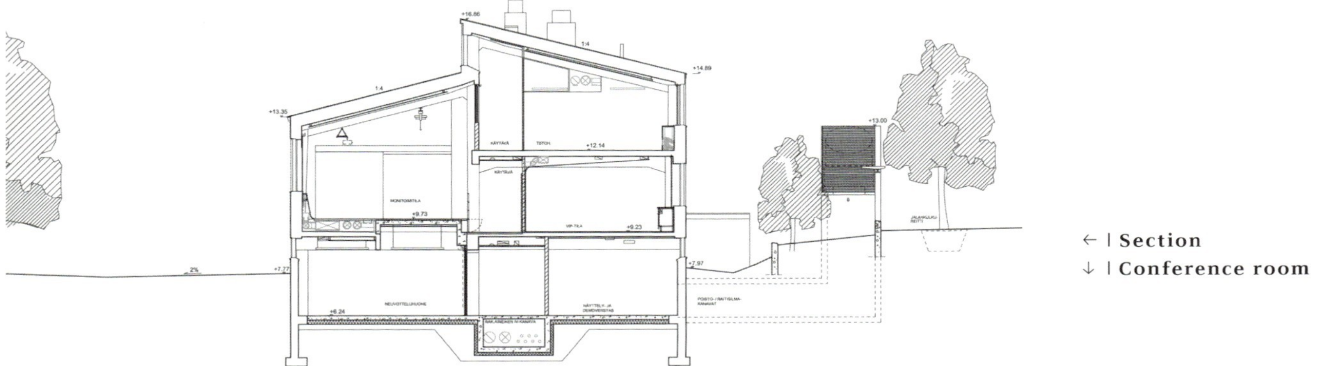

← | Section
↓ | Conference room

Aleks Istanbullu Architects / Corinna Gebert, Aleks Istanbullu

↑ | **Main project room from entrance**
↓ | **First floor plan,** historic and new

Harris & Ruble Law Offices

Los Angeles

Layers of scabbed-on finishes were carefully stripped away, exposing original fenestration, ironwork, columns and beams. All fenestration was freed from layers of paint, plastic, blinds, and other encumbrances. Windows were partially re-glazed and original frames and hardware restored. The concrete floor, cut and patched beyond repair, was covered with an epoxy topcoat, restoring the feel of generous open flow throughout the ground level. Office and work areas were covered with carpet of a neutral color. The structure and new walls were painted in a minimalist palette of white and grays while the original brick wall in the project room was exposed to mark the industrial heritage of the building.

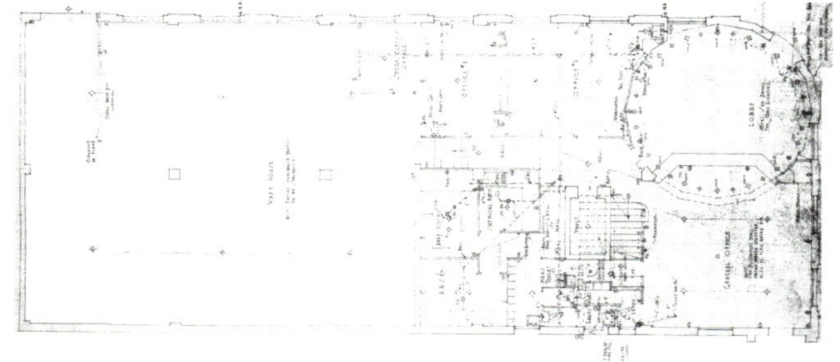

PROJECT FACTS

Address: 6424 Santa Monica Blvd, Los Angeles, CA 90038, USA. **Client:** Harris & Ruble. **Completion:** 2009. **Building type:** law office building. **Gross floor area:** 561 m².
Original building: Theodore H. Pettit. **Client:** Agfa-Ansco. **Completion:** 1937. **Building type:** warehouse. **Gross floor area:** 561 m².

↑ | Main project room from filing area
↓ | Stair and safe vault from rotunda

↑ | Entrance rotunda and gallery
← | Hallway from conference room

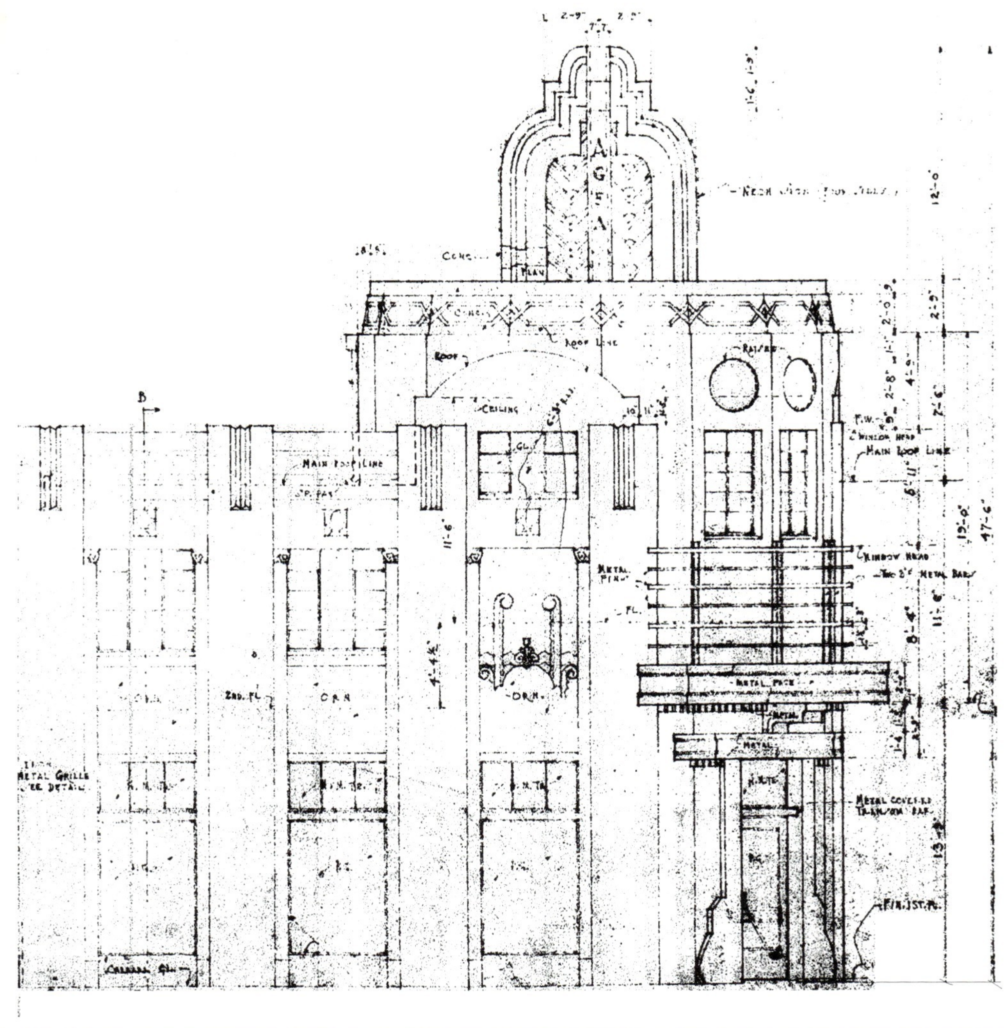

← | **Historic north elevation**

↑ | **Exterior view north,** present

↓ | **Kitchen,** upper level

chartier-corbasson

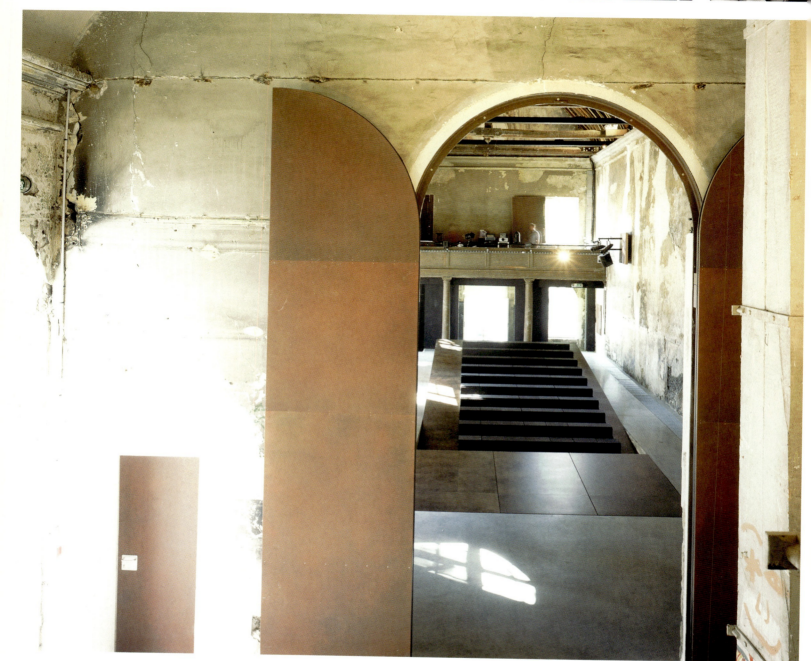

↑ | Entrance to the chapel
↗ | The scene
→ | The metal plate

Maison de l'Architecture

Paris

The current building displays vestiges of strata laid down at different points in the past. The architects proposed that the form of the operation be carried out on the existing building in such a way as to be easily legible foreveryone, as a logical consequence of the history of the site. They have drawn on features of religious architecture for references, and propose to punctuate the space using a series of 'patches' integrating all the components that ensure the 'Maison de l'Architecture' will be a veritable architectural tool. In order to create overall coherence, they chose to work with one single material, corten steel, which has a chronological dimension and is informed by the history of the location.

PROJECT FACTS

Address: 148, Rue du Faubourg, Saint Martin, 75010 Paris, France. **Engineering:** Cotec. **Client:** CROAIF Conseil regional de l'ordre des architectes d'ile de france. **Completion:** 2004. **Building type:** office, showroom. **Gross floor area:** 1,000 m^2.

Original building: architect unknown. **Client:** Recollets convent. **Completion:** 17th and 18th century. **Building type:** convent. **Gross floor area:** unknown.

↑ | **Interior view,** office area
↓ | **Section**

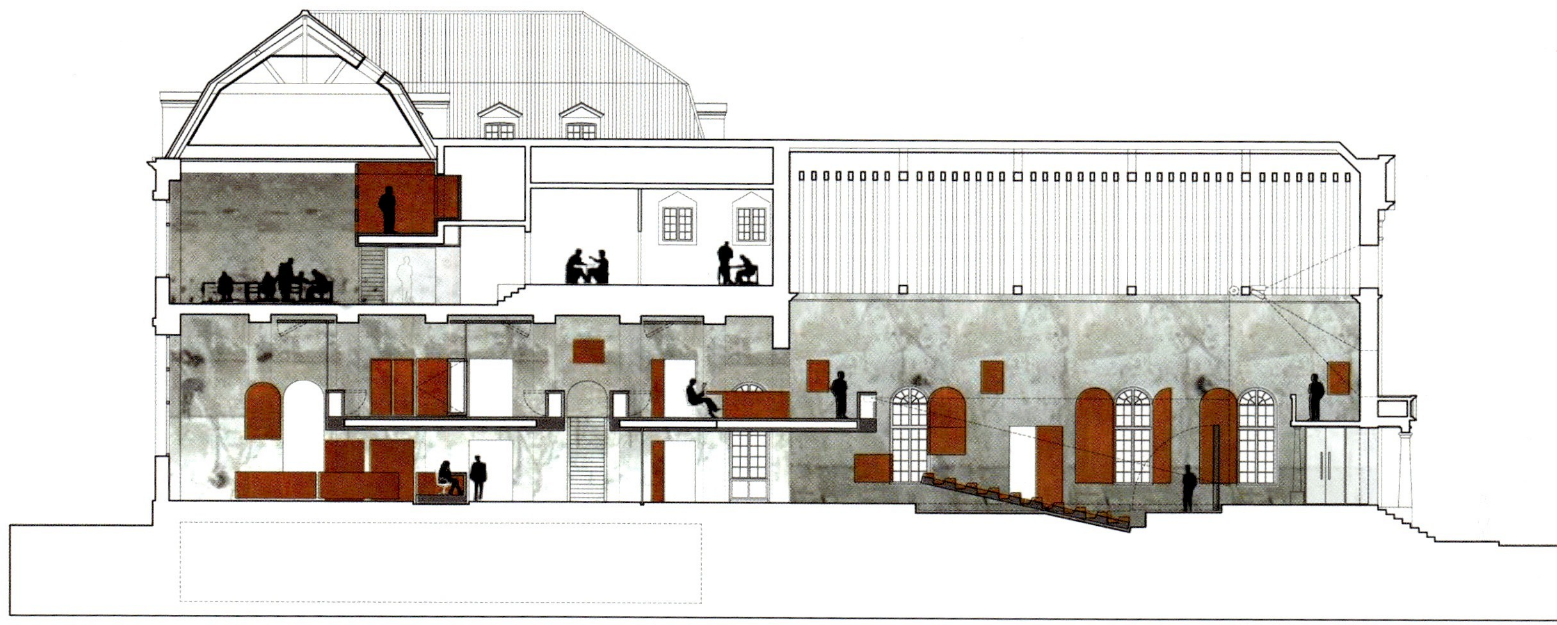

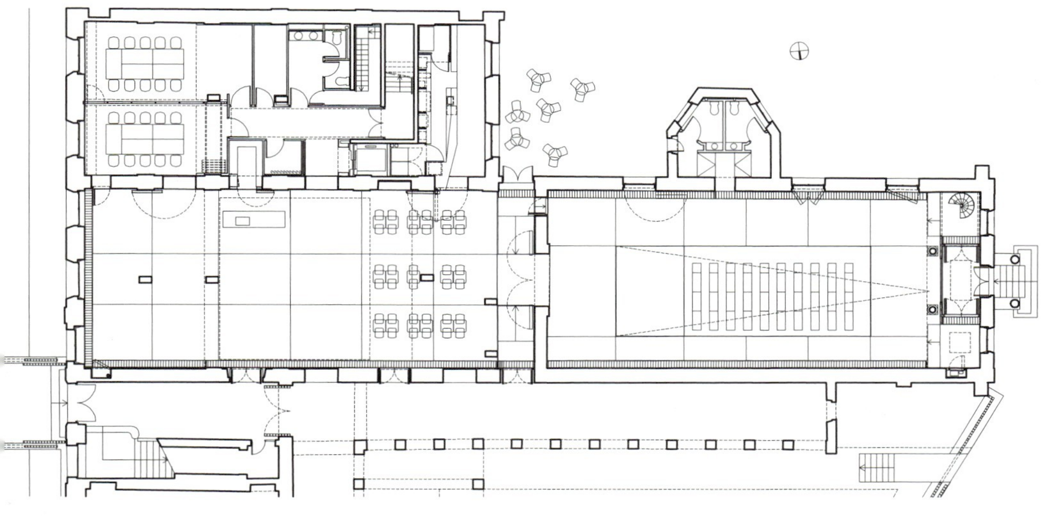

← | **Ground floor plan**
↓ | **Interior view,** the bar

VARIOUS FUNCTIONS

ARX PORTUGAL, Arquitectos Lda. / Nuno Mateus, José Mateus

↑ | **Exterior,** chapel
↗ | **Entrance,** library
→ | **Exterior,** youth forum

Ílhavo City Library

Ílhavo

Of the original building, only the main façade and the chapel, both in ruins, were left. The preliminary program specified building three autonomous nuclei: library, chapel and youth forum. The limits of the manor and the line of the old façade were chosen as an anchorage point, where administrative areas and areas compatible with the façade's rhythm were placed. The design of the reading rooms and youth forum, establishes direct morphological relations with the surroundings, thus creating architectural closure in a context that incorporates the physiognomy and traces of the surroundings. The chapel, deprived of its most important decorative elements, like tiles, woodwork, tomb stones and furniture, was restored.

PROJECT FACTS

Address: Avenida General Elmano Rocha Alqueidão, 3830 - 198 Ílhavo, Portugal. **Client:** City of Ílhavo. **Completion:** 2005. **Building type:** library, chapel, youth forum. **Gross floor area:** 3,200 m².
Original building: architect unkown. **Client:** Visconde de Almeida. **Completion:** 17th century. **Building type:** manor. **Gross floor area:** 1,300 m².

↑ | **Chapel**, altar
← | **Ground floor plan**

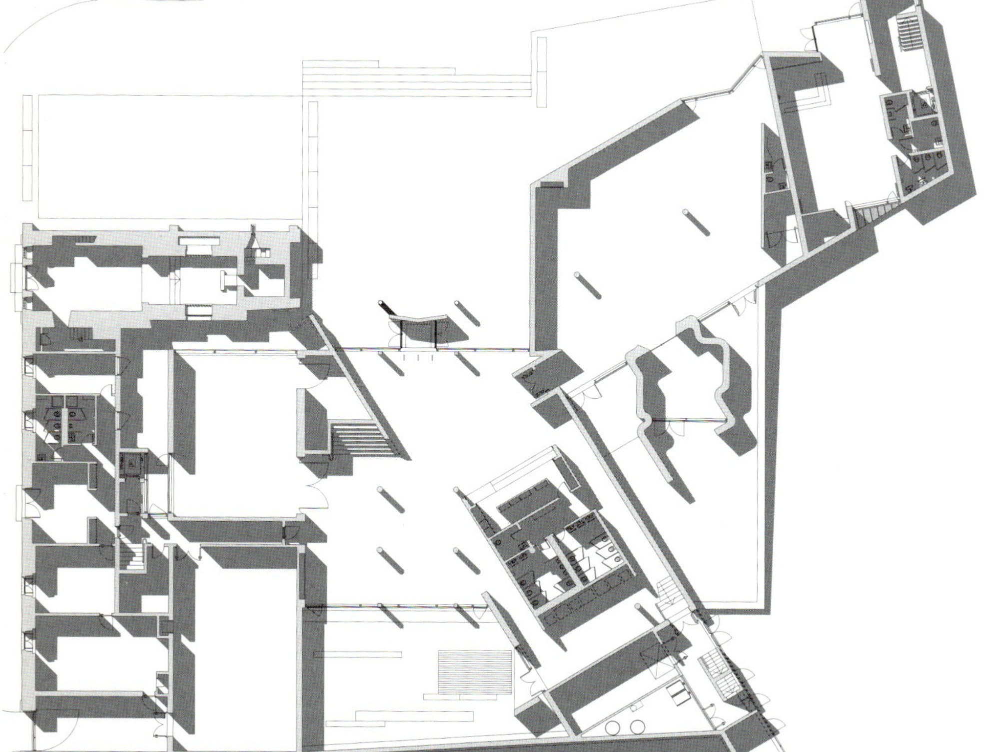

← | **Interior,** staircase system
↓ | **Elevation,** north
↓↓ | **Elevation,** west

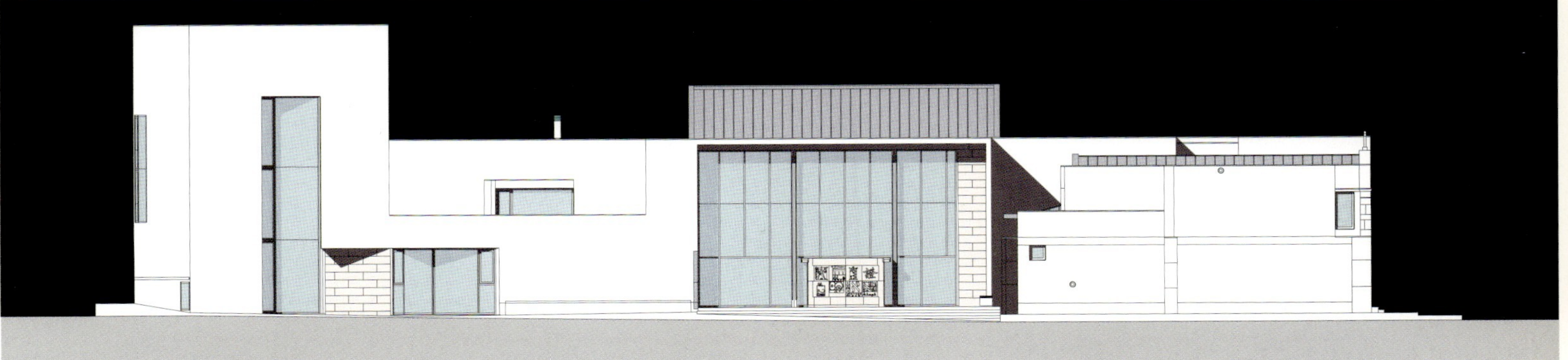

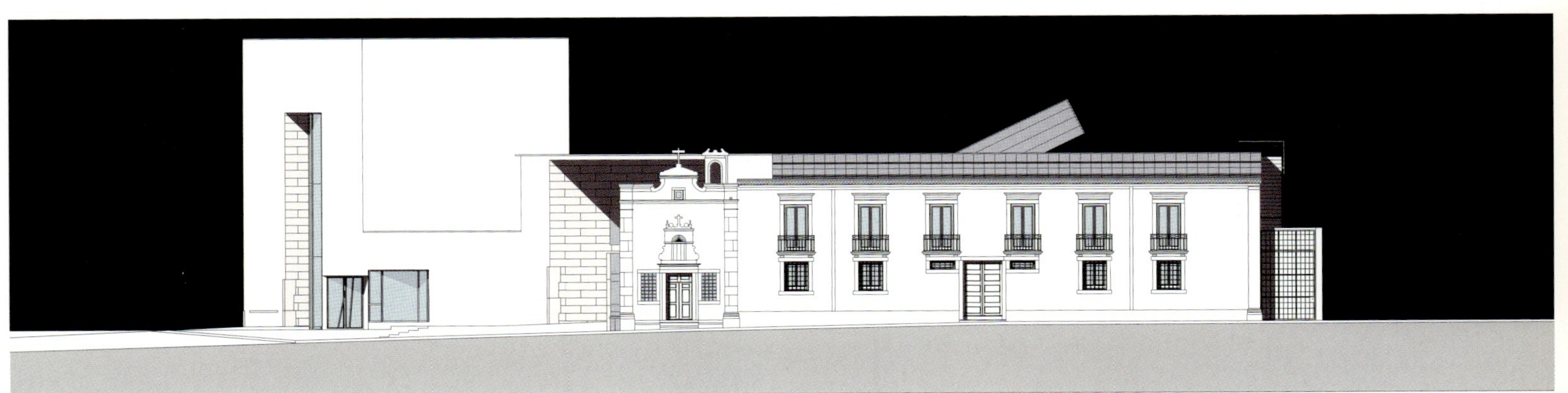

Sarah Wigglesworth Architects

↑ | Overview
↗ | Detail of ribbon roof
↗↗ | Ground floor plan
→ | Rehearsal studio

Siobhan Davies Company

London

The Siobhan Davies Company found their perfect potential headquarters in Southwark, south London, in a former school annex which had exactly the same footprint as a standard performance space. Extensive remodeling and conversion made it a suitable home for this leading contemporary dance company. The central core was stripped out at the ground and first-floor levels to create a double-height space which becomes the heart of the building, linking & organizing occupied spaces with the central circulation zone providing additional space for functions. To accommodate the new 5 meter high studio, the only location possible was at roof level. The existing roofs were removed and a new room was built within the ruins of the existing structure.

PROJECT FACTS

Address: s85 St Georges Road, London, SE1 6ER, United Kingdom. **Client:** Dancers' Studio Trust. **Completion:** 2005. **Building type:** mixed use. **Gross floor area:** 789 m². **Original building:** architect unknown. **Client:** School Board for London. **Completion:** 1898. **Building type:** school. **Gross floor area:** 761 m².

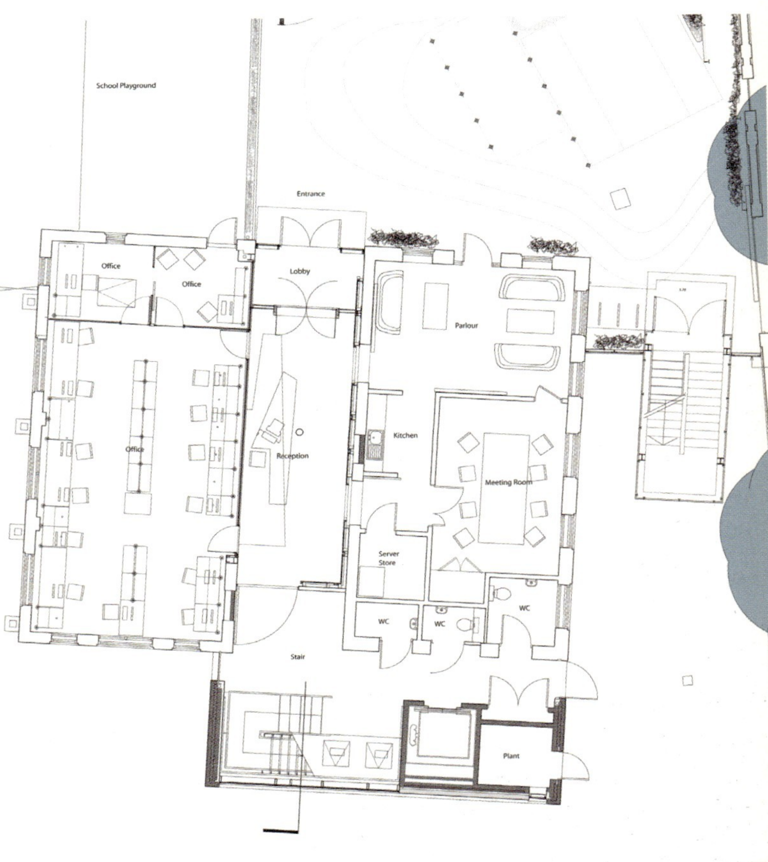

m2r architecture

↑ | **Entrance and welcome zone**

↓ | **Original building**

L'OREAL Academy

Kiev

After completing the new head office at the same building, L'OREAL invested 2008 with a rather small budget into its first hair dressing academy within Ukraine. Since the premises was rather small, a flexible use of space was key to transform the academy for master classes, lectures and shows for up to 200 people. Movable glass and mirror walls, integrated light box elements, product displays and presentation screens are part of a flexible and creative environment. In order to maintain the original industrial spirit of the building, the architects exposed the concrete structure and used slick and shiny materials such as glass, mirrors and painted MDF in contrast. The colors black and white create a minimalistic but very distinctive world of beauty and cosmetic.

PROJECT FACTS

Address: Horizon Business Center, Kiev 03038, Vul Mykoli Grinchenka 4, Ukraine. **Client:** L'OREAL Ukraine. **Completion:** 2008. **Building type:** training center. **Gross floor area:** 234 m^2 (converted part). **Original building:** architect unknown. **Client:** unknown. **Completion:** 1938. **Building type:** factory. **Gross floor area:** 7,500 m^2.

↑ | **Impression**
↓ | **Wet zone and coloration lab**

↑ | **Teaching area**
← | **Interior view**

↑ | **Interior master classroom**
← | **Plan,** workstations
↙ | **Plans,** master classroom and teaching

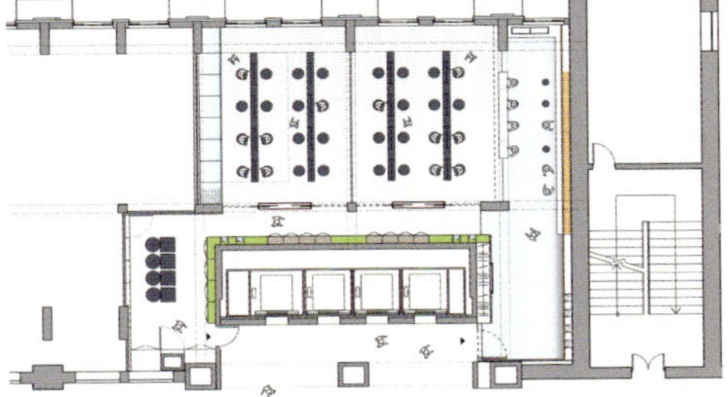

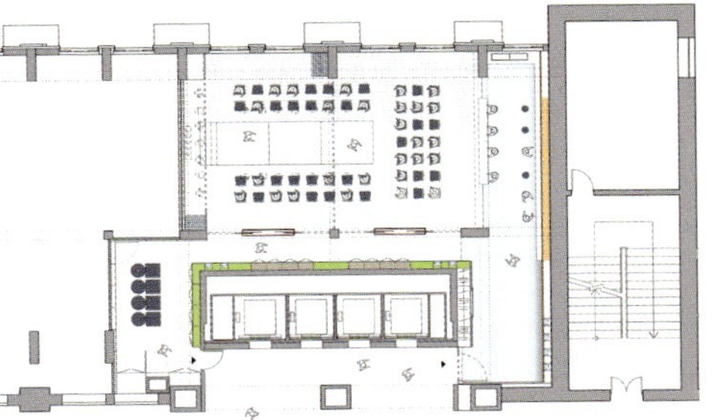

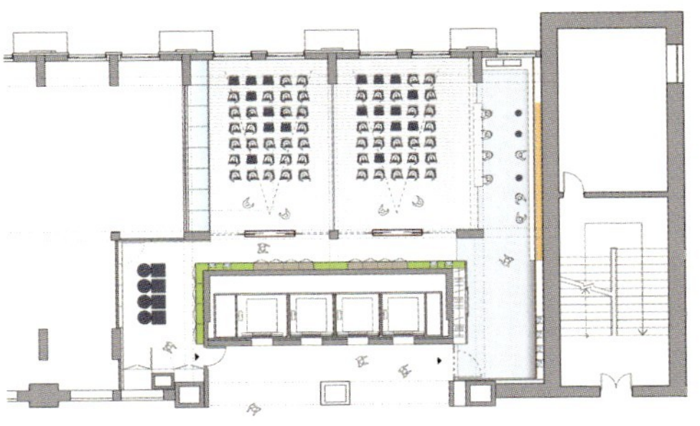

↑ | **Bird's-eye view**
→ | **The Hot Bath,** built in 1775, manifests itself to passers-by and sets the alignment of the New Royal Bath behind

Thermae Bath Spa

Bath

Thermae Bath Spa marks the revitalization of the city's spa quarter. The spa complex comprises one new building – the New Royal Bath – and the sensitive restoration and adaption of another five Grade 1 and 2 listed buildings. Requirements for the new spa facility and listed building parameters have inevitably lead to a very closely integrated design with a direct and intimate interplay between new and old. The difference in levels between existing buildings has been carefully resolved with the use of split level planning and the clear articulation of the connecting spaces as transparent bridge links which open up vistas along, across and through the complex.

Address: Thermae Bath Spa Ltd, The Hetling Pump Room, Hot Bath Street, Bath BA1 1SJ, United Kingdom. **Client:** Bath & North East Somerset Council & Thermae Development Co. **Completion:** 2006. **Building type:** leisure. **Gross floor area:** 3,650 m^2.

Original building: Thomas Baldwin. **Client:** unknown. **Completion:** 1789. **Building type:** healthcare. **Gross floor area:** unknown.

↑ | Second floor steam rooms
← | Exterior view of rooftop pool

← | **Interior view** of the oculus above the old hot bath
↓ | **Section**

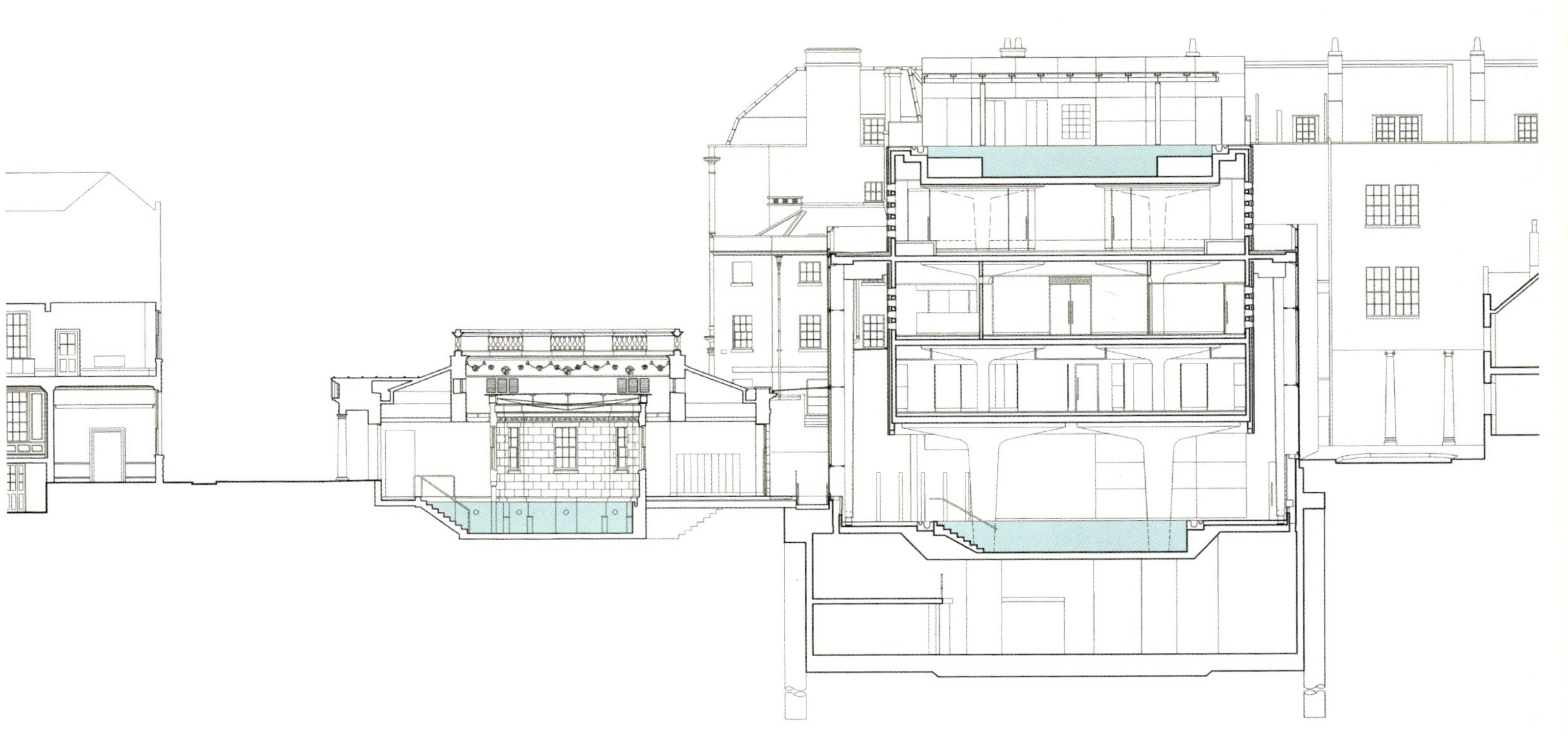

Rafael Moneo

↑ | **Archive** with working places
↓ | **Original building**

Royal and General Archive of Navarra

Pamplona

The restored building contains the administrative and academic activities, with the new tower providing the required archive space. While the original buildings have been restored using contemporary construction methods, the Gothic windows and the scale of the rooms have been respected in order to evoke the character of the former Palace. The crypt is composed of six ribbed vaults in which the simplicity of the ribs gives rise to a severe space with the light entering through six windows as a powerful break in the wall. This impressive piece of Gothic architecture that has survived in its original condition now serves as an exhibit space with glass display cases and natural light where the public can view period documents.

PROJECT FACTS

Address: Calle del Dos de Mayo, Pamplona, Spain. **Client:** Government of Navarra. **Completion:** 2006. **Building type:** archive. **Gross floor area:** 12,000 m².
Original building: architect unknown. **Client:** Kings of Navarra. **Completion:** medieval. **Building type:** palace. **Gross floor area:** 3,100 m².

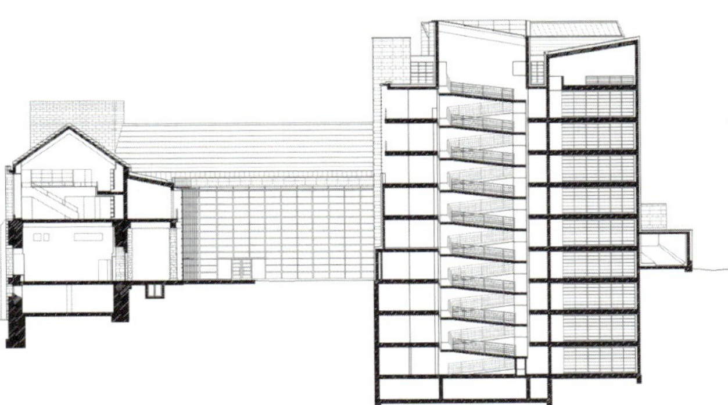

↑ | **Section**
↓ | **Ramp** in the book storage tower

↑ | **Reading room**
↓ | **Inner courtyard**

Max van Aerschot architect bv

↑ | **North-west façade,** new thermal skin behind original façade
↓ | **Sections**

MTV Networks Benelux

Amsterdam

In 2007 the carpentry workshop on the former NDSM shipyard was transformed into the bustling headquarters of MTV Networks Benelux. The 1927 monument was to be fused with today's high tech world. Inside the stripped hall a detached concrete frame consisting of four layers is placed with a new thermal wall, about one meter behind the existing masonry and single glass walls. One half of the new building contains the recording studio with the directors' offices on top, between the roof structure and skylights. The other half contains the various business units, on four floors around the entrance hall with a large void. The cantilevered glass restaurant gives the building a new front to the river IJ.

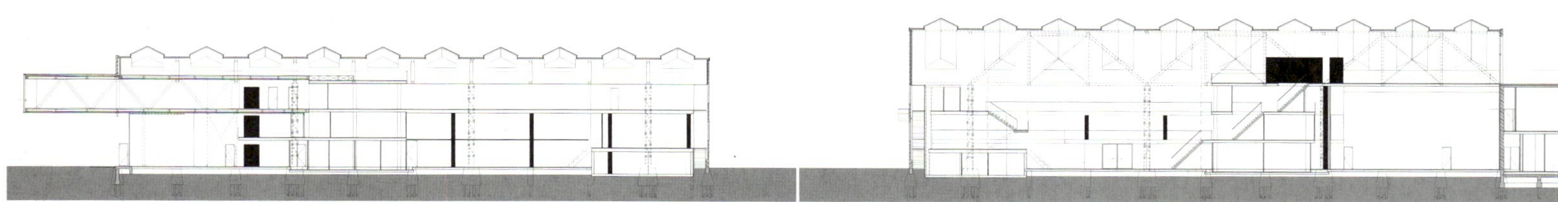

PROJECT FACTS

Address: TT Neveritaweg 6, 1033WB Amsterdam, The Netherlands. **Interior Design:** QuA Associates bv. **Structural Design:** EversPartners. **Client:** MediaWharf BV. **Completion:** 2007. **Building type:** offices, restaurant, recording studio. **Gross floor area:** 6,500 m².

Original building: architect unknown. **Client:** NDSM-wharf. **Completion:** 1927, rebuild 1935. **Building type:** shipyard carpentry workshop. **Gross floor area:** 3,000 m².

↑ | **North-west façade** with cantilevered glass restaurant

↓ | **East corner,** entrance

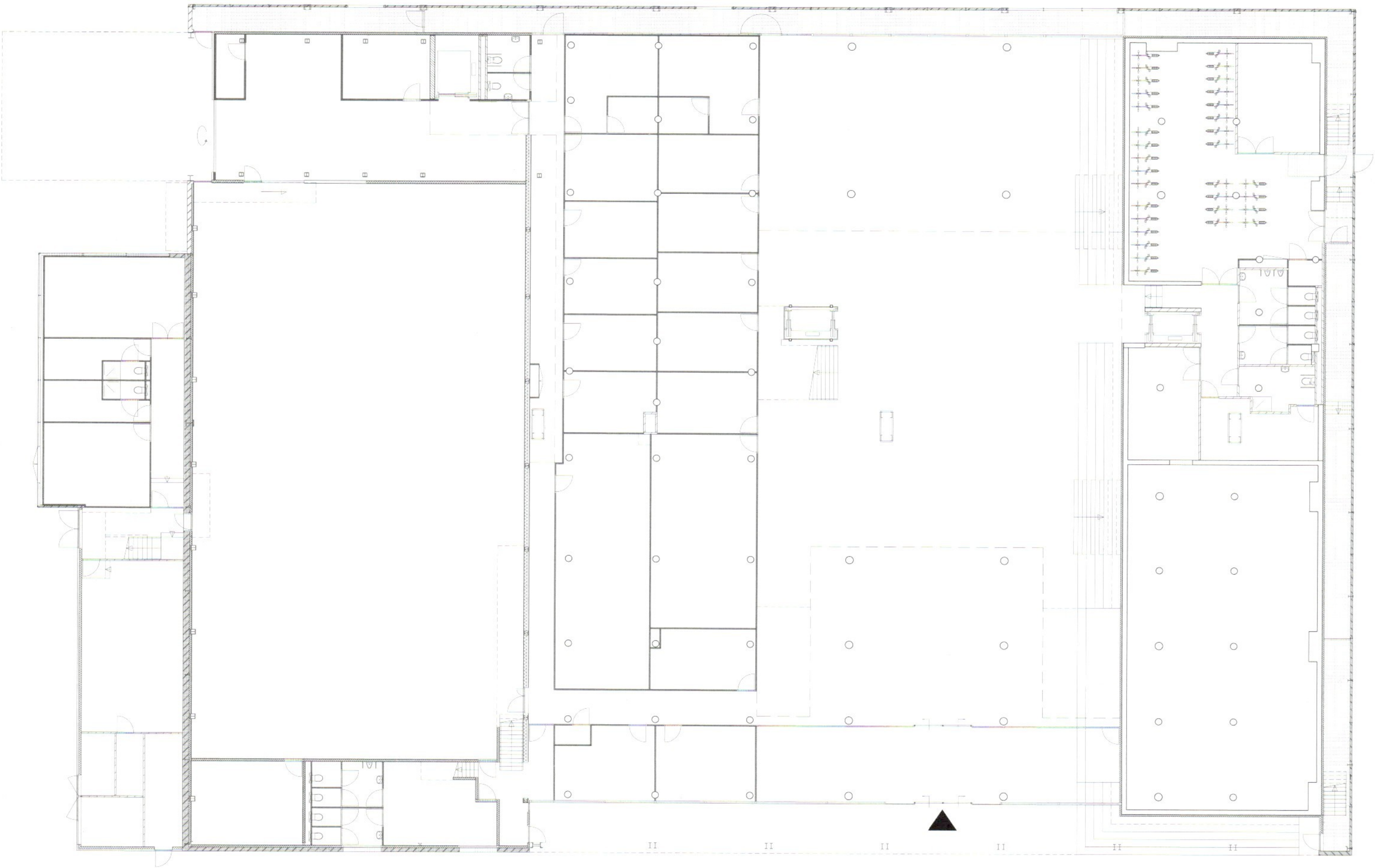

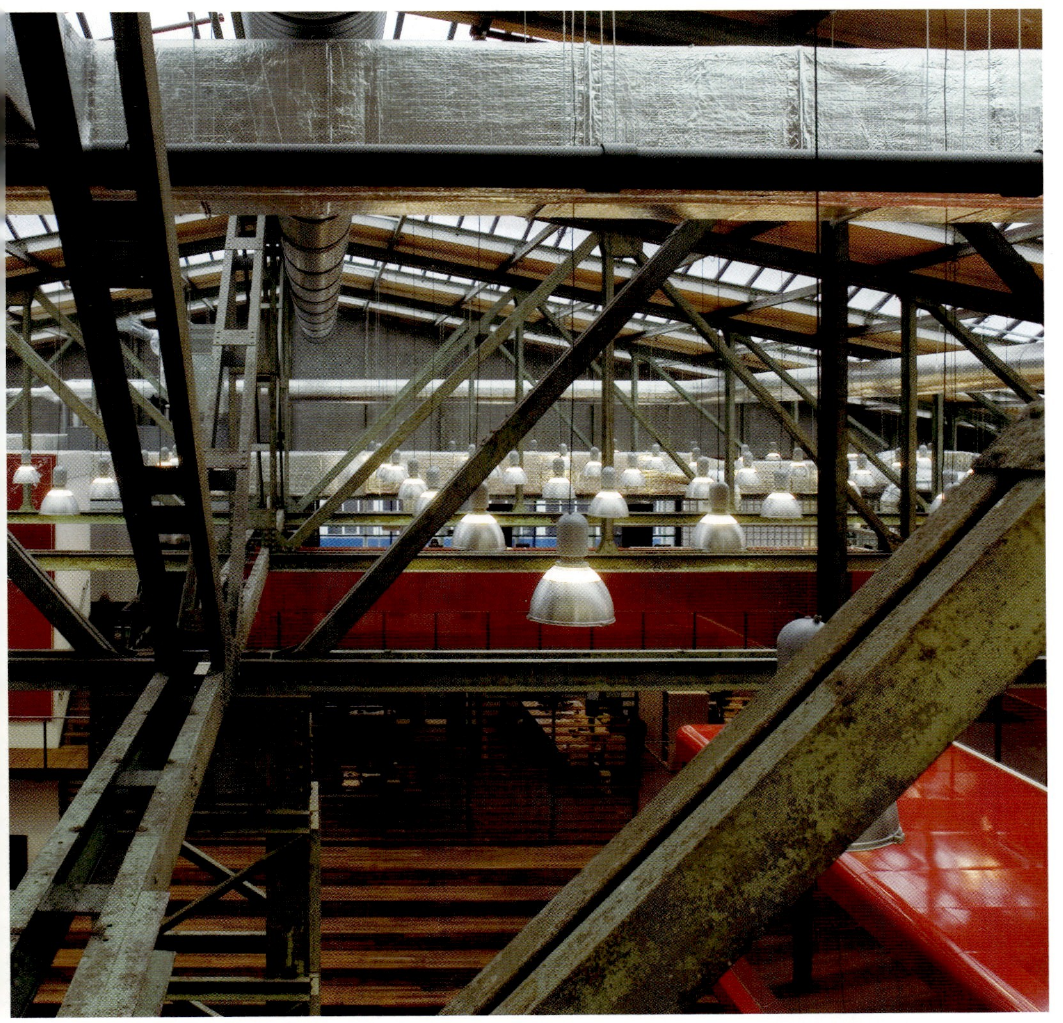

←←| **Central hall,** original roof construction and skylights
↙ | **Ground floor plan**
← | **Original roof construction**
↓ | **Central hall**

UTARCHITECTS / Tim Bauerfeind, Henning von Wedemeyer

↑ | **Workshop building**
→ | **Sheltered area** and manor house

Restoration Center

Berlin

In accordance to its 18th century ambiance a manor was converted to a new use as training center for restorers and cabinet makers. Personnel and training rooms were located in the old manor house. A new workshop where the hands-on training takes place was erected in the courtyard. The façade and roof of the hall constitute a continuous building envelope, which opens up in glass to the weather sheltered area in the front, the courtyard and the old building. A workshop on two levels, consisting of a machine shop on the ground floor and work room on the upper floor, is located beneath the hall. The sightlines allow for unencumbered communication and offer views into the courtyard from all work areas. The street side façade is for the most part closed to protect against noise.

Address: Richterstraße 6, 12524 Berlin, Germany. **Client:** Restaurierungszentrum Berlin e. V. **Completion:** 2009. **Building type:** restoration center. **Gross floor area:** 1,010 m^2.
Original building: architect unknown. **Client:** unknown. **Completion:** 1900. **Building type:** manor house. **Gross floor area:** 360 m^2.

↑ | **View from street** with manor house
↙ | **View from court yard** with manor house
↓ | **Site plan**

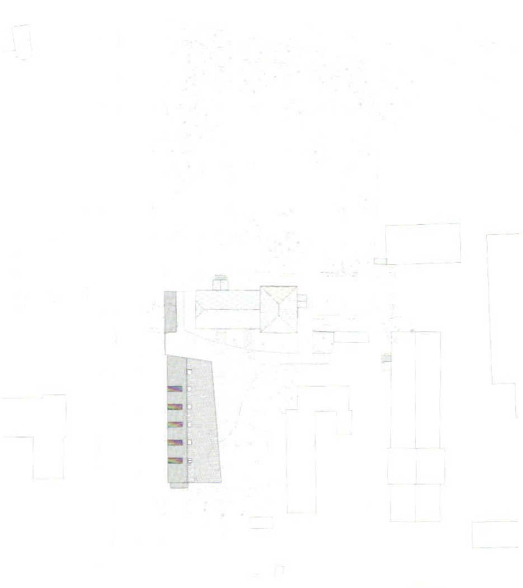

← | Interior
↙ | Ground floor plan
↓ | First floor plan

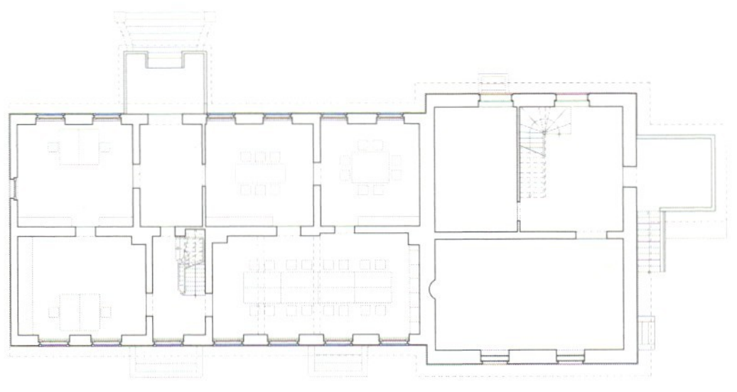

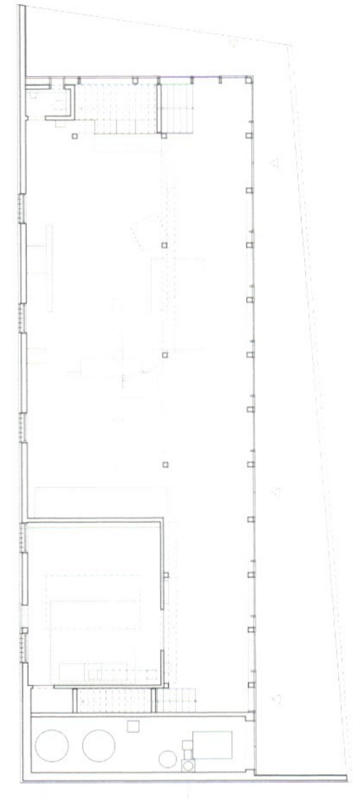

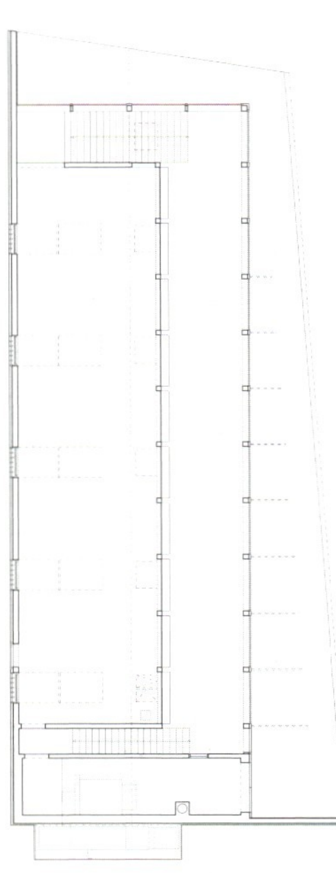

Sergei Tchoban Architekt BDA nps tchoban voss
A. M. Prasch, S. Tchoban, E. Voss

↑ | Main façade
→ | Prayer room

Synagogue Münstersche Straße

Berlin

The 1922 building did service as a transformer station, substation and illumination laboratory for street lighting. With its classicistic façade the building fits in well in the neighborhood of wealthy homes. Purchased by a Jewish foundation in 2004, the building was placed at the disposal of the orthodox Jewish "Chabad Lubawitsch" organization. The exterior was retained to a great extent, except for the addition of a prestigious portal opening up to the street. The orthodox synagogue was built in the former transformer hall with a traditional ritual bath (mikvah) located in the cellar. In addition there are rooms for seminars and childrens' services, a library, café and ballroom with kosher kitchen for the community members and visitors.

PROJECT FACTS

Address: Münstersche Str. 6, 10709 Berlin, Germany. **Architect in charge:** Frederik-Sebastian Scholz. **Client:** Chabad Lubawitsch Berlin e. V. **Completion:** 2007. **Building type:** sacred building. **Gross floor area:** 2,050 m^2.

Original building: Otto Hanke. **Client:** Elektrizitätswerk Südwest AG. **Completion:** 1922. **Building type:** transformer station. **Gross floor area:** 2,100 m^2.

↖ | **Interior of entrance area**

↑ | **Lobby,** organic formed interior decoration

← | **First floor plan**

← | Façade
↙ | Woman's gallery
↓ | Detail of the boarding

↑ | Entrance area

St. Elisabeth

Aachen

The goal of the project was to provide space for non-ecclesiastical use in a church building which had become too large for the shrinking parish, in order to bring life into the building during times when services are not being held. The entry area of the church was spatially detached from the nave. A non-ecclesiastical area was created with a central meeting zone, an adjoining parish office and separate conference rooms. The glass vestibule is placed in slices in the space as a four-wing door installation, followed immediately by the central access to the church. Glass partitions seal off the parish office from the sacral chamber and the meeting area. A new window creates mutual between the inside and outside and a source of natural light.

PROJECT FACTS

Address: Blücherplatz 2, 52068 Aachen, Germany. **Client:** Catholic Church St. Elisabeth. **Completion:** 2005. **Building type:** mixed-use. **Gross floor area:** 148 m^2.

Original building: E. Endler. **Client:** Catholic Church St. Elisabeth. **Completion:** 1907. **Building type:** church.

SCHIFF

BESPRECHUNG

BEGEGNUNG

← | **Sections**

↙ | **Pastor's office**

↓ | **View** from the entrance towards the choir

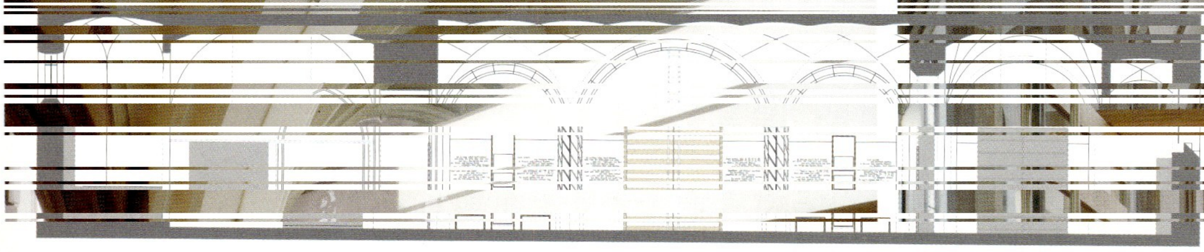

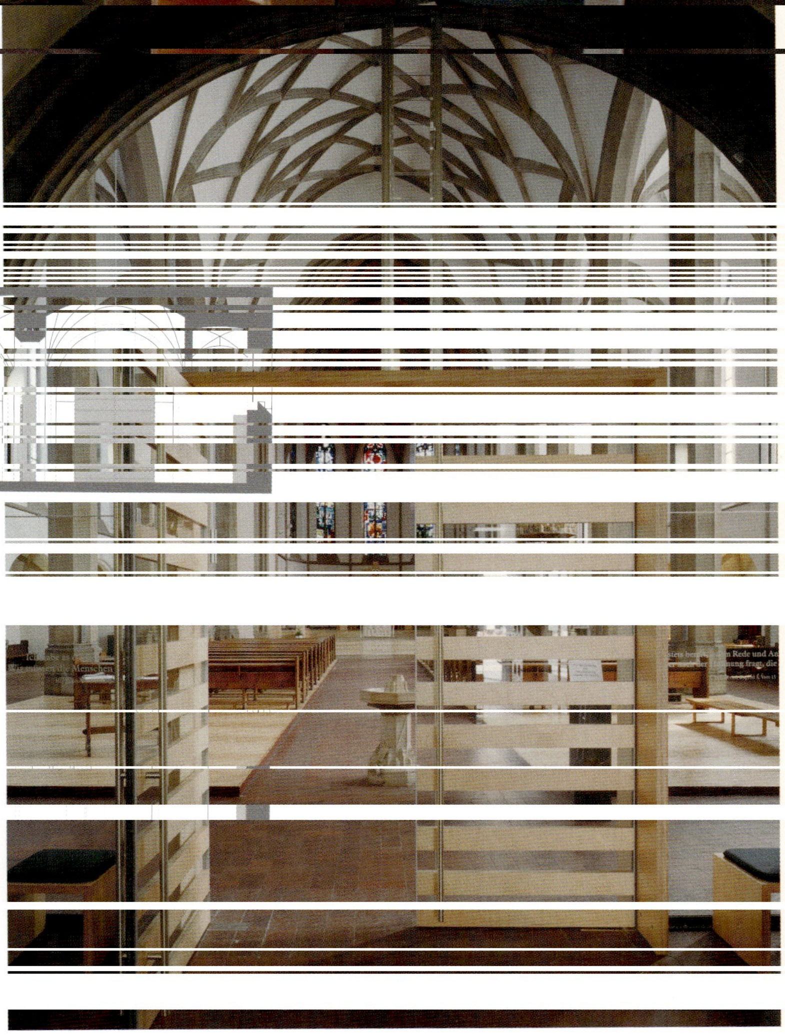

4of7 architecture

↑ | Interior view
→ | Fitness room

WellnessSky

Belgrade

The main volume of the building, triangular in plan, is elevated some fifteen meters above the river and the ground level with the pedestrian esplanade. It is supported solely by the central core, which contains two elevator shafts and a double spiral staircase. The concrete floor-slab and ceiling shell are not connected at the perimeter of the building, allowing for the continuity of the glass façade to the full extent. An uninterrupted glass strip, with a total length of 150 meters, is wrapped around the building. The ceiling design consists of a sequence of geometric transformations and subdivisions applied to the original grid. As a result, approximately 390 backlit panels with the finite variation in shape and size are suspended from the triangular steel construction.

PROJECT FACTS

Address: Dunavski Kej, 32, Belgrade 11000, Serbia. **Client:** Wellness. **Completion:** 2008. **Building type:** wellness center. **Gross floor area:** 1,200 m².

Original building: Iva Antic. **Client:** State of Yugoslavia. **Completion:** 1973. **Building type:** restaurant. **Gross floor area:** 1,200 m².

↑ | **Exterior view**
← | **Floor plan**

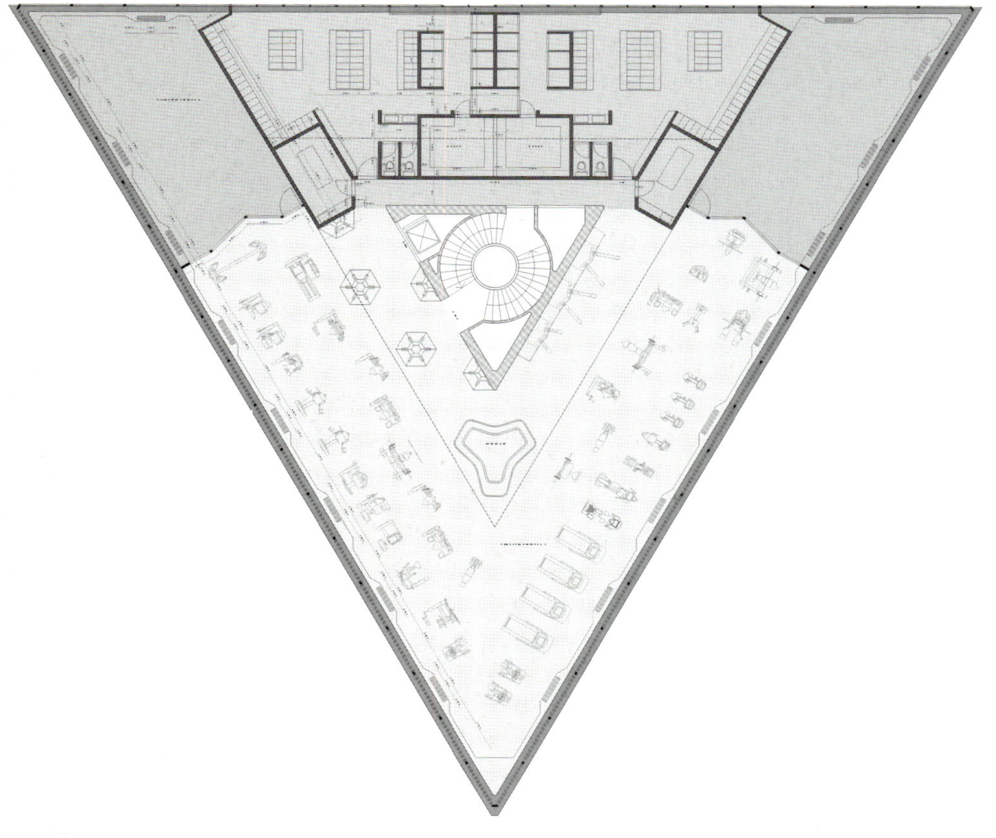

← | Ceiling plan
↓ | Interior view

LAN Architecture

↑ | Street elevation
→ | Exterior view

Children's Toy Library

Bonneuil sur Marne

This design of a children's toy library resulted from an approach that aimed to simultaneously resolve a number of problems and develop new ideas. The library makes use of an existing building to create a children's play area. In spite of the difficulties of a very restricted budget, a small-scale public facility was created to give an identity to a socially unstable area, occupied by large housing complexes. The architects decided to design a building with no sense of scale, one which would appear timeless, a dense solid mass, an urban symbol, standing out from its environment as a shell protecting its contents. The result is a volume with a bunker-like appearance, reminiscent of a vernacular construction.

PROJECT FACTS

Address: 14 Rue M. Goutier, 94380 Bonneuil sur Marne, France. **Client:** City of Bonneuil sur Marne. **Completion:** 2008. **Building type:** library. **Gross floor area:** 380 m².
Original building: architect unknown. **Client:** France Telecom. **Completion:** 1960s. **Building type:** social housing. **Gross floor area:** 203 m².

↖ | Entrance area
↑ | Street elevation
← | Interior view
↓ | Axonometry

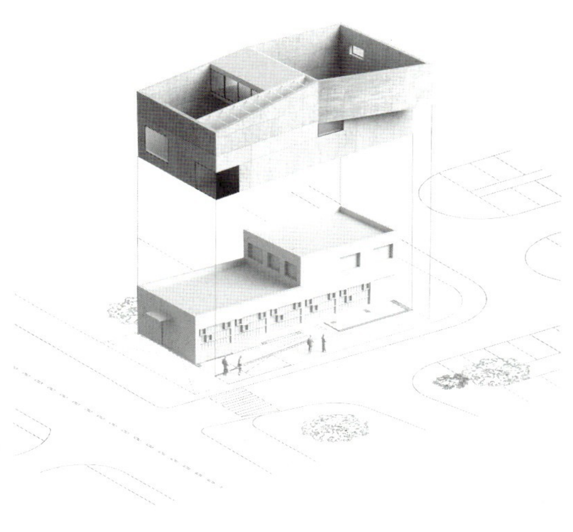

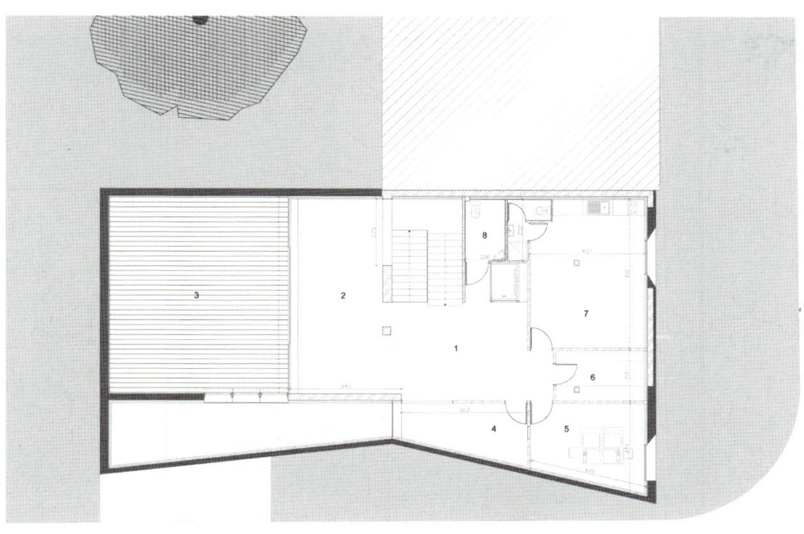

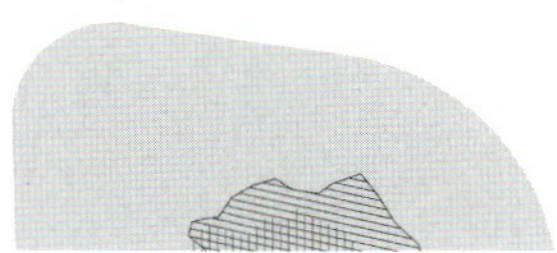

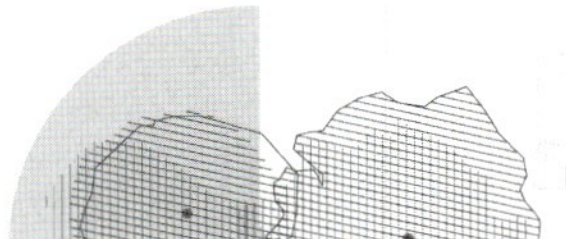

← | **First floor plan**
↓ | **Interior view,** playground

studiometrico / Francesca Murialdo, Lorenzo Bini

↑ | Showroom

bastard store

Milano

Bastard store is the new headquarters of a company that conceives, produces and distributes clothing for skateboarders under the bastard brand. The building, designed by Mario Cavallé in the 1940s, is an adapt environment to host the activities of the company. At the bastard store it is possible to create, develop, produce, communicate and test bastard products. All the new elements have been inserted within the existing building as an independent construction and put in continuous physical and visual communication with each other. New elements are clearly distinguished from the existing building structure with their materials, geometries and level of detail constituting a newly added discrete layer.

PROJECT FACTS

Address: Via Scipio Slataper 19 20125 Milano, Italy. **Structures:** Atelier LC. **Client:** COMVERT S.r.l. **Completion:** 2008. **Building type:** mixed use. **Gross floor area:** 1,400 m².
Original building: Ing. Mario Cavallé. **Client:** unknown. **Completion:** 1950s. **Building type:** cinema theater. **Gross floor area:** 1,400 m².

↑ | **Storage and bastard bowl**

↓ | **Bastard bowl**

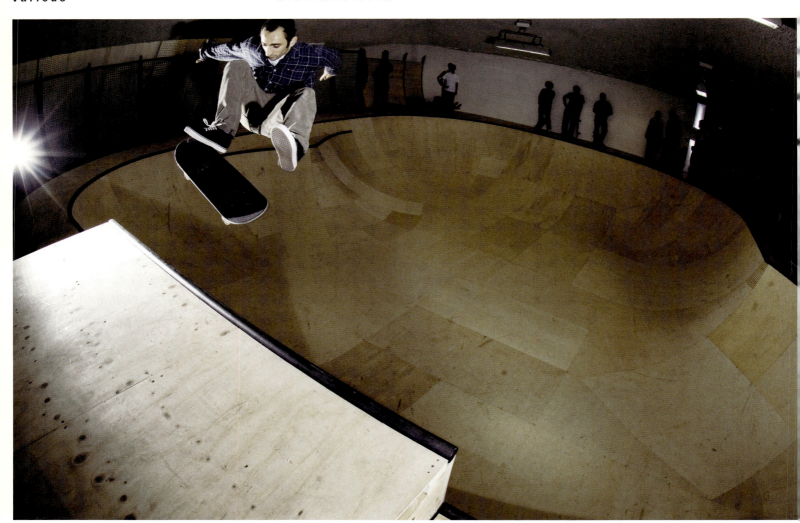

↑ | **Skater in bastard bowl**
↓ | **Longitudinal section**

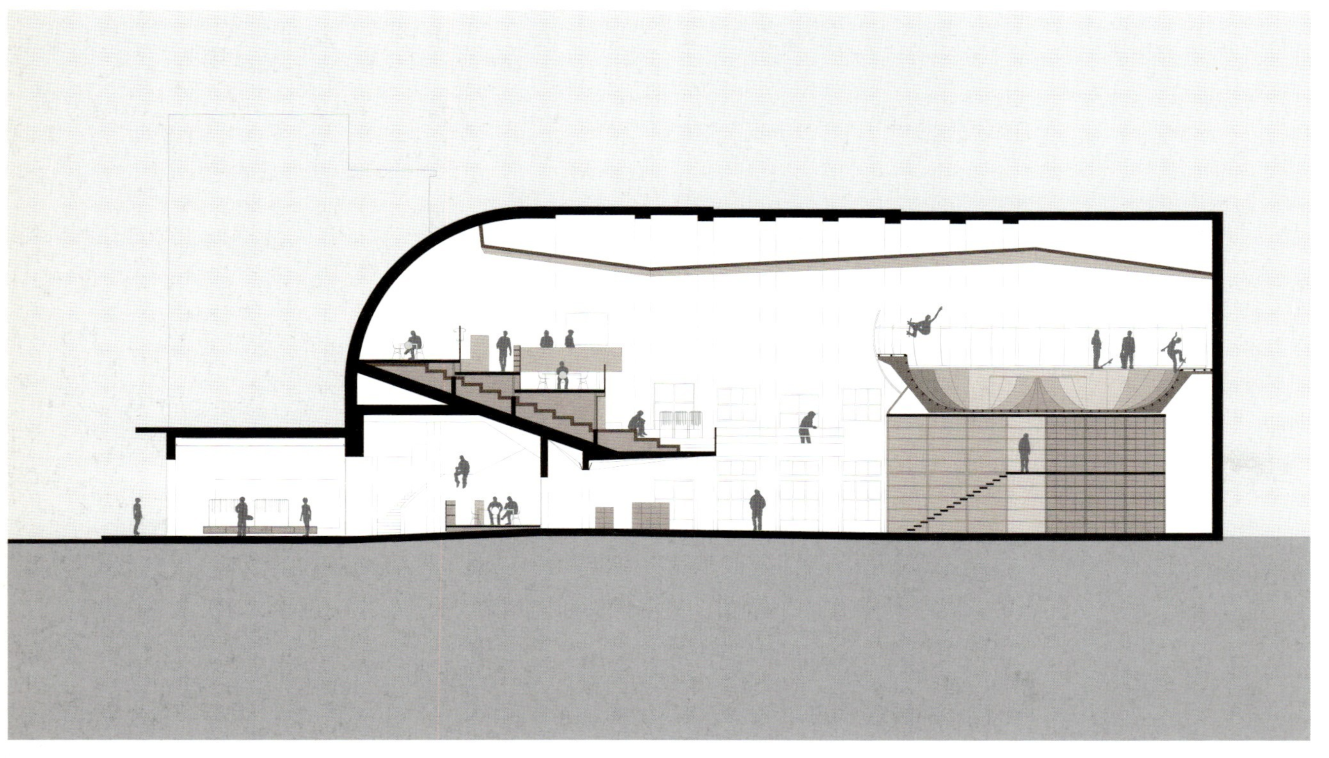

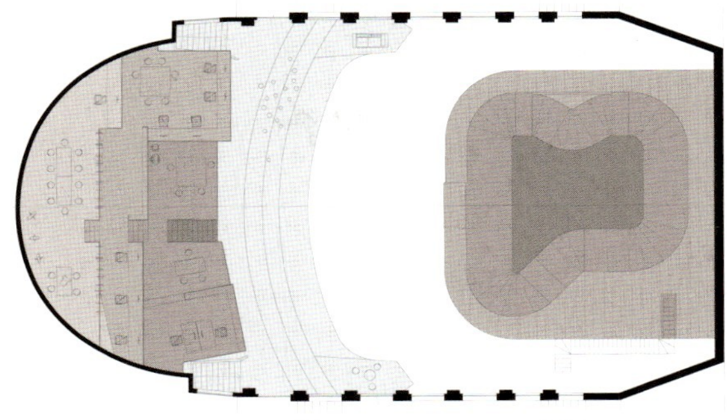

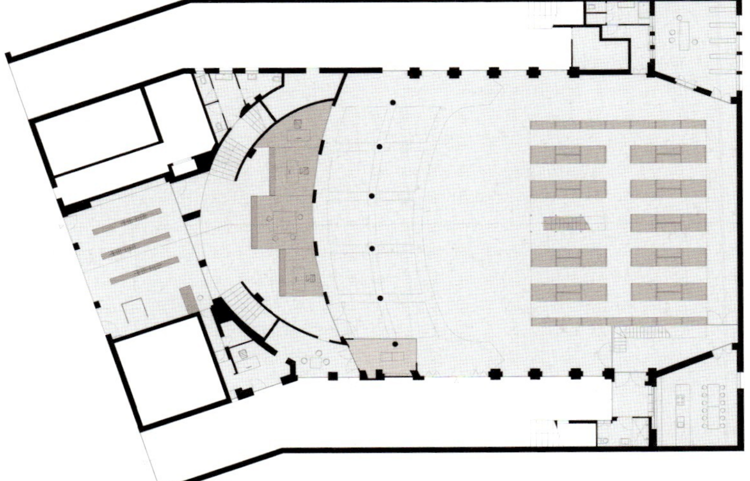

← | **Plans,** upper level and ground floor

↓ | **Administration department**

Emilio Marin + Murúa-Valenzuela / Emilio Marin, Rodrigo Valenzuela, Benjamín Murúa

↑ | Exterior view

Licantén Public Library

Licantén

In spite of its condition of abandonment and deterioration, the metal shop has its place in the history of Licantén. Through the incorporation of a new program and in keeping certain essential elements of the existing building, the proposal is to recover the building and give it a new meaning. It has been considered essential, as part of the recovery operation of the building, to preserve the main space of the old metal shop in addition to its exterior volume. Based on this idea, the proposal preserves the height of the space and its lighting conditions, and transforms it into the main reading room of the new library. The idea that is addressed with the incorporation of the two new volumes is to form a single new unified space.

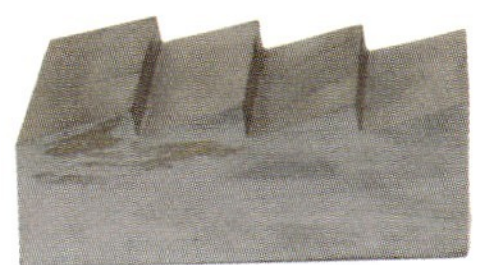

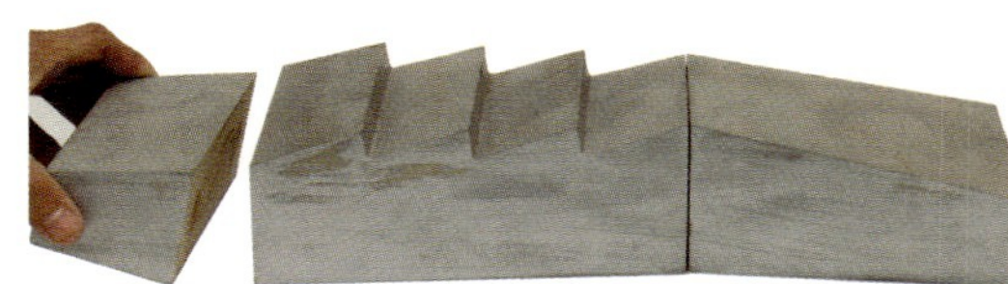

PROJECT FACTS

Address: Calle Alejandro Rojas, Licantén, VII Región del Maule, Chile. **Associate Architect:** Enrique Browne. **Collaborating Architect:** Juan Carlos Lopez. **Client:** Dirección de Bibliotecas, Archivos y Museos, Chile. **Completion:** 2009. **Building type:** library. **Gross floor area:** 490 m^2.
Original building: architect unknown. **Client:** unknown. **Completion:** 1937. **Building type:** metal shop for trains. **Gross floor area:** 308 m^2.

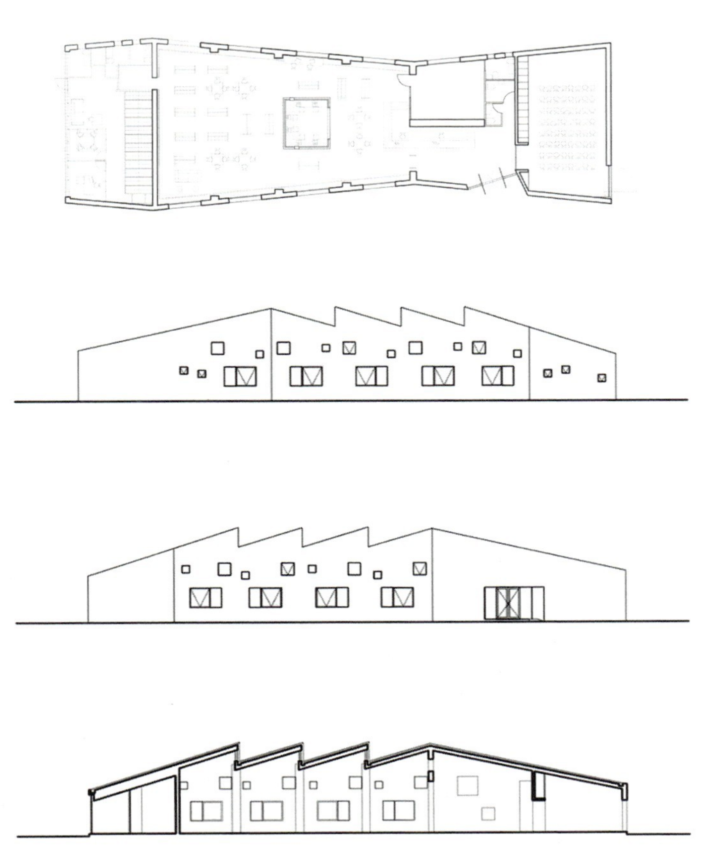

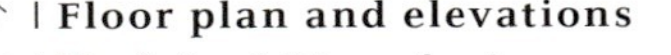

↑ | **Floor plan and elevations**
↙ | **Model,** addition of volumes

↑ | **Interior**
↓ | **Interior**

Ipro Dresden, Büro Böhme + Schönfeld

↑ | Bird's-eye view

Hubertusburg

Wermsdorf

On behalf of the SIB, NL Leipzig II Ipro Dresden was commissioned to undertake the architectural planning for the renovation of the building façades and the installation of the central workshops for the restoration of archive and library assets (ZErAB) that were compatible with the existing building substance. The exterior walls and façades were restored on the castle courtyard site in the style of the 18th century. Historical colors were tested on sample grids. Windows and doors were recreated according to the Baroque model and outfitted with the necessary technical equipment. The planned archive and workshop required the installation of the most demanding restoration technology while maintaining the Baroque castle grounds.

Address: Hubertusburg, Geb. 71–79, 04779 Wermsdorf, Germany. **Client:** Staatsbetrieb Sächsisches Immobilien- und Baumanagement (SIB), NL Leipzig II. **Completion:** 2009. **Building type:** restoration studios (ZErAB). **Gross floor area:** 13,500 m² (only ZErAB).
Original building: Johann Christoph Knöffel. **Client:** King August II. von Sachsen. **Completion:** 1753. **Building type:** hunting lodge. **Gross floor area:** 48,600 m² (whole area).

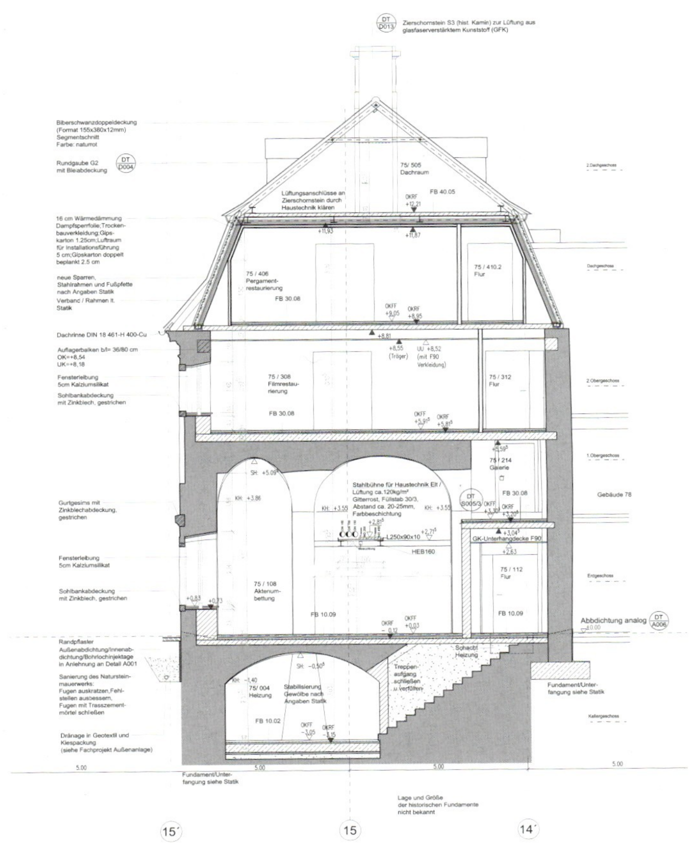

↑ | **Section**

↓ | **Baroque outbuildings,** restoration studios and state archives

↑ | **Baroque stairs,** building 73

Gijs van Thienen Architecten

Lieven de Key-building Handicraft School

Amsterdam

↑ | Entrance
↓ | Original exterior

The architects believe that sustainability is not only dependant on the implementation of new technologies, but has to start with making conscious decisions in terms of orientation and organization. The building was part of a complex originally build as a educational facility for the crafts trades. In collaboration with the end-users the architects selected the part that was most suitable for the specific function. The building itself consists of two layers. With a loading area on the ground floor and offices on the first floor. This distinction is reflected in the use of materials and details. Re-using the existing structure it has been possible to transform the former machine shops into a landscaped office with a transparent but friendly atmosphere.

PROJECT FACTS

Address: Turbinestraat 6, 1014 AV Amsterdam, The Netherlands. **Client:** Housing Association 'De Key'. **Completion:** 2009. **Building type:** workshop, office. **Gross floor area:** 2,100 m². **Original building:** architect unknown. **Client:** unknown. **Completion:** 1650s. **Building type:** handicraft school. **Gross floor area:** unknown.

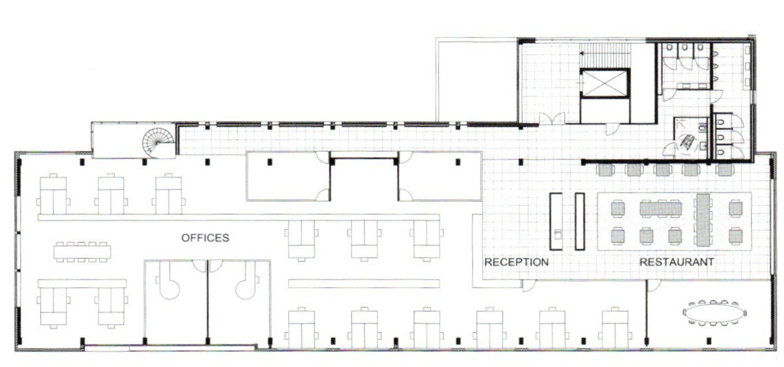

↑ | First and ground floor plan
↓ | New exterior

↑ | Entrance from inside
↓ | Cafeteria

Atelier PRO architekten

↑ | **Courtyard façade** follows the existing medieval building line
→ | **Seventeenth-century brick** arch at the entrance of library

Library of Special Collection

Amsterdam

This complex includes the University Museum and the Special Collections belonging to the university library. The crux of the plan is an "interior street" which gives the complex a new main structure. This feature endows the cluttered rear of the buildings on the side of the Binnengasthuis grounds with an ambience worthy of a traditional court. The solar court doubles as a glass case for displaying the obliquely placed back section of the building – a physical reminder of the site's medieval land division. The narrow old gateway, the Gasthuishofpoort, has become the new, architecturally spruced up, entrance with a tall, narrow light court topped off with a glass roof.

PROJECT FACTS

Address: Oude Turfmarkt 129, 1012 GC Amsterdam, The Netherlands. **Interior architect:** Merkx + Girod Architecten. **Client:** College van Bestuur Universiteit van Amsterdam. **Completion:** 2007. **Building type:** university library and museum. **Gross floor area:** 6,151 m^2.
Original building: P. F. Laarman and Phillip Vingboons. **Client:** unknown. **Completion:** 1645, 1884. **Building type:** monastery / hospital. **Gross floor area:** 2,920 m^2.

↑ | **The Rosenthaliana Library**
← | **Stairs and bridges** intersect the atrium, connecting various parts of the building
↓ | **Section**

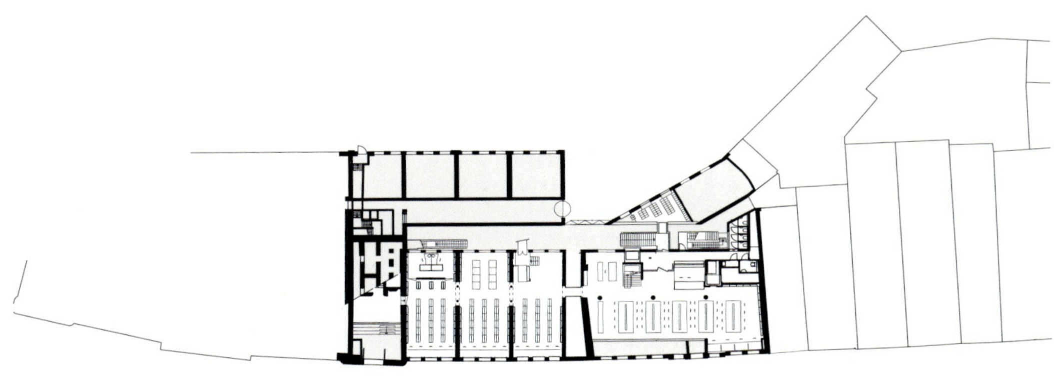

↖ | **First floor plan**
↙ | **Ground floor plan**
↓ | **Exterior view,** façade

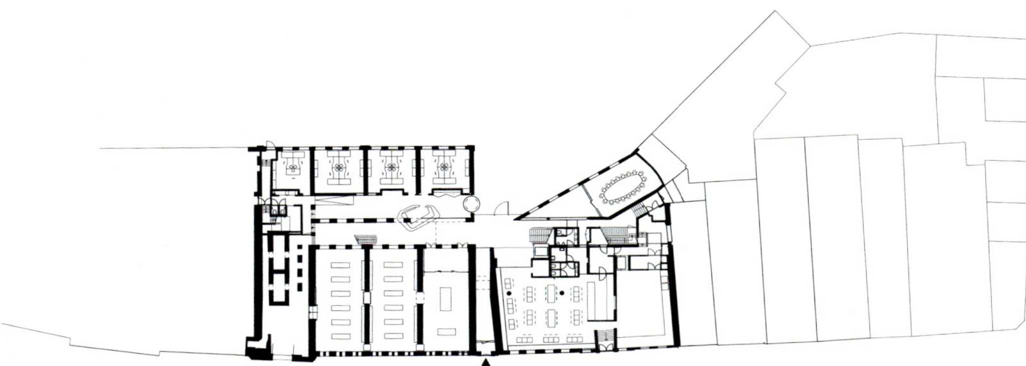

Pugh + Scarpa Architects / Gwynne Pugh, Angela Brooks, Lawrence Scarpa

↑ | View toward kitchen along pool
→ | View along pool toward desk

Jigsaw

Los Angeles

The film editing profession requires small, dark environments free from distraction and light reflection. Yet, a film editing company must exist in a stimulating, socially interactive workspace. Within a rough 1940s warehouse, the architects created discrete environments with gradients of privacy. Hovering over a large, placid reflecting pool, the central design elements are the two oblong curvilinear boxes, which enclose the editing studios and offices. Facing the lobby, the ends present luminous textured façades, filled respectively with ping-pong balls and acrylic beads. Bathing the rooms in softly diffused light, they afford the users privacy and minimize distractions. The design creates a delicate balance between flow and calm focus.

PROJECT FACTS

Address: 2223 S. Carmelina Ave., Los Angeles, CA, 90064, USA. **Client:** Jigsaw. **Completion:** 2005. **Building type:** creative office building. **Gross floor area:** 520 m². **Original building:** architect unknown. **Client:** unknown. **Completion:** 1940. **Building type:** bow-truss warehouse. **Gross floor area:** 520 m².

↑ | **View of office cubes and pool from common area**
← | **Sections**
↓ | **Existing interior**

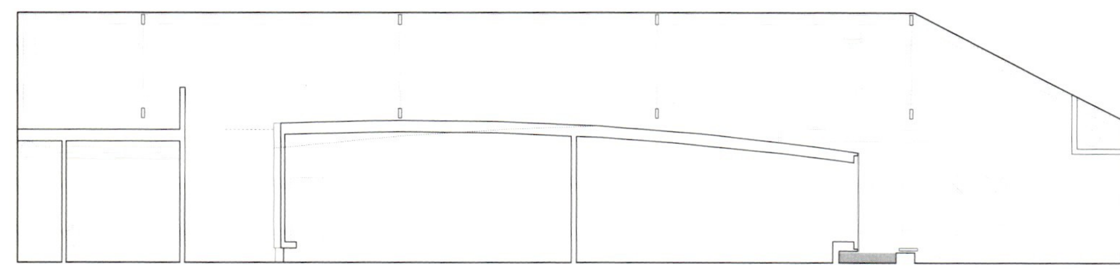

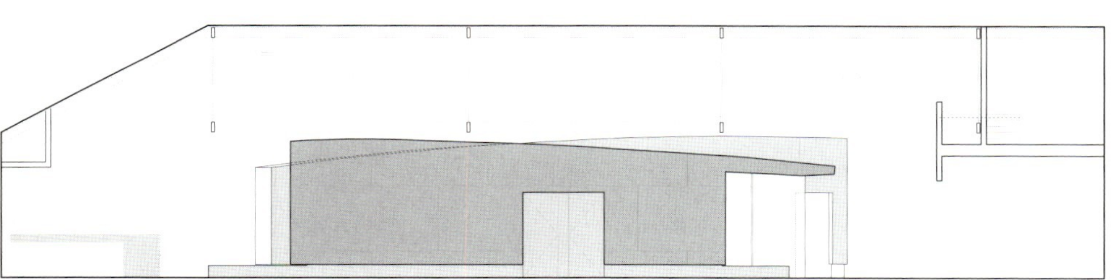

← | **Passageway,** adjacent to edit cube
↓ | **Plan**

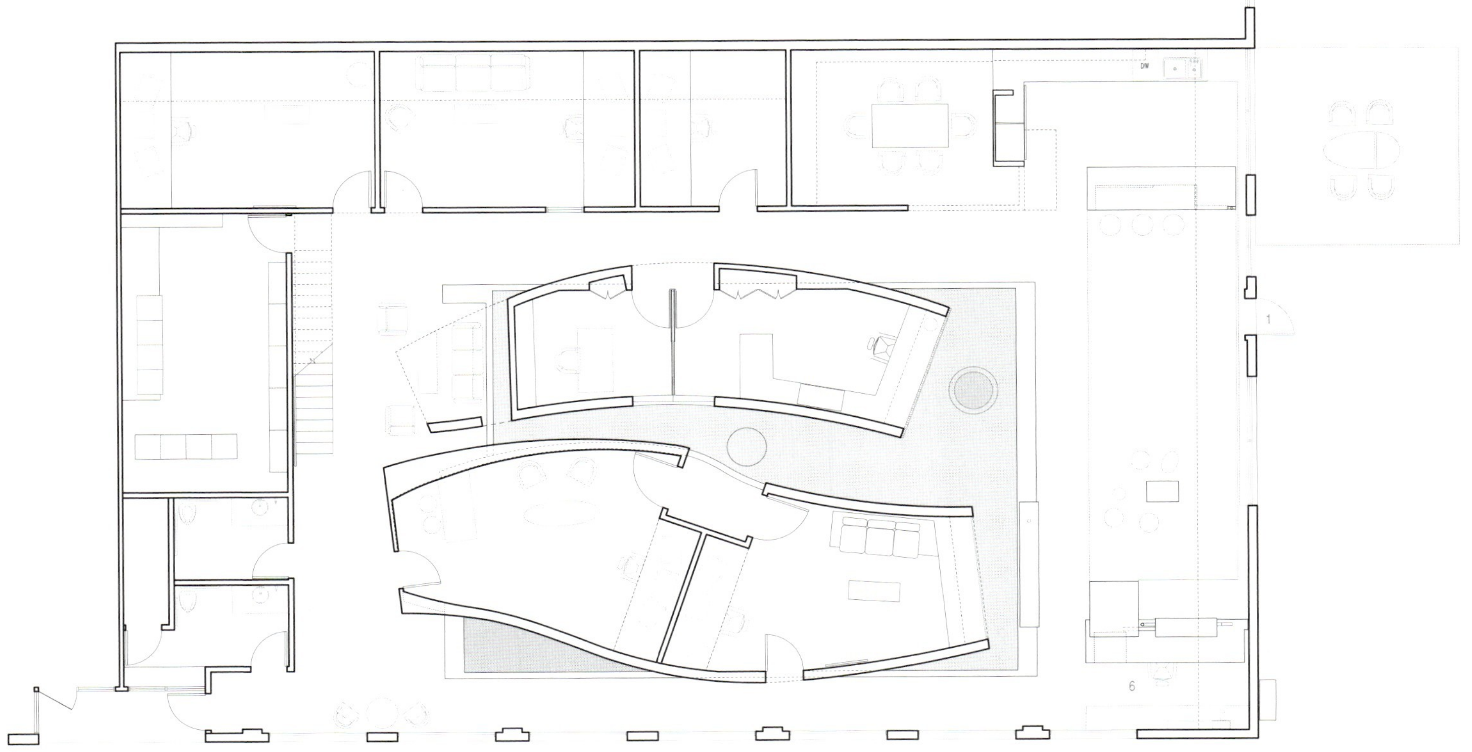

Aidlin Darling Design /
David Darling, Joshua Aidlin

↑ | Night view of building's apertures
→ | View of perforated shadows from exterior skin
↓ | Original building

355 11th Street: Matarozzi / Pelsinger Building

San Francisco

355 11th Street is a LEED Gold adaptive reuse of a derelict, turn-of-the-century historic warehouse. A collection of metal and glass apertures, sensitively inserted into the original structural frame, provide the requisite functions of entry, exit, light and view. On the east and west façades, the new metal skin is perforated with areas of small holes that allow light and air to pass through new, hidden windows. The original fenestration of the building's north façade was preserved and refurbished. The existing timber and concrete frame was carefully sandblasted to reveal the warmth and texture of the original materials. As day turns to evening, the perforations in the new skin reveal the historic interior.

PROJECT FACTS

Address: 355 11th Street, San Francisco, CA 94103. **Client:** Matarozzi / Pelsinger Builders. **Completion:** 2008. **Building type:** mixed use commercial. **Gross floor area:** 1,301 m².
Original building: architect unknown. **Client:** Jackson Brewery. **Completion:** 1912. **Building type:** bottling plant and warehouse. **Gross floor area:** 1,301 m².

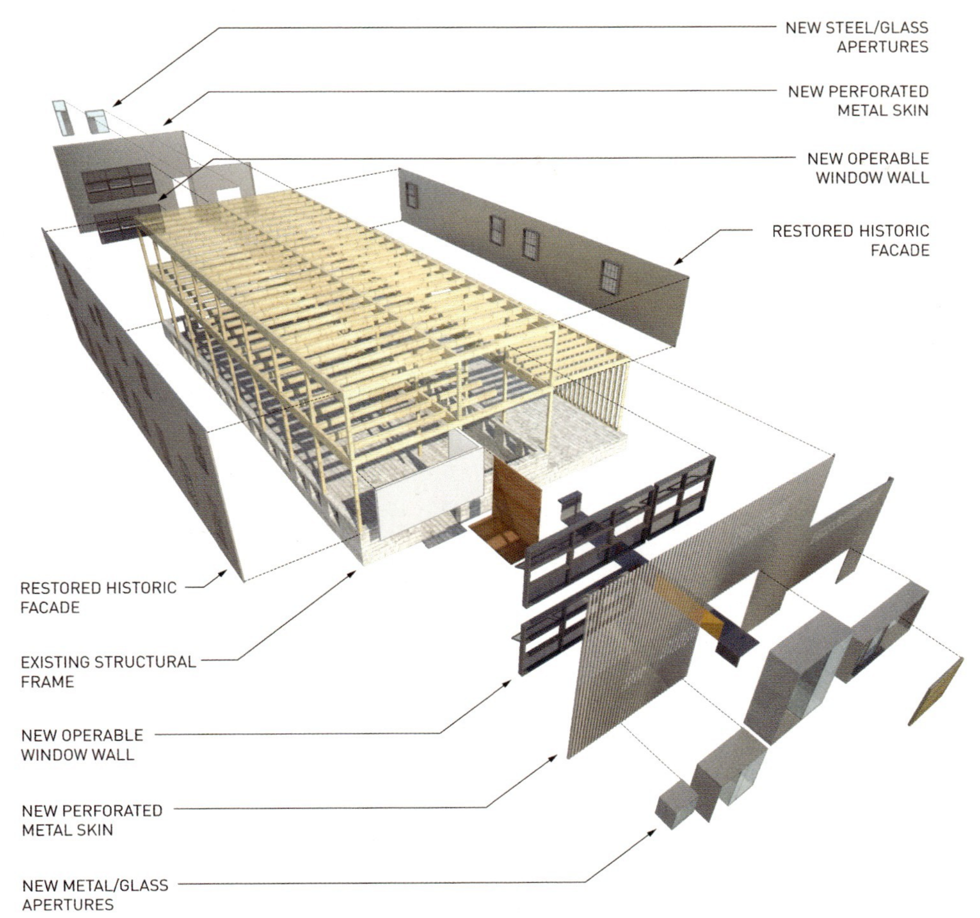

←←| View of reception area
← | Diagram of structural and esthetic changes
↓ | Reception area

Dok architecten (Liesbeth van der Pol) and AEQUO Architects (Aat Vos)

↑ | **Art gallery** on the first floor
→ | **Entrance area**

Mediatheek

Delft

Durability through transformation was the idea behind the DOK Delft, a multi-media center, that merges the former Disco Take, the Public Library of Delft and the Art Center Delft housed in the completely renovated Hoogovenpand. The ultra-modern final result is characterized by colorand light, caused by the sharp contrast between contemporary and traditional materials, as well as the different atmospheres, which simultaneously form a inextricable unity. Liesbeth van der Pol, the architect, and Aat Vos, the interior architect, joined forces in a unique form of co-operation, in which both decided to cede to each other part of their assignments. They not only adapted the 1970s building for the new use but made this modern usage visible as well.

PROJECT FACTS

Address: Vesteplein 100, 2601 CX Delft, The Netherlands. **Client:** City of Delft. **Completion:** 2007. **Building type:** public building. **Gross floor area:** 9,940 m².

Original building: Groosman. **Client:** unknown. **Completion:** 1970. **Building type:** office. **Gross floor area:** 7,000 m².

↑ | Kids library
← | Kids comic book room
↓ | Section

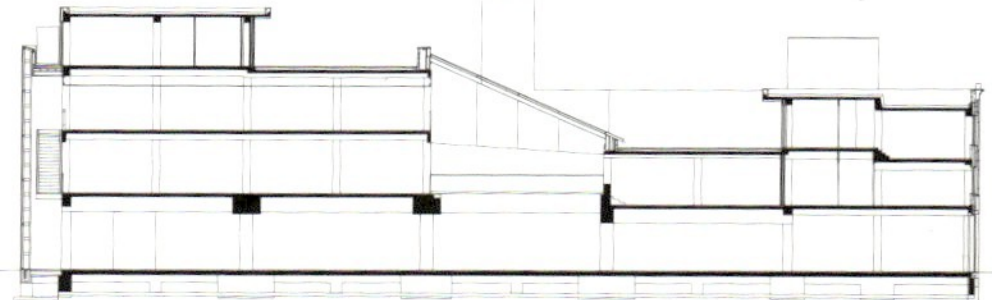

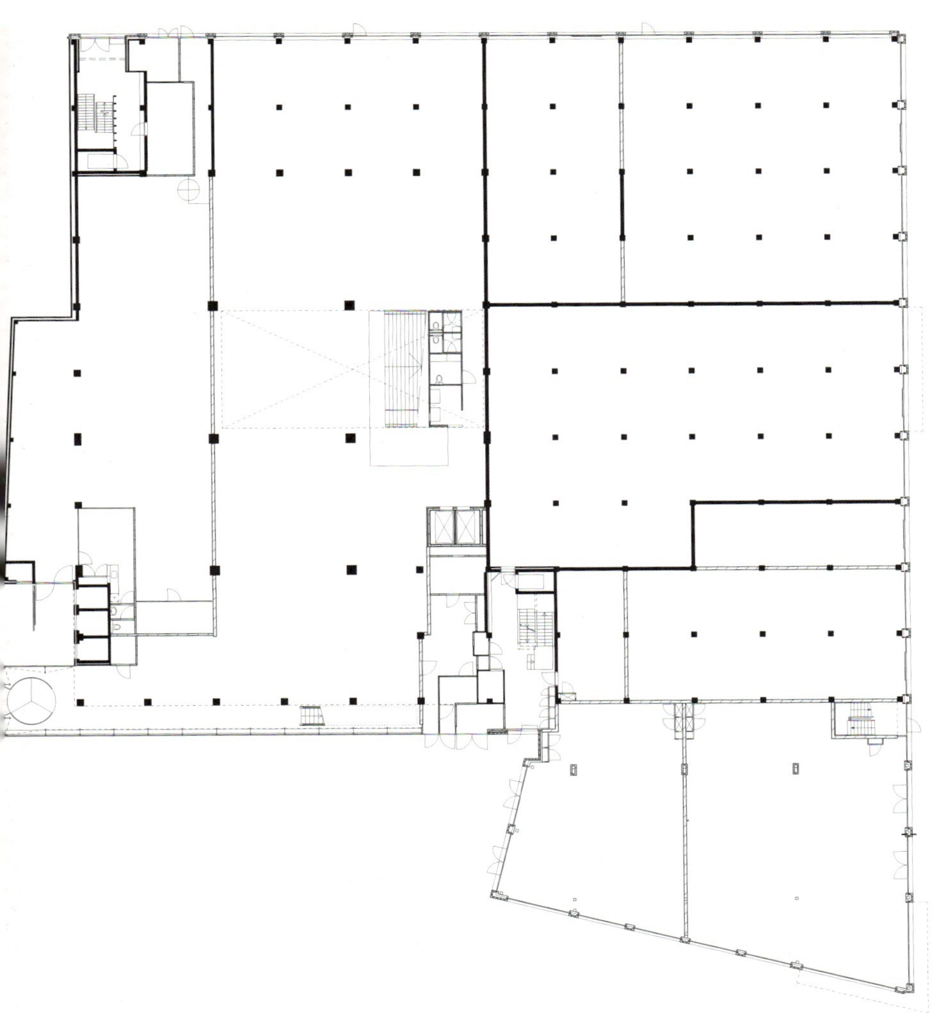

← | **Ground floor plan**
↓ | **Main stairs,** central view

SAC Federal Credit Union Ames Branch

Omaha

↑ | **Public lobby**
→ | **Entrance view**, at night
↓ | **Original building**, exterior and interior

Located in Omaha, the original 465 square meter Hollywood Video Store, abandoned for over two years, was converted into a fully functional credit union branch. It was important to the client that the building encourages growth within the community through a functional and sustainable transformation. The decision was made to create a drive-thru within the existing space. A walkway was created for pedestrians and a corner of the structure was removed to provide a covered entrance. The primary cladding of the building is a 100 % natural exterior poplar siding that forms spaces within. The poplar was thermally modified, providing a maintenance-free exterior that is resistant to mold, insects, and deterioration.

PROJECT FACTS

Address: 3161 Ames Avenue, Omaha, NE 68111, USA. **Client:** SAC Federal Credit Union. **Completion:** 2010. **Building type:** financial. **Gross floor area:** 269 m^2.
Original building: DJR Architecture Inc. **Client:** Hollywood Video. **Completion:** 2001. **Building type:** retail. **Gross floor area:** 465 m^2.

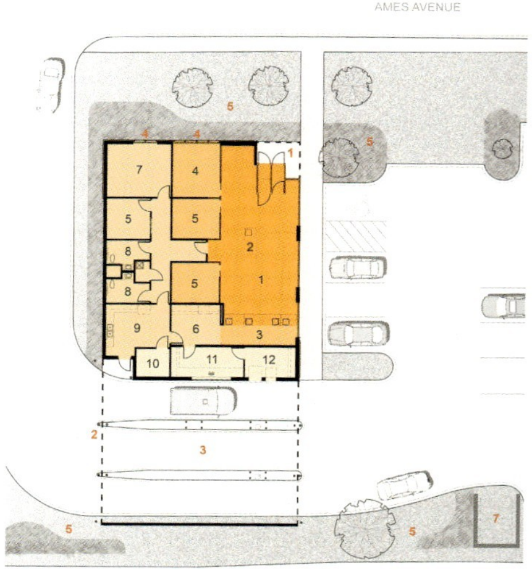

↑ | **Exterior view**
← | **Façade**
↓ | **Floor plan**

← | Internet kiosk
↓ | Teller line

Inde
Arch
Ar

tects Index

24H architecture

Hoflaan 132
3062 JM Rotterdam (The Netherlands)
T +31.10.4111000
F +31.10.2827287
info@24h.eu
www.24h.eu

→ 102

3LHD Architects

Nikole Božidarevica 13/4
10000 Zagreb (Croatia)
T +385.1.2320200
F +385.1.2320100
info@3lhd.com
www.3lhd.com

→ 52

4of7 architecture

Molerova 12
11000 Beograd (Serbia)
T +381.2441217
http://4ofseven.com

→ 358

51N4E

58, rue Delaunoy
1080 Brussels (Belgium)
T +32.2.503.50.89
F +32.2.410.58.03
mail@51N4E.com
www.51N4E.com

→ 250

AEQUO Architects

Prinses Irenestraat 7
9401 HH Assen (The Netherlands)
T +31.592.555051
F +31.592.555073
assen@aequo.nl?
www.aequa.nl

→ 389

Max van Aerschot architect bv

Jansstraat 53
2011RV Haarlem (The Netherlands)
T +31235316419
F +31235511380
info@vanaerschot.nl
www.vanaerschot.nl

→ 342

Aidlin Darling Design

500 Third Street, Suite 410
San Francisco, CA 94107 (USA)
T +1.415.974.5603
F +1.415.974.0849
info@aidlindarlingdesign.com
www.aidlindarlingdesign.com

→ 384

Angelis+Partner Architekten

Peterstraße 38
26121 Oldenburg (Germany)
T +49.441.265650
F +49.441.26550
mail@angelis-partner.de
www.angelis-partner.de

→214

David Archer

Böckh J. Street 1
7625 Pécs (Hungary)
T +36.30.5201064
moto354@freemail.hu

→ 150

Architekturbüro [lu:p]

Ringstraße 21
96271 Grub am Forst (Germany)
T +49.9560.8122
F +49.9560.8121
info@lu-p.de
www.lu-p.de

→ 282

ARX PORTUGAL, Arquitectos Lda.

argo de Santos, 4 / 1º
200-808 Lisbon (Portugal)
+ 351.21.3918110
+ 351.21.3918119
xportugal@arx.pt
ww.arx.pt

326

telier PRO architekten

erkhoflaan 11a
585 JB The Hague (The Netherlands)
+31.70.3506900
+31.70.3514971
fo@atelierpro.nl
ww.atelierpro.nl

194, 376

aurmann.dürr architekten

rschstraße 120
6137 Karlsruhe (Germany)
+49.721.91435350
+49.721.91435370
ontakt@bdarchitekten.eu
ww.bdarchitekten.eu

168

IG

ørrebrogade 66D, 2nd floor
200 Copenhagen N (Denmark)
+45.72217227
ww.big.dk

78

binnberg design

Steinstraße 28
81667 Munich (Germany)
T +49.89.48088630
F +49.89.48088650
info@binnberg.com
www.binnberg.com

→ 158

Blackburn Architects

1820 N Street NW
20036 Washington, DC (USA)
T +1.202.3371755
F +1.202.3375271
jab@blackburnarch.com
www.blackburnarch.com

→ 134

Blok Kats van Veen architects

Wilgenweg 22b
1031 HV Amsterdam (The Netherlands)
T +31.20.4227233
info@bkvv.nl
www.bkvv.nl

→ 212

Brasil Arquitetura Studio

Rua Harmonia, 101, Vila Madalena
São Paulo Sp, 05435 000 (Brasil)
T +55.11.38159511
F +55.11.38159511
brasilarquitetura@brasilarquitetura.com
www.brasilarquitetura.com

→ 74

BURO II & ARCHI+I

Hoogleedsesteenweg 415
8800 Roeselare (Belgium)
T +32.51.211105
F +32.51.224674
info@buro2.be
www.buro2.be

→ 112, 240

chartier-corbasson

3, rue Ambroise Thomas
75009 Paris (France)
T +33.1.48010298
F +33.1.48010347
agence@chartier-corbasson.com
www.chartier-corbasson.com

→ 320

DAP studio

via Gian Battista Brocchi 7/a
20131 Milan (Italy)
T +39.02.70631511
F +39.02.2361496
info@dapstudio.com
www.dapstudio.com

→ 28

Davidsson Tarkela Architects

Pälkäneentie 19 A
00510 Helsinki (Finland)
T +358.9.4342060
F +358.9.43420615
ark@arkdt.fi
www.arkdt.fi

→ **202, 321**

de Architekten Cie.

Keizersgracht 126
1015 CW Amsterdam (The Netherlands)
T +31.20.5309300
F +31.20.5309399
info@cbp.de
www.cbp.de

→ **20, 92, 278**

diederendirrix

Dommelstraat 11
5611 CJ Eindhoven (The Netherlands)
T +31.40.2606740
F +31.40.2606760
info@diederendirrix.nl
www.diederendirrix.nl

→ **246**

Dok architecten

Entrepotdok 86
1001 ME Amsterdam (The Netherlands)
T +31.20.3449700
F +31.20.3449799
post@dokarchitecten.nl
www.dokarchitecten.nl

→ **389**

Dow Jones Architects

39 Calbourne Road
London SW12 8LW (United Kingdom)
T +44.20.87720507
F +44.20.86756892
mail@dowjonesarchitects.com
www.dowjonesarchitects.com

→ **12, 132**

Erick van Egeraat

Calandstraat 23
3016 CA Rotterdam (The Netherlands)
T +31.10.4369686
F +31.10.4369573
info@erickvanegeraat.com
www.erickvanegeraat.com

→ **72,**

EMBAIXADA

Rua des Remolares n*35 1 *Esq
1299-370 Lisboa (Portugal)
T +351.918727250
F +351.211524293
geral@embaixada.net
www.embaixada.net.

→ **44**

fischerarchitekten

Lothringerstraße 61a
52070 Aachen (Germany)
T +49.241.99760
F +49.241.9497620
mail@fischerarchitekten.de
www.fischerarchitekten.de

→ **354**

FloS und K architektur + urbanistik

Bleichstraße 24
66111 Saarbrücken (Germany)
T +49.681.3799710
F +49.681.3799714
info@flosundk.de
www.flosundk.d

→ **56**

form, environment, research (fer) studio LLP

1159 East Hyde Park Blvd.
Inglewood, CA 90302 (USA)
T +1.310.6724749
F +1.310.6724733
inquiry@ferstudio.com
www.ferstudio.com

→ **272**

Format Architektur

Kaiser Wilhelm Ring 40
50672 Cologne (Germany)
T +49.221.7880170
F +49.221.78801719
konopek@format-architektur.de
www.format-architektur.de

→ **124**

Albert France-Lanord Architects

ehnsgatan 3
13 57 Stockholm (Sweden)
+46.8.6645664
+46.8.6645664
fo@af-la.com
ww.af-la.com

296

rturo Franco Architect

Ventura Rodrigues 22. Bajo.
)08 Madrid (Spain)
+34.91.7583760
+34.91.7583761
studio@arturofranco.es
ww.arturofranco.es.

36, 40

ranke Rössel Rieger Architekten

chwanthalerstraße 12
3336 Munich (Germany)
+49.89.75940050
+49.89.75940070
fo@franke-roessel-rieger.de
ww.franke-roessel-rieger.de

118

ung + Blatt Architects, Inc.

927 N. Figueroa Street
os Angeles CA 90065 (USA)
+1.323.2255865
+1.323.2227599
ontact@fungandblatt.com
ww.fungandblatt.com

300

Grimshaw

57 Clerkenwell Road
London EC1M 5NG (United Kingdom)
T +44.20.72914141
F +44.2072914194
info@grimshaw-architects.com
www.grimshaw-architects.com

→ 336

Hacin + Associates, Inc.

112 Shawmut Avenue, Studio 5A
Boston, MA 02118 (USA)
T +1.617.4260077
F +1.617.4260645
info@hacin.com
www.hacin.com

→ 184, 254

Halle 58 Architekten GmbH

Marzilistrasse 8a
3005 Berne (Switzerland)
T +41.31.3021030
F+41.31.3029889
info@halle58.ch
www.halle58.ch

→ 162

Hamonic + Masson

93, rue Montmartre
75002 Paris (France)
T +33.1.53629943
F +33.1.53629938
contact@hamonic-masson.com
www.hamonic-masson.com

→ 234

Haworth Tompkins

19–20 Great Sutton Street
London EC1V 0DR (United Kingdom)
T +44.20.72503225
F +44.20.72503226
info@haworthtompkins.com
www.haworthtompkins.com

→ 24

hks Architekten + Gesamtplaner

Puschkinstraße 18
99084 Erfurt (Germany)
T +49.361.3460366
F +49.361.3460367
ef@hks-architekten.de
www.hks-architekten.de

→ 128

Inbo

Scherpakkerweg 15
5600 AT Eindhoven (The Netherlands)
T +31.40.2434045
info@inbo.com
www.inbo.com

→ 258

Ipro Dresden, Büro Böhme + Schönfeld

Schnorrstraße 70
01069 Dresden (Germany)
T +49.351.46510
F +49.351.4651554
ipro@ipro-dresden.de
www.ipro-dresden.de

→ **372**

Aleks Istanbullu Architects

1659 11th Street, Suite 200
Santa Monica CA 90404 (USA)
T +1.310.4508246
F +1.310.3991888
@ai-architects.com
www.ai-architects.com

→ **208, 316**

Architektur Büro Jäcklein

Erlachhof 5
97332 Volkach (Germany)
T +49.9381.71070
F +49.9381.710715
info@jaecklein.de
www.jaecklein.de

→ **148**

Jensen Architects, Jensen & Macy Architects

833 Market Street, 7th floor
San Francisco, CA 94103 (USA)
T +1.415.3489650
F +1.415.3489651
info@jensen-architects.com
www.jensen-architects.com

→ **268**

Jestico + Whiles

1 Cobourg Street
London NW1 2HP (United Kingdom)
T +44.20.73800382
F +44.20.73800511
jw@jesticowhiles.com
www.jesticowhiles.com

→ **108**

Christoph Kalb Architekt ARB DipArc BSc

Färbergasse 15 Schwarz 5
6850 Dornbirn (Austria)
T +43.5572.890137
F +43.5572.89013715
office@architekturwerk.at
www.architekturwerk.at

→ **292**

Klous + Brandjes Architecten bna

Zijlweg 199
2015 CK Haarlem (The Netherlands)
T +31.23.5320840
F +31.23.5423741
info@klousbrandjes.nl
www.klousbrandjes.nl

→ **304**

L6 studio

6, ul. Listopad
Sofia 1202 (Bulgaria)
T +359.2.8311379
F +359.2.8311379
mail@L6studio.com
www.L6studio.com

→ **302**

LAN Architecture

25, rue d'Hauteville
75010 Paris (France)
T +33.1.43700060
F +33.1.43700121
info@lan-paris.com
www.lan-paris.com

→ **362**

Leo A Daly

8600 Indian Hills Drive
Omaha, NE 68114 (USA)
T +1.402.3918111
F +1.402.3918564
info@leoadaly.com
www.leoadaly.com

→ **392**

Studio Daniel Libeskind

Rector Street, 19th Floor
w York, NY 10006 (USA)
1.212.4979100
1.212.2852130
o@daniel-libeskind.com
vw.daniel-libeskind.com

80, 84

N Finn Geipel + Giulia Andi

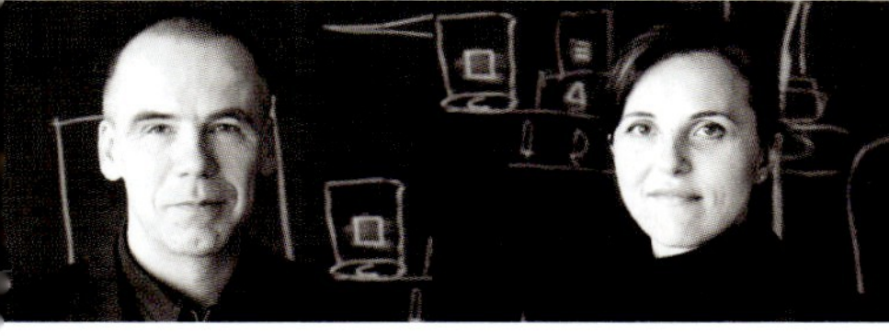

lmholtzstraße 2–9
587 Berlin (Germany)
49.30.39800900
49.30.39800909
fice@lin-a.com
vw.lin-a.com

42

uczak Architekten

nefelder Straße 42
825 Cologne (Germany)
+49.221.513050
+49.221.513051
o@luczak-architekten.de
vw.luczak-architekten.de

190

2r architecture

Bentinck Street, Suite 12797
ndon W1U 2EL (United Kingdom)
+44.20.77887449
+44.20.32921547
ndon@m2r.eu
vw.m2r.eu

332

MANIFOLD.Architecture Studio

10 Jay Street #309B
11201 Brooklyn, NY (USA)
T +1.347.2235975
F +1.347.7565046
contact@mani-fold.com
www.mani-fold.com

→ 138

Emilio Marin

Santiago de Chile (Chile)
T +56.2.7695107
hola@emiliomarin.cl
www.emiliomarin.cl

→ 370

C. F. Møller Architects

Europaplads 2, 11
8000 Århus C (Denmark)
T +45.87305300
F +45.87305399
cfmoller@cfmoller.com
www.cfmoller.com

→ 176

Rafael Moneo

Cale Cinca 5
Madrid 28002 (Spain)
T +34.915.642257
F +34.915.635217
r.moneo@rafaelmoneo.com

→340

Murúa-Valenzuela

Enrique Nercasseaux 2370
Providencia, Santiago de Chile (Chile)
T +56.2.7898727
mail@murua-valenzuela.com
www.murua-valenzuela.com

→ 370

oliv architekten

Sonnenstraße 6
80538 Munich (Germany)
T +49.89.20019802
F +49.89.20019803
office@oliv-architekten.de
www.oliv-architekten.de

→ 286

OTH, Ontwerpgroep Trude Hooykaas

Kruithuisstraat 23
1018 WJ Amsterdam (The Netherlands)
T +31.20.6274576
F +31.20.6273649
info@oth.nl
www.oth.nl

→ 308

Tomas Pejpek

Na zakope 62
77200 Olomouc (Czech Republic)
T +420.58.5315964
pejpek@iol.cz

→ 200

Personal Architecture BNA

Graaf Florisstraat 62a
3021CJ Rotterdam (The Netherlands)
T. +31.10.8865093
info@personal-architecture.nl
www.personal-architecture.nl

→ 118

Thomas Pink | Petzinka Pink Architekten

Cecilienallee 17
40474 Düsseldorf (Germany)
T +49.211.478710
F +49.211.4787110
sekretariat@petzinka-pink.de
www.petzinka-pink.de

→ 16, 224, 228

Dirk Jan Postel (Kraaijvanger • Urbis)

Watertorenweg 336
3063 HA Rotterdam (The Netherlands)
T +31.10.4989292
mail@kraaijvanger.urbis.nl
www.dirkjanpostel.nl

→ 232

Pugh + Scarpa Architects

2525 Michigan Avenue F1
Santa Monica, CA 90404 (USA)
T +1.310.8280226
F +1.310.4539606
info@pugh-scarpa.com
www.pugh-scarpa.com

→ 264, 380

RCR Arquitectes

Fontanella, 26
17800 Olot (Spain)
T +34.972.269105
F +34.972.267558
rcr@ rcrarquitectes.es
www.rcrarquitectes.es

→ 104

RE-ACT NOW Studio

9–11 Strada Selari
Bucharest, 030068 (Romania)
T +40.21.3103420
F +40.21.3103420
office@re-act.ro
www.re-act.ro

→ 242

John Ronan Architects

320 West Ohio Street 4e
Chicago, IL 60654 (USA)
T +1.312.9516600
F +1.312.9516544
ronan@jrarch.com
www.jrarch.com.

→ 186

rooijakkers + tomesen architecten

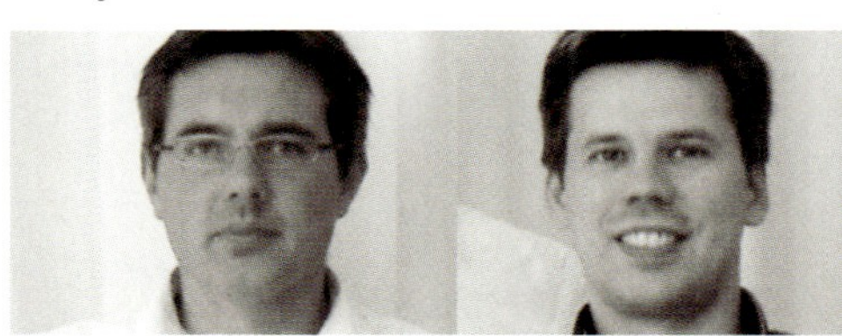

WG-Plein 105
1054 SC Amsterdam (The Netherlands)
T +31.20.6152262
F +31.20.6127884
architectenbureau@rooijakkers-tomesen.com
www.rooijakkers-tomesen.com

→ 180

Szymon Rozwaka (C+HO_aR)

Mahlerova 15
77900 Olomouc (Czech Republic)
T +420.606.372962
olomouc@cplushoar.com
www.cplushoar.com

→ 200

SATIJNplus Architecten

Kasteelhof 1
6121 XK Born (The Netherlands)
T +31.46.4205555
F +31.46.42205566
info@satijnplus.nl
www.satijnplus.nl

→ 100

erie Architects

it 2P Leroy House, 436 Essex Road
ndon N1 3QP (United Kingdom)
+44.20.72260022
'o@serie.co.uk
v www.serie.co.uk.

114

harlotte Skene Catling

; Bloomsbury Street, Bedford Square
ndon WC1B 3QT (United Kingdom)
+44.20.76314887
ail@scdlp.net
vw.scdlp.net.

164

MO Architektur

cilienstrasse 48
)667 Cologne (Germany)
+49.221.2574132
+49.221.2574134
10.architektur@t-online.de
vw.smoarchitektur.com

48

tudioinges Architektur und tädtebau

ubbenkammerstraße 4
)437 Berlin (Germany)
+49.30.27496921
+49.30.27496922
ɔst@studioinges.de
vw.studioinges.de

220

studiometrico

via Fontanesi 4
20146 Milan (Italy)
T +39.02.45498389
mail@studiometrico.com
www.studiometrico.com

→ 366

Swaney Draper Architects (Sally Draper Architects)

45 Watkins Street
3068 North Fitzroy, VIC (Australia)
T +61.3.9486 6606
F +61.3 9486 6607
mail@sallydraperarchitects.com.au

→ 142

Takenouchi Webb

17 Woking Road, #03-05 Tangier
138696 Singapore (Singapore)
T +65.64754005
info@takenouchiwebb.com
www.takenouchiwebb.com

→ 90

Sergei Tchoban Architekt BDA nps tchoban voss – A. M. Prasch, S. Tchoban, E. Voss

Rosenthaler Straße 40–41
10178 Berlin (Germany)
T +49.30.2839200
F +49.30.283920200
berlin@npstv.de
www.npstv.de

→ 172, 236, 290, 350

Tham & Videgård Arkitekter

Blekingegatan 46
11662 Stockholm (Sweden)
T +46.8.7020046
F +46.8.7020056
info@tvark.se
www.tvark.se

→ 68

Gijs van Thienen Architecten

Cruquiusweg 111-A
1019 AG Amsterdam (The Netherlands)
T +31.20.4190251
F +31.20.4190252
info@gvt-architecten.nl
www.gvt-architecten.nl

→ 374

Tonkin Zulaikha Greer

117 Reservoir Street
Surry Hills NSW 2010 (Australia)
T +61.2.92154900
F +61.2.92154901
info@tzg.com.au
www.tzg.com.au

→ 64, 204

TOR 5 Architekten

Alleestraße 144
44793 Bochum (Germany)
T +49.234.6406190
F +49.234.6406199
info@tor5.de
www.tor5.de

→ 32

UTARCHITECTS

Glogauer Straße 6; 2. HH Aufgang links
10999 Berlin (Germany)
T +49.30.81492891
F +49.30.81492890
mail@utarchitects.com
www.utarchitects.com

→ 346

van den Valentyn Architektur

Aachener Straße 23
50674 Cologne (Germany)
T +49.221.9257870
F +49.221.92578730
valentyn@vandenvalentyn.de
www.vandenvalentyn.de

→ 48, 154

Vertex Architectuur en Stedenbouw

Pelgrimstraat 5b
3029 BH Rotterdam (The Netherlands)
T +31(0)10.4766512
F +31(0)10.4766615
mail@vertex-online.nl
http://vertex-online.nl

→ 60

Studio Ramin Visch

Groenhoedenveem 18
1019 BL Amsterdam (The Netherlands)
T +31.20.6710902
F +31.20.7781620
info@raminvisch.nl
www.raminvisch.nl.

→ 96

Paulus van Vliet architects

Zwaardemakerlaan 17
3571 ZA Utrecht (The Netherlands)
T +31.30.2312763
F +31.30.2369015
vlietvan@paulusarch.nl
www.paulusarch.nl

→ 212

Werkgemeinschaft Quasten + Berger

Lindenstr. 31
41515 Grevenbroich (Germany)
T +49.2181.61025
F +49.2181.9492
info@quasten-berger.de
www.quasten-berger.de

→ 146

Sarah Wigglesworth Architects

9/10 Stock Orchard Street
London N7 9RW (United Kingdom)
T +44.20.76079200
F +44.20.76075800
mail@swarch.co.uk
www.swarch.co.uk

→ 330

XTEN Architecture

201 S. Santa Fe Avenue, Suite 202
Los Angeles, CA 90012 (USA)
T +1.213.6257002
F +1.213.6257004
info@xtenarchitecture.com
www.xtenarchitecture.com

→ 260

ervé Abadie 230 (portrait), 230, 231
genturDuL 286
ITPROP / Missirkov & Bogdanov, Sofia 302, 303
oos Aldershoff 374, 375 b.l.
iep van Apeldoorn (beeldsmaak
tografie), Amersfoort 258 (portrait)
't Gray 260–263
'thur Bagen 242 (portrait), 242–245
chard Barnes, San Francisco 269 b., 270, 384–387
n Bartelsman 390
oban Basic 326
ank Bauer 330 (portrait)
ephan Baumann | bild_raum | Karlsruhe 168–171
uliano Berarducci / Milan 366–369
elene Binet 25, 26 b., 27 b.r.
atrick Bingham-Hall 64 (portrait)
204 (portrait), 204–207
tter Bredt Fotografie, Berlin 80 a. , 81, 83, 84–87
ertram Bölkow Fotodesign, Leipzig 373
ijn Bollaert 250
m Bonner, Los Angeles 208–211
arion Brenner, Oakland 271
ight / fotolia.com 6 a.l.
ristiaan de Bruijne 308 (portrait r.), 308, 309, 310 b., 311
chard Bryant / Arcaid 330, 331
rl Carter, Melbourne 142–145
ego Castellanos 36 (portrait), 40 (portrait)
na Cavar, Zagreb 52 (portrait)
dy Chopping 24 (portrait)
eith Collie 150 (portrait), 150–153
ark Darley, Mill Valley 80 b., 82 a.
i Davidsson 312 b.
atthew Deboer, LEO A DALY, Omaha 392 (portrait), 392–395
efan Dewickere, Antwerpen 112 (portrait), 236 (portrait)
ermester & Lindner 286 (portrait), 287, 288, 289
riejuni 212 b., 213
riejuni / VIA Drupsteen 212 a.
ichael Falco 140 a.
lbert Fastenaekens 251, 252, 253
rlos Fernandez Piñar 36–41
+SG - Fotografia de Arquitectura 326–329
oto+Co. Peter Schubert, Dresden 372 (portrait), 372
anc100 / fotolia.com 6 b.
ristian Gahl 232–235, 291
ercês Gomes (MG) 47
m Grafft, Boston 184 (portrait)
avid Grandorge, London 12–15, 132, 133
arc de Haan 96 (portrait)
oland Halbe 290
ax Hampel, Düsseldorf 224, 225 a., 226, 227
arcus Hanschen, San Francisco 384 (portrait)
ob 't Hart, Rotterdam 60, 61, 62 a., 63
son Hawkes 338 b.
rg Hempel Photodesign, Aachen 128 a., 129, 130, 131
ea van den Heuvel, Nijmegen 197
ené Hoch 353
ob Hoekstra 92–95, 310 a.
artin Hogeboom 308 (portrait l.)

Lee Homes staff, Los Angeles 267
Caren Huygelen fotografie 118 (portrait)
Aleks Istanbullu, Los Angeles 319 b.
Jeremy Jachym, San Francisco 268
Susanne Jager 56 (portrait)
Ulrik Jantzen 78 (portrait r.)
Ben Johnson 336 (portrait)
Guy Jost, Berne 162, 163
Jack Journey, Bodega Bay 269 a.
Julia Jungfer 350, 351, 352
Ales Jungmann, Prague 108, 109, 110, 111 b.r.
Dean Kaufman 138, 139, 140 b., 141
Angelo Kaunat, Großgmain 158–161
Taufik Kenan 225 b., 332–335
P. Kers 212 (portrait r.)
Nathan Kirkman, Chicago 186–189
Michael Klinkhamer Photography 80 (portrait), 84 (portrait)
Bruno Klomfar, Wien 292–295
Mirek Kolcava, Wojciech Krynski,
Szymon Rozwalka 200, 201
Nelson Kon, São Paulo 74–77
Ana Kostic 358–361
Luuk Kramer, Amsterdam 20 (portrait), 92 (portrait), 278 (portrait), 342–345
Hilbert Krane 72 (portrait)
Christoph Kraneburg 220, 221
Jan-Oliver Kunze, LIN 43 a.
Andre Lansel 272 (portrait)
Sandro Lendler, Zagreb 52–55
Ralph Lerner 114 (portrait)
John Edward Linden, Woodland Hills 264, 265 ,266
Åke E:son Lindman, Stockholm 68–71, 296–299
Michelle Litvin, Chicago 186 (portrait)
A. A. Lodder 212 (portrait)
Marcel Loermans, Den Haag 194 (portrait), 376 (portrait)
Renee Lorenz, Grub am Forst 282–285
Rainer Mader 48 (portrait), 48–51, 154–157
Olaf Mahlstedt, Düsseldorf 32 (portrait), 32–35, 354–357
Daniel Malhão (DMF) 44 (portrait), 44–46
Andrei Margulescu 238–241
Bruce T. Martin Photography, Natick 254a., 255, 256, 257
Andrea Martiradonna, Milano 28–31
Hans van der Mast, Beverwijk 258, 259 a.
Romain Meffre & Yves Marchand 320 (portrait)
Philipp Meuser 172 (portrait), 232 (portrait), 290 (portrait), 350 (portrait)
MEW 176 (portrait)
Constantin Meyer, Cologne 190 a., 191–193), 246–249
Stefan Meyer, Berlin 148 a., 149
Jean-Marie Monthiers 362–365
Michael Moran 340, 341
James Morris 164–167
Stefan Müller-Naumann, Munich 198, 199
Jeroen Musch, Rotterdam 96–99, 376–379
Michael Nicholson 64–67
Rob Niemantsverdriet, Rotterdam 228 (portrait)
Petr Nosal 200 (portrait r.)

Cristobal Palma, Santiago 370, 371
Josh Perrin Photography, Los Angeles 300, 301
Fram Petit 114–117
Heikki Pulsa 202, (portrait), 312 (portrait)
Marvin Rand, Venice 380–383
RED POINT, Sofia 302 (portrait)
Christian Richters, Münster 42, 43 b., 228,229
Tomas Riehle 16–19
Val Riolo, Los Angeles 316, 317, 318, 319 a.
Sabrina Rothe, Cologne 154 (portrait)
Erkki Rousku 202,203
Zuzana Rozwalka 200 (portrait l.)
Philippe Ruault 320–323
Peter de Ruig, The Hague 194, 195, 196
Sabine Saam, Würzburg 148 (portrait)
Daniel Sahlberg 296 (portrait)
Daria Scagliola & Stijn Brakkee,
Rob Hoekstra, Allard van der Hoek 20–23
Daria Scagliola & Stijn Brakkee 278–281
Lawrence Scarpa, Venice 380 (portrait m.), 264 (portrait m.)
SCDLP 164 (portrait)
Etiënne van Sloun, Maastricht 100 (portrait), 100, 101
Anke Schlüter, Cologne 190 (portrait)
Arjen Schmitz 388, 389, 391
Peter Schürch 162 (portrait)
Ulrich Schwarz , Berlin 346–349
Shaheen Seth, Los Angeles 208 (portrait), 316 (portrait)
Christoph Stieber 56–59
Dietmar Strauß, Besigheim 216–219
Edmund Sumner / View 336, 337, 338a., 339
Hisao Suzuki 104–107
Sybille Thomé, Königsberg 282 (portrait)
Jussi Tiainen 312 a., 313, 314, 315
Jeremy San Tzer Ning, Singapore 90, 91
Chris van Uffelen 6 a.r., 9
Kris Vandamme, Gent 112, 113, 236, 237
Pieter Vandermeer 102 (portrait)
Philip Vile, London 24, 26 a., 27 b. l.
Peter Vincent 374 (portrait)
Visarc Incorporated [3D visualization] 185 b.l.
Ger van der Vlugt, Amsterdam 304–307
c/o Warimpex and Andel's Hotel 111 b.l.
Ted Wathen/Quadrant, Louisville 272–275
Clemens von Wedemeyer, Berlin 346 (portrait)
Taco van der Werf, PA 118, 120, 121
Julian Weyer 176–179
Andreas Winkler 168 (portrait)
Luke Wooden, Los Angeles 264 (portrait l., r.), 380 (porträt l., r.)
Frank Wurzer, Düsseldorf 16 (portrait), 220 (portrait), 222, 223, 224 (portrait)
Kenneth M Wyner Photography Inc 134–137
Jan Zappner, Berlin 42 (portrait)

All other pictures, especially portraits and plans, were made available by the architects.

Cover front: Ales Jungmann, Prague
Cover back: left: Ted Wathen / Quadrant, Louisville; right; Jeremy San Tzer Ning, Singapore

IMPRINT

The Deutsche Bibliothek lists this publication in the Deutsche Nationalbibliographie; detailed bibliographical information can be found on the Internet at http://dnb.ddb.de

ISBN 978-3-03768-064-3

www.braun-publishing.ch

1st edition 2011

Editorial office van Uffelen
Editorial staff: Sarah Schkölziger, Chris van Uffelen
Translation: Geoffrey Steinherz
Graphic concept: ON Grafik | Tom Wibberenz
Layout: Sarah Schkölziger, Natascha Saupe
Reproduction: Bild1Druck GmbH, Berlin